A *Dune* Comp

CW00673836

A *Dune* Companion

Characters, Places and Terms in Frank Herbert's Original Six Novels

DONALD E. PALUMBO

CRITICAL EXPLORATIONS IN
SCIENCE FICTION AND FANTASY, 62

Series Editors Donald E. Palumbo *and* C.W. Sullivan III

McFarland & Company, Inc., Publishers
Jefferson, North Carolina

The author and publisher gratefully acknowledge permission to reprint excerpts from the following:
"'Plots Within Plots ... Patterns Within Patterns': Chaos-Theory Concepts and Structures in Frank Herbert's Dune Novels." *The Journal of the Fantastic in the Arts* 7:1.
"The Monomyth as Fractal Pattern in Frank Herbert's Dune Novels." *Science-Fiction Studies* 25: 76 (November 1998).
Dune by Frank Herbert, copyright© 1965 by Frank Herbert. Used by permission of G.P. Putnam's Sons, an imprint of Penguin Publishing Group, a division of Penguin Random House LLC. All rights reserved.

LIBRARY OF CONGRESS CATALOGUING-IN-PUBLICATION DATA

Names: Palumbo, Donald, 1949– author.
Title: A Dune companion: characters, places and terms in Frank Herbert's original six novels / Donald E. Palumbo.
Description: Jefferson, North Carolina : McFarland & Company, Inc., Publishers, 2018. | Series: Critical explorations in science fiction and fantasy ; 62 | Includes bibliographical references and index.
Identifiers: LCCN 2018026946 | ISBN 9781476669601 (softcover : acid free paper) ∞
Subjects: LCSH: Herbert, Frank. Dune. | Herbert, Frank—Encyclopedias. | Dune (Imaginary place)—Encyclopedias. | Science fiction, American—Encyclopedias.
Classification: LCC PS3558.E63 Z84 2018 | DDC 813/.54—dc23
LC record available at https://lccn.loc.gov/2018026946

BRITISH LIBRARY CATALOGUING DATA ARE AVAILABLE

ISBN (print) 978-1-4766-6960-1
ISBN (ebook) 978-1-4766-3329-9

Front cover illustration by Charline Forns

Printed in the United States of America

McFarland & Company, Inc., Publishers
  Box 611, Jefferson, North Carolina 28640
  www.mcfarlandpub.com

Table of Contents

Introduction

Ecology, Chaos-Theory Concepts and Structures, and the Monomyth in Frank Herbert's Dune Novels

In addition to Frank Herbert's original six Dune novels—*Dune* (1965), *Dune Messiah* (1975), *Children of Dune* (1981), *God Emperor of Dune* (1981), *Heretics of Dune* (1984), and *Chapterhouse: Dune* (1985)—Herbert's son Brian Herbert and his collaborator Kevin J. Anderson have since added an additional thirteen novels as prequels and sequels to the Dune series: *Dune: House Atreides* (1999), *Dune: House Harkonnen* (2000), *Dune: House Corrino* (2001), *Dune: The Butlerian Jihad* (2002), *Dune: The Machine Crusade* (2003), *Dune: The Battle of Corrin* (2004), *Hunters of Dune* (2006), *Sandworms of Dune* (2007), *Paul of Dune* (2008), *The Winds of Dune* (2009), *Sisterhood of Dune* (2011), *Mentats of Dune* (2014), and *Navigators of Dune* (2016). However, while the prequels and sequels to the initial six-volume series exhibit a remarkable, almost unerring faithfulness to the numerous and intricate details of Frank Herbert's original novels—and while many of them, like *Dune: House Harkonnen* in particular, are good reads—the prequels and sequels do not exhibit quite the same extremely-high level of aesthetic integrity as does the original series. What differentiates Frank Herbert's original Dune novels from the thirteen prequels and sequels to follow—a characteristic that lends a special unity to these first six novels—is an unusually deep interrelationship between form and content in the initial series that derives from the relationship between these six novels' explicit ecological theme and their less obvious fractal structure. An ecology is a dynamical system, ecology is a dynamical-systems-analysis or chaos-theory science, and chaos theory phenomena exhibit a fractal structure (which is characterized by repetition of detail on the same and on descending scales). Consonant with its being a series of ecological novels, Frank Herbert's initial Dune series articulates all of the axioms of chaos theory while exhibiting a fractal structure in several ways—chief among them being its overall trilogy-within-a-trilogy-within-a-trilogy structure (repetition of detail on descending scales), its recapitulation in each of the six volumes of the monomyth (repetition of detail on the same scale), and the surprising fact that the monomyth itself exhibits a thoroughly fractal structure. This introduction's consideration of chaos-theory concepts and structures in Frank Herbert's six original Dune novels illuminates the inter-relationship of numerous major elements to reveal this initial series' deep aesthetic integrity.

However, Herbert's initial six Dune novels are not themselves artistically equal. *Dune, Dune Messiah,* and *God Emperor of Dune* are more successful novels than are *Children of Dune, Heretics of Dune,* and *Chapterhouse: Dune. Dune,* an epic masterpiece and the most popular science fiction novel ever published, *Dune Messiah,* which contains one of the most stunning surprises in the history of science fiction, and *God Emperor of Dune,* which is in large part an extended meditation on power, exhibit more-comprehensible plots and more well-realized characters than do the other three novels in the original series, and the final two novels in the original series would have benefited as well from more-rigorous editing. While the major characters and events in *Dune, Dune: Messiah,* and *God Emperor of Dune* stick in the mind, many characters and events in the other three novels of the original series do not. Readers of these other three novels need to be reminded who is who, what is happening, and where it is happening—not only after each work is finished, but also while each is being read. Thus, this introduction is followed by a companion of the characters, places, and terms in the six initial Dune novels, which I hope will be useful to those who have read or are reading Frank Herbert's entire original series. While a volume titled *The Dune Encyclopedia* (1984) already exists, it was published prior to the publication of the last two novels in the original Dune series, so it contains no reference to those two novels whatsoever, and it is essentially a work of fiction in any case, as the vast majority of its content is just made up; it is not, nor is it intended to be, a faithful encyclopedia of the content in Frank Herbert's Dune novels. This companion, by contrast, draws its information exclusively from Frank Herbert's original six Dune novels and contains no extrapolations.

The Ecological Theme and Chaos Theory in Frank Herbert's Dune *Novels*

Although the principles of chaos theory are reviewed in greater detail as they arise in the following discussion, a brief overview is appropriate here. Chaos theory is the popularized term for dynamical systems analysis—the study of orderly patterns in turbulent, dynamical, or erratic systems. The "chaos" in chaos theory refers back, past the nineteenth-century view of chaos as "the antagonist of order," to the classical view of chaos as that formlessness from which order emerges, "the stuff from which the world was made" (Hayles, 21, 20). Chaos theory begins where "classical science stops," in investigating "the irregular side of nature, the discontinuous and erratic side" (Gleick, 3). Just as Euclidean geometry is mathematically convenient yet does not describe reality (in which there are no perfect circles), so, too, has classical science studied what was mathematically convenient—linear systems, whose behaviors can be predicted without laborious computations—even though linearity is the exception rather than the rule in the real world, which is essentially nonlinear because everything in it is part of the whole, interrelated and mutually interdependent. Classical physics can predict accurate results only in the simplest systems, such as two particles colliding in a cloud chamber, but reality is so thoroughly integrated (nonlinear) that "if an effect as small as the gravitational pull on an electron at the edge of the galaxy is neglected, the trajectories of colliding billiard balls become unpredictable *within one minute*" (Hayles, 13). Classical science studied parts in isolation from the whole because that is all its tools would permit, but in the 1970s the "computer enabled scientists to probe the complex interior of nonlinear equations" (Briggs and Peat, 23), which enabled the study of whole systems as they exist in nature. Chaos theory posits that the irregularity and complexity of real-world systems are neither random nor unfathomable but have discoverable laws that govern a wide range of phenomena: population dynamics, biological systems, the spread of epidemics, weather patterns, thought processes, the structures of the universe, and the origins of life.

"Part of its importance comes from its re-visioning of the world as dynamic and nonlinear, yet predictable in its very unpredictability" (Hayles, 143). Complex dynamical (nonlinear) systems are composed of numerous interlocking feedback loops, mechanisms of interdependence through which the behavior of one element affects the behaviors of others. Nonlinearity indicates feedback, a process through which mutually interdependent elements in nonlinear systems interact; part of the system's output returns as input, which then modifies that output, which returns again as modified input, ad infinitum. Thus, dynamical systems are recursive (i.e., nonlinear), and feedback is an essential characteristic of this nonlinearity. Similarly, "one difference between linear and nonlinear equations is feedback—that is, nonlinear equations have terms which are repeatedly multiplied by themselves" (Briggs and Peat, 24). Chaos theory's best-known manifestation is fractal geometry, which uses such recursive equations or reiterated geometric procedures to generate images that replicate similar (but not necessarily identical) structures across the same scale and on smaller and smaller scales, ad infinitum. The Mandelbrot set, no part of which exactly resembles any other part, is a fractal image generated from a nonlinear equation. Fractal images generated by reiterating a geometric procedure, like a Koch curve, however, replicate identical structures on the same and descending scales. To build a Koch curve, which resembles an infinitely detailed snowflake, start with an equilateral triangle and add new triangles one-third the original's size to the middle of each side, creating a six-pointed star; then add new triangles one-ninth the original's size to the middle of each of these twelve sides; and so on. Both the Koch curve and Mandelbrot set exhibit the paradoxical quality of containing an infinitely lengthy line in a finite space.

While scale is irrelevant to Euclidean geometry and Newtonian mechanics, this "self-similarity" on the same and descending scales is a definitive quality of fractal geometry that mirrors the self-similarity of many objects in our nonlinear world; self-similarity across the same scale is obvious in nature's ubiquitous reiteration with variation of everything, from subatomic particles, to microbes, to people, to galaxies, while self-similarity on descending scales is evident in turbulence, in the shapes of coastlines, clouds, and earth faults, and in branching in circulatory and bronchial systems as well as in plants. Because they are generated by recursive procedures or by feeding results back into nonlinear equations to replace initial terms, fractal images are visual representations of feedback; fractal geometry is indispensable to dynamical systems analysis because fractals replicate the self-similar structures of dynamical (nonlinear) systems: "Wherever chaos, turbulence, and disorder are found, fractal geometry is at play" (Briggs and Peat, 95), for "the structures that provide the key to nonlinear dynamics prove to be fractal" (Gleick, 114). The reiteration of a compact function like $Z^2 + C$, which yields the Mandelbrot set, can generate infinite complexity, just as finite information in the human genome can produce a highly complex organism; nonlinearity and feedback are the mechanisms through which simple processes produce nonrandom complexity in nature. In addition to being self-similar, both fractals and dynamical systems demonstrate "sensitive dependence on initial conditions," which means that a small change in an initial situation can yield dramatically different results when that change is magnified by feedback as it iterates upward through ascending levels of scale. Thus, "you can generate vastly different fractals by a slight alteration of the iterated complex function" (Laplante, 29); and, unlike Koch curves, no two snowflakes in the real world are identical due to minute variations in their initial conditions.

In nature, fractal structures—replications of self-similar patterns on the same and descending scales—signify the presence of dynamical systems, those nonlinear, recursive, seemingly "chaotic" organizations of mutually inter-dependent elements that chaos theory investigates. This is the case in the original Dune series as well. Its fractal architecture and fractal reiteration of plot structure, themes, and motifs across and within its component volumes mirror its scientific premise in representing its universe as a dynamical system; as any ecology is a dynamical system, Herbert's depiction of a dynamical universe reinforces his ecological theme. Herbert's ecological theme implies that the structure of the initial Dune series' reality is fractal, and it is—as is reflected in the structure of its architecture, plots, themes, and motifs.

As the architecture, plots, themes, and motifs of Herbert's initial Dune series all exhibit the fractal's definitive characteristic of self-similarity, as fractal structures are essential to chaos theory, and as the central theme of the series, ecology, is in itself a chaos theory science, then the series echoes its core concept—chaos theory, the scientific idea underlying its ecological theme—in both its form and content (and thus also echoes its form in its content). One would associate such a rarified level of aesthetic sophistication with elite literature—not with science fiction. Herbert's artistry is still at least one order of magnitude beyond even this, however, for while this aesthetic effect of mirroring concept in both form and content per se could potentially be achieved given *any* concept, mirroring is the essence of *this* concept. One of chaos theory's fundamental insights is precisely that the structure of the whole is mirrored in the structure of its parts; this is another way to describe the fractal image's self-similarity. Thus, this aesthetic effect of mirroring concept in both form and content (which is also a mirroring of form in content) in itself exhibits the fractal's definitive quality of self-similarity, pattern-within-pattern; the fractal image is a visual metaphor for this aesthetic effect, which is therefore yet another reflection of the chaos theory model that supports Herbert's ecological theme—but on a higher scale, beyond content and form, on the plane of aesthetics. Form echoes content echoes concept in this series in which an aspect of the core concept is that form echoes content. Herbert's artistry is heightened exponentially through this reiteration of concept in self-similar structures containing self-similar contents, producing a mirrors-within-mirrors effect on the plane of aesthetics (visual feedback as metaphor for aesthetic feedback) that in itself replicates the fractal's characteristic self-similarity. And the artistry of Frank Herbert's initial Dune series is compounded even further, not only in that the plot structure (form) replicated in each component novel is the monomyth, which is polymorphously fractal per se, but also in that the monomyth itself symbolizes the process of attaining spiritual enlightenment, which also turns out to be polymorphously fractal per se.

Frank Herbert published the first Dune novels—and certainly established the seminal chaos-theory axioms and dynamics in *Dune*—before "scientists ... invented 'chaos theory' in the 1970s and 1980s" (Briggs and Peat, 16). In this series that is crucially concerned with the motif of foreseeing the future, Herbert prophetically presents his series' basic underlying concept, ecology, as an extrapolation of what was *only in the process of becoming* dynamical systems analysis, the scientific field now popularly termed "chaos theory"; and the series persistently mirrors both in its narrative structure and in its themes and motifs what can *only in retrospect* be seen as its basic concept's dynamical-systems model. Looking at Herbert's initial Dune novels from the perspective of chaos theory demonstrates, not only that both the artistry and the unity of these six novels are far more compelling than has been supposed, but also that the science fiction writer (in the specific instance of Herbert) can articulate at great length and complexity a world-view that presupposes and is unified by certain scientific concepts, from which his work extrapolates, *prior* to any formal articulation of those same concepts by the scientific community—that is, while science can investigate only what it first imagines, this crucial visionary step is often taken by the artist, not the scientist: science follows a path that art has already envisioned, and mapped for the culture as a whole.

Herbert acknowledges that *Dune* "was to be an ecological novel ... with many overtones" (*Heretics*, v), and this ecological theme is integrated with many of the Dune series' other most prominent elements, the "overtones," through mutual connections to chaos-theory concepts and structures. Dune's Imperial Planetary Ecologist, Dr. Liet Kynes, is obsessed with the desert planet's ecology and with the prospect of "using man as a constructive ecological force ... to transform the water cycle, to build a new kind of landscape" (*Dune*, 274). His working hypothesis—that "if we can get three per cent of the green plant element on Arrakis [Dune] involved in forming carbon compounds as foodstuffs, we've started the cyclic system" that will transform Arrakis from an arid to an arable planet (*Dune*, 139)—perceives Dune's ecology, via a chaos-theory model, as a dynamical system that might be radically altered through a minimal change in a key variable affecting its interlocking feedback loops. For chaos theory is the study of orderly patterns in turbulent, erratic, or dynamical systems, and "mathematical biologists of the twentieth century built a discipline, ecology, that ... treated populations as dynamical systems ... used the elementary tools of mathematical physics to describe life's ebbs and flows" (Gleick, 59). Thus, the assumptions behind Kynes' (and his father's) scheme "to tip the entire structure over into our self-sustaining system" by exploiting the knowledge that "life improves the capacity of the environment to sustain life" (*Dune*, 276, 272) are echoed by chaos-theory proponents of the Gaia hypothesis, who assert that "the conditions necessary for life are created and maintained by life itself in a self-sustaining process of dynamical feedback" (Gleick, 279).

As in the specific instance of an ecology, key elements in any dynamical system are by definition mutually interdependent: the behavior of one variable affects the behavior of other variables. Thus, a dynamical system is fundamentally recursive, rather than linear; and feedback is an aspect of this characteristic nonlinearity. This recursive characteristic of nonlinear equations generates feedback loops, which exist everywhere in real-world systems—as well as in nonlinear equations that attempt to describe such systems—and are a prominent characteristic "in the evolution of the ecology" (Briggs and Peat, 26) precisely because of intra-systemic interdependency. Feedback loops "can stabilize a system as well as destabilize it" (Gleick, 193). Negative feedback loops—such as those created by setting a thermostat or those that govern the population dynamics between predators and prey—regulate elements within a system to maintain the system's stability; positive feedback loops—such as those that create "ear-splitting screeches ... in a public address system"—can magnify "the smallest effects" into "indeterminate results" to destabilize a system (Briggs and Peat, 24–28 passim; *see also* Gleick, 61–63).

As they are generated by repeatedly feeding the result back into a nonlinear equation to replace one of the initial terms, fractal geometry images are a visual representation of feedback; thus, fractal geometry is indispensable to the analysis of dynamical systems because "the structures that provide the key to nonlinear dynamics prove to be fractal" (Gleik, 114). "A visual representation of chaotic behavior," a fractal is an image "with an infinite amount of self-similarity" generated in "the realm of dynamical systems" by the "repeated application of an algorithm" or by the reiteration of recursive geometric procedures (Laplante, 20, 3–4, 14–15). "Above all, fractal [means] self-similar" (Gleick, 103). And "'self-similarity' ... means a repetition of detail at descending scales" (Briggs and Peat, 90)—"pattern inside of pattern" (Gleick, 103)—as well as duplication across the same scale. Thus, "the structure of the whole is often reflected in every part," and any part—although similarly rather than identically, when certain algorithms are used—might appear to be both "a small reproduction of the larger image" and a near-clone of innumerable like structures on the same scale (Laplante, 3).

This precis of the interrelationship of dynamical systems, feedback loops, and fractal geometry points to a deep inter-connectedness between the Dune series' ecological theme and many of its "overtones"—the series' plot structure and recurring metaphors as well as its other motifs and themes *per se*—and also between this ecological theme *with* all its "overtones" and the frequent reiteration of these and other structures, themes, motifs, and metaphors throughout the course of the series. The fractal's characteristic "pattern inside of pattern" structure is realized in the relentlessly recurring "patterns within patterns" (*Chapterhouse*, 207), "plans within plans within plans" (*Dune*, 18), "feint within a feint within a feint" (*Dune*, 43), "plots within plots" (*Messiah*, 37) structure of the various characters' schemes interacting repeatedly within the overarching plot of the Dune series; because these numerous sub-plots are interlinked and characteristically interfere with one another, thus creating feedback loops that move the main plot forward, the larger plot structure in which they interact itself emulates within each book in the series a dynamical system that echoes the dynamical-systems model explicit in the series' treatment of its ecological theme.

Of course, chaos-theory equations, and thus the fractal images they generate, are "just metaphors" that imperfectly "represent reality," actual dynamical systems (Gleick, 77). And Herbert's controlling "patterns within patterns" metaphor is reiterated through numerous variations—like a fractal image—to describe the complex schemes, frequently working at cross-purposes, of the Harkonnens, the Atreides, the Emperor, Princess Irulan, the Bene Gesserit, the Tleilaxu, the Spacing Guild, the Fremen, and, ultimately, the Honored Matres. Herbert's many variations of this metaphor include, to give still more examples, "tricks within tricks ... plans within plans" (*Dune*, 285), "vision-within-vision" (*Messiah*, 39), "meanings within meanings" (*Messiah*, 136), "trickery within trickery" (*Children*, 207), "wheels within wheels" (*Children*, 209; *God Emperor of Dune*, 245), "hidden shells within hidden shells" (*Emperor*, 375), "a cage within a cage" (*Chapterhouse*, 94), "a box within their box" (*Chapterhouse*, 197), "contingencies on contingencies" (*Chapterhouse*, 349), and the numerous repetitions of the ubiquitous "feint within a feint within a feint" (*Dune*, 43, 332, 372; *Children*, 140, 322). Each variation, like the motif of schemes nested within schemes that each usually signifies, underscores the series' fractal plot structure and thus echoes its ecological theme. Wonderfully, Leto I tells Paul, very early in *Dune*, that politics "is like single combat ... only on a larger scale—a feint within a feint within a feint ... seemingly without end" (43), a variation that is also a perfectly apt description of the infinite depth of the archetypal fractal image.

Dune is dedicated "to the dry land ecologists." Its explicit theme is the proposition that "the highest function of ecology is understanding consequences" (272; repeated on 498). Schmitt-v. Muhlenfels argues that "Herbert is remarkably successful in ... [describing] an ecological system that functions with perfection" because he "created his fictional world on the basis of solid and genuine scientific facts" and that Leto II's transformation into a sandworm is an objective correlative of "the symbosis of human beings and animals" that symbolizes "the perfectly functioning ecosystem of Arrakis" (28, 30). Duke Leto's cryptic dying thought, *"the day the flesh shapes and the flesh the day shapes"* (*Dune*, 183), is but a more enigmatic expression of life's interdependence, humanity's oneness, with its environment: The individual affects the environment, but the environment in turn makes the individual what it is; both are interrelated elements of the same system and constantly affect one another through a process of interactive, mutual feedback. Thus does Paul think, later, *"I am a theatre of processes"* (380). And the Dune series' first three prequels—Brian Herbert's and Kevin J. Anderson's *Dune: House Atreides*, *Dune: House Harkonnen*, and *Dune: House Corrino*—take as their theme the nearly-identical thesis that everyone (and most specifically Duke Leto) is what life makes him.

Yet, just as its fractal, "pattern inside of pattern" plot structures and metaphors mirror its chaos-theory premise, ecology, by mimicking the structure of a dynamical system, so too does the Dune series echo its chaos-theory premise by exhibiting a similar trilogies-within-trilogies-within-trilogies architecture, even though the series contains only six volumes. A brief synopsis of the Dune novels may be helpful at this point. In *Dune* the inhospitable desert planet Arrakis or Dune is of crucial economic and political importance because it is the only source of mélange, the addictive "spice" that is indispensable to interstellar travel because it makes navigation at trans-light speeds possible by enabling Guild Navigators to foresee the future. After the assassination of Duke Leto, his father, Paul Atreides acquires unprecedented prescient powers through genetics, training, and mélange use; he then leads the revolt of Dune's native Fremen that deposes the evil Harkonnen usurpers, brings down the Corrino dynasty that had backed them, and establishes Paul as Emperor of the known universe and the Atreides as the new imperial family. In *Dune Messiah* Paul is blinded and forced to abdicate his throne as the result of a conspiracy that also takes the life of his wife, Chani, as she gives birth to their twins, Leto II and Ghanima; that Hayt, loyal Atreides retainer Duncan Idaho's ghola (a duplicate of an individual cloned from cells harvested from a cadaver), regains the original Idaho's persona immediately after Chani dies is a crucial element of this conspiracy, for the Tleilaxu thus demonstrate their ability to restore to a ghola its original persona at the moment they offer to provide Paul with a perfect ghola duplicate of Chani in return for control of the empire, a temptation Paul resists.

In *Children of Dune* prepubescent Leto II acquires his father's prescient abilities and merges symbiotically with Dune's sand trout (a stage in the sandworm life-cycle) while thwarting a series of assassination attempts; bonding with the sandtrout gives Leto II invulnerability, great longevity, and superhuman speed and strength, but it also effects his gradual metamorphosis into a sandworm. In *God Emperor of Dune* a transformed Leto II orchestrates his own assassination 3,508 years later at the hands of Idaho ghola number 3 and Siona Ibn Faud al-Seyefa Atreides, Paul's descendant, as the culmination of his millennia-spanning scheme to assure humanity's survival by manipulating it into "scattering" explosively throughout the universe. In *Heretics of Dune*, 1,500 years after that, Bene Gesserit Mother Superior Alma Mavis Taraza raises Idaho ghola number 4 to be the bait in her successful plot to break Leto II's lingering hold on humanity's future by luring the Honored Matres, perverse shadows of the Bene Gesserit who have returned from the "Scattering" to conquer and enslave the Old Empire, into destroying Dune and its worms. And in *Chapterhouse: Dune* Taraza's successor, Reverend Mother Superior Darwi Odrade, uses both Idaho ghola number 4 and a clone of Bene Gesserit Supreme Bashar Miles Teg, another Atreides, as instruments in her successful scheme to co-opt the Honored Matres and thus end their systematic extermination of the Bene Gesserit.

These six novels constitute a trilogy-within-a-trilogy-within-a-trilogy. The three volumes that precede and the two volumes that follow *God Emperor* make up two distinct sets of books, each of which occupies a relatively brief period of time and contains the same characters, yet each set is separated from the remaining books in the series by vast gulfs of time. *Dune, Messiah*, and *Children*, the Paul Atreides books, cover a thirty-year period and focus on Paul and his family. *Heretics* and *Chapterhouse*, the Bene Gesserit books, occupy an even shorter period and focus on the Bene Gesserits and their agents. *God Emperor* occupies the briefest time period, occurs 3,508 years after the Atreides books and 1,500 years before the Bene Gesserit books, and focuses on Leto II and the circumstances surrounding his assassination. Of course, the three Atreides books constitute the trilogy within this larger trilogy; and *Dune* itself is the trilogy within this trilogy in that it is subdivided into three "Books": "Book I—DUNE," "Book II—MUAD'DIB," and "Book III—THE PROPHET." This fractal view of the Dune series foregrounds its demonstration of the intermittency of time, for "periods of stability and predictability in the midst of random fluctuations are called 'intermittency.' ... something inherent in the complexity of networks that contain nonlinear feedback loops ... islands of order in a sea of randomness" (Briggs and Peat, 62): Leto II's 3,508 years of tyranny, the period between *Children* and *God*

Emperor, is an island of order bounded by periods of chaos; preceded by Paul's conquest of Dune, the subsequent 12-year Jihad, and the conspiracy that deposes him and kills Chani, it is followed by the "Scattering." Similarly, on a smaller scale, Paul foresees his period of "happiness" with Chani that follows his seizure of the throne and precedes his Jihad as being "a moment of peace between periods of violence" (*Dune*, 362).

In mirroring its ecological theme, the initial Dune series' dynamical-systems plot structure echoes the fractal's definitive quality of "self-similarity" in both its aspects. The "pattern inside of pattern" structure *in* the entire series, *in* each of its constituent novels, and *in* each character's particular scheme within each novel *per se* is analogous to the fractal's characteristic of "repetition of detail at descending scales." Its repetition with variations *across* the volumes, as it reiterates Joseph Campbell's monomyth in book after book, and *across* the characters, as character *after* character pursues his or her own scheme within a scheme, corresponds to the fractal's characteristic of duplication across the same scale. Moreover, nearly all of the characters or groups embroiled in their schemes within schemes reveal themselves to be *de facto* chaos theorists in the recurring similarity of their statements or actions to chaos-theory axioms. This circle of nascent chaos theorists includes not only Kynes, but also Paul Atreides, Emperor Leto II, the Bene Gesserit, the Mentats, and the Fremen; and their declarations or representations of chaos-theory maxims reinforce the series' ecological theme both implicitly and explicitly. As a consequence, the series' conceptions of history, time, and pre-science—as expressed by these characters—likewise exhibit affinities to chaos theory that further reinforce this theme. The fractal quality of self-similarity as duplication across the same scale is exhibited as well in the repetition of ancillary themes—metamorphosis into the Other, addiction, secrecy and disguise, and rebellion—as well as in its repetition of the interrelated themes of tests and trials, death and rebirth, and apotheosis or revelation, all of which are subsumed into the encompassing monomyth structure that recurs (with *bildungsroman* overtones) in each volume.

Like Kynes' hypotheses, precepts or actions ascribed to the Mentats, Paul, Leto II, the Fremen, and the Bene Gesserit also mirror the thinking of chaos theorists. Paul, several of the Bene Gesserit, many of the Idaho gholas, and Miles Teg—like *Dune*'s Thufir Hawat and Piter de Vries—are all Mentats. "The first chaos theorists … had an eye for pattern … a taste for randomness and complexity, for jagged edges and sudden leaps…. They feel that they are turning back … the analysis of systems in terms of their constituent parts … that they are looking for the whole" (Gleick, 5), and Mentats too are "trained to sense patterns, to recognize systems and wholeness" (*Heretics*, 110). Just as chaos theorists realize that "a system can never be sealed in a box" (Briggs and Peat, 148), so too does "the First Law of Mentat" state that "a process cannot be understood by stopping it. Understanding must move with the flow of the process" (*Dune*, 31–32), cannot be achieved through analysis of constituent parts in isolation. This is the point Kynes makes in asserting that "laboratory evidence blinds us to a very simple fact ... we are dealing here with matters that originated and exist out-of-doors" (139). *The Mentat Handbook* prescribes that, "above all else, the mentat must be a generalist, not a specialist.... The mentat-generalist ... looks for living principles, knowing full well that such principles change.... It is to the characteristics of change itself that the mentat-generalist must look" (*Children*, 221). Thus, "Mentats accumulated questions the way others accumulated answers. Questions created their own patterns and systems. This produced the most important *shapes*" (*Chapterhouse*, 71).

Paul teaches that "there is in all things a pattern ... in the way sand trails along a ridge, in the branch clusters of the creosote bush or the pattern of its leaves. We try to copy these patterns in our lives and our society, seeking the rythms, the dances, the forms that comfort" (*Dune*, 380). It is just such irregular, "random," "jagged" patterns that chaos theorists study, and Herbert too tries "to copy" this pattern in the Dune series' fractal structures and themes, and particularly in its reiteration of the monomyth. Leto II writes, "If patterns teach me anything it's that patterns are repeated"; he tells his Major Domo, Moneo, that "there are no closed systems" and that "paradox is a pointer telling you to look beyond it. If paradox bothers you, that betrays your deep desire for absolutes. The relativist treats a paradox merely as interesting, perhaps ... educational" (*Emperor*, 165, 67, 277)—as do chaos theorists, who study the anomalous, paradoxical data that science has historically marginalized and ignored. Leto II agrees with the Mentats, and with the Bene Gesserit's "Panoplia Prophetica," that "nothing remains in its state," that the only constant in the universe is "change" (*Children*, 267). But—again like the chaos theorists, who demonstrate that "chaos ... [is] a subtle form of order," that "chaos, irregularity, unpredictability ... have laws of their own" (Briggs and Peat, 45, 14)—he notes that "chaos ... has predictable characteristics" (*Emperor*, 28) and seeks "a universe of recognizable regularities within its perpetual changes" (*Children*, 338), order within apparent chaos.

The "unnatural, broken pattern" of the Fremen way of walking on sand so as not to attract the sandworms, which is "like the natural shifting of sand ... like the wind" (*Dune*, 264), and the ritual dance of the Museum Fremen into which it evolves are objective correlatives of order existing within the appearance of chaos that explicitly imitate this fractal pattern as it exists in nature. Chaos theorists attempt to discover just this type of "broken pattern," a distinctive feature of the fractal image. And Odrade recognizes that the Museum Fremen's dance, "an unrhythmic and seemingly uncoordinated display, which came around periodically to a repeated pattern ... was related to the Ancient Fremen way of sandwalking" (*Heretics*, 185), that "the dance had been deliberately unrhythmic but the progression created a long-term rhythm that repeated itself in some two hundred ... steps," and that this "stretched" rhythm is also an aspect of the sexual technique through which Honored Matres enslave men (413), which makes use of "feedback keyed to the sexual response" (*Chapterhouse*, 290). Odrade believes that "chaos existed as raw material from which to create order" (380). Her Bashar, Miles Teg, agrees that from "chaos ... *we must make our own order*," an axiom he incorporates into his battle strategies (*Heretics*, 191). The Bene Gesserit often articulate Herbert's general principle "that the existence of chaos makes order possible" (McLean, 151), which anticipates Prigogine's and Stengers' admonition to see "*chaos as that which makes order possible*" (Hayles, 100). The "Bene Gesserit Way" is to "begin by recognizing the essential, raw instability of our universe" and create "relative stability ... with your own belief" (*Children*, 250–51). Thus do the Bene Gesserit theorize that "*belief structure creates a filter through which chaos is sifted into order*" (*Heretics*, 123; *see also* 279). Obsessed with patterns, they study "the pattern of history" (*Dune*, 23) only to discover that "we repeat history and repeat it and repeat it" (*Chapterhouse*, 308).

Leto II, who has lived for over 3500 years and has "genetic memories" that go back to the origins of humanity, agrees; he notes that the economic/social/political "cycle repeated itself with such persistence that ... anyone should have seen how it must be built into long forgotten survival patterns," and he complains of having "seen people and their fruitless societies in such repetitive posturings that their nonsense fills me with boredom" (*Emperor*, 273, 41). For Leto II history repeats itself most specifically in the behavior of his Idaho gholas, whose "pattern" has "become boringly repetitive" (87) over the millennia in which the Tleilaxu have manufactured them. Emblematic of both this recapitulant "pattern of history" and of the suggestion that Leto's "Golden Path" is designed to terminate it, to replace it with "a new kind of time without parallels" (418), the Idaho gholas have almost always ultimately rebelled against Leto II, only to be "crushed and crushed and crushed ... time and again" (*Heretics*, 425).

Ilya Prigogine argues that "in bifurcations the past is continuously recycled ... by stabilizing through feedback the bifurcation path it takes ... thus the dynamics of bifurcations reveal that time is ... recapitulant"; yet, as "each decision made at a branch point involves an amplification of something small

... branching takes place unpredictably" (Briggs and Peat, 144–45). Paul discerns time's bifurcations in his prescient visions, which usually foresee the timescape of the future in terms of "paths" and "branchings" (*Dune*, 194, 197, 199, 218, 295). As early chaos theorist Doyne Farmer points out, this concept of a chaotic system that is both recapitulant and unpredictable can "reconcile free will with determinism" (Gleick, 251). And to see history as recapitulant yet unpredictable because each branch point amplifies some small change is to see it as a chaotic system, for "chaotic systems are in unstable equilibrium ... have *sensitive dependence* on initial conditions" (Laplante, 2). As "fractals are chaotic in that they're very sensitive to changes in initial conditions" as well (20), time or history can be unpredictable and yet may be fractal in any case, may still possess this fractal self-similarity; and Paul perceives time's fractal character in his prescient visions, which frequently (as in his duel with Jamis) reveal myriad subtle variations of the same event encroaching on one another.

The Dune series is *like* a time-travel story without any time travel in that its protagonists attempt to use knowledge of possible futures (gained through prescience) to alter the future. Herbert is in step with chaos theorists in that he consistently presents history as being both fractal and chaotic. Mentats *can* predict the future to some extent in terms of probabilities (*see Dune*, 18–19), and Paul uses "higher-order mathematics and dimensions to predict the future" (DiTommaso, 320; *see Dune*, 508); in fact, the Fremen traitor Palimbasha "had attempted to explain Muad'Dib through mathematics" (*Children*, 198; *see also* 234). And Paul's prescience is sometimes so complete that he can use it as a substitute for his lost eyesight, as at *Messiah*'s conclusion, even though there are also many "gaps" in his perception of the "time-wall" (*Dune*, 467). Yet Paul realizes prior to his duel with Jamis that "anything could tip the future" (302). While still somewhat paradoxical, time and history exhibit "sensitive dependence on initial conditions" in Frank Herbert's original Dune series.

In fact, *Dune*'s first sentence is a Bene Gesserit precept cited by Princess Irulan that is also a corollary to the chaos-theory concept of sensitive dependence on initial conditions: "*A beginning is the time for taking the most delicate care that the balances are correct*" (3). This is echocd by Paul "remembering his mother's teaching: '*Beginnings are such delicate times*'" and by Jessica herself thinking that "*beginnings are times of such great peril*" at "*the delicate moment*" of their first encounter with Stilgar's troop (286, 293, 282). Irulan also writes, "*Does the prophet see the future or does he see a line of weakness, a fault or cleavage that he may shatter with words or decisions as a diamond-cutter shatters his gem with a blow of a knife?*" (277). This conception of prophecy is consonant with a chaos-theory view of time as a chaotic system—one that prescience can dramatically affect with minimal effort because at "critical pressure points ... a small change can have a disproportunately large impact" (Briggs and Peat, 24). Irulan reports *"that a single obscure decision of prophecy, perhaps the choice of one word over another, could change the entire aspect of the future"* (*Dune*, 218). This is the "butterfly effect" as it pertains to time and history, as "a bifurcation in a system is a vital instant when something ... small ... is swelled by iteration to a size so great that a fork is created and a system takes off in a new direction" (Briggs and Peat, 143). What Paul's prescience may do to the future echoes what Kynes hopes his plan "to transform the water cycle" on Arrakis will do to its ecology, nudge it into a new equilibrium through a minimal change in a key variable. Throughout the Dune series Herbert abandons the "classical paradigms," in which "a small cause is generally associated with a small effect," for a chaos-theory paradigm, in which "small changes ... in initial conditions can result in very large changes in the final state" (Hayles, 211).

Paul's duel with Jamis is one such "critical pressure point" that is replete with such potential "small changes": "a boiling of possibilities focused here, wherein the most minute action—the wink of an eye, a careless word, a misplaced grain of sand—moved a gigantic lever across the known universe. He [Paul] saw violence with the outcome subject to so many variables that his slightest movement created vast shiftings in the pattern" (*Dune*, 296). A comparable "pressure point" in *Messiah* is Paul's meeting with Bijaz the dwarf in Otheym's house: "They walked occam's razor in this room. The slightest misstep multiplied horrors—not just for themselves, but for all humankind" (195). And in *Children* Paul (disguised as The Preacher) explicitly articulates to Prince Farad'n the concept of sensitive dependence on initial conditions as it applies to history: "Governments may rise and fall for reasons which appear insignificant, Prince. What small events! An argument between two women ... which way the wind blows on a certain day ... a sneeze, a cough, the length of a garment or the chance collision of a fleck of sand and a courtier's eye ... dictate the course of history" (89).

During Paul's duel with Jamis "variable piled on variable—that was why this cave lay as a blurred nexus in his path. It was like a gigantic rock in the flood, creating maelstroms in the current around it" (*Dune*, 304). The Dune series reiterates this turbulence similie in numerous passages in which water-current, wind-current, and storm metaphors are similarly used to describe prescience, which reveals to Paul "the strongest currents of the future ... as though he rode within the wave of time, sometimes in its trough, sometimes on a crest" (302, 320). As the study of turbulence, like ecology, is "a subset of

... chaos theory" (Briggs and Peat, 47), this association of prescience with turbulence echoes the Dune series' chaos-theory view of time. When Paul's "prescient awareness" first awakens in the desert, it is "as though his mind ... sampled the winds of the future.... He sensed the future as though it twisted across some surface as undulant and impermanent as that of the windblown kerchief"—and Jessica notes later that Fremen "kerchiefs fluttered like ... butterflies" (*Dune*, 193, 289). Paul and Jessica escape from the Harkonnens after Duke Leto's death by flying into a sandstorm; Paul survives this ordeal, and foreshadows his later use of prescience, by "sorting out the interwoven storm forces ... dust fronts, billowings, mixings of turbulence, an occasional vortex" (241).

Foreseeing his duel with Jamis, Paul senses "time's movement everywhere complicated by shifting currents, waves, surges, and counter surges, like surf against rocky cliffs" (195–96). As she advises Paul to accept the water recovered from Jamis' corpse, Jessica thinks, "we must find the currents and patterns in these strange waters" (311). The more Paul fights "against the coming of the jihad, the greater the turmoil that wove through his prescience. His entire future was becoming like a river hurtling toward a chasm" (388). And just before his duel with Feyd, another "critical pressure point" that his duel with Jamis had prefigured, Paul "sampled the time-winds, sensing the turmoil, the storm nexus that now focused on this moment place" (482). In *Messiah* Edric, the "fish mouth" Guild Navigator, tells his fellow-conspirators that, "as water creatures stir up the currents in their passage, so the prescient stir up Time"; and Paul later pauses to consider "the waters of Time through which this oracular Steersman moved" (16, 76). Paul compares himself as a prescient being like the Steersman to "a chip caught in the wave," musing that "there's no cause and effect in the oracle. Causes become occasions of convections and confluences, places where the currents meet" (63). And he later perceives "the vast migrations at work in human affairs" as "eddies, currents, gene flows" (135).

The turbulence caused by "critical pressure points" in time and space limits Paul's prescient vision. He sees the future only intermittently; many stretches are blank to him, chaotic, with many "gaps visible to him in the time-wall" (*Dune*, 467). Irulan describes "the limits of this power" by comparing it to the line of sight of a man standing "on the floor of a valley" whose view of the "terrain" is blocked by surrounding hills (218). One image that can represent simultaneously both Paul's many references to time's "branchings" and the limited scope of his prescience as indicated by his perception of "gaps" in the "time-wall" is the phase-space bifurcation diagram generated by reiterating the simplest ecological equation used to model population dynamics, x_{next}=rx(1-x), which describes how single populations behave over time. Like Paul's intermittent visions of the future, this diagram reveals "windows of order inside chaos"—areas containing recurring branching patterns, in which population fluctuations are predictable, alternating with large areas of randomness, in which no prediction is possible (Gleick, 74).

"You can see the chaos of nature in the study of population dynamics, particularly in the relationship between predator and prey" (Laplante, 41), and this phase-space diagram is the simplest representation of feedback in population dynamics. Paul (as The Preacher) declares in *Children* that young Leto II "is the ultimate feedback on which our species depends [because] he'll reinsert into the system the results of its past performance" (373). And Leto II, who states that his "purpose is to be the greatest predator ever known," writes in his journals that, "given enough time for the generations to evolve, the predator produces particular survival adaptations in its prey which, through the circular operation of feedback, produce changes in the predator which again change the prey—etcetera, etcetera, etcetera" (*Emperor*, 16, 353). Leto II sees himself as a benevolent predator who, via the operation of a feedback loop, will ensure the survival of humankind, his prey; he will "teach" humanity a lasting appreciation of freedom, which will motivate it to spread forever across the universe, through the calculated oppression of his 3,508-year reign as The Tyrant. He writes, "Liberty and Freedom are complex concepts…. These ideals owe their very existence to past examples of oppression. And the forces that maintain such ideas will erode unless renewed by dramatic teaching or new oppressions. This is the most basic key to my life" (*Heretics*, 190). Perhaps what Paul's shifting, limited prescient visions reveal to him is not so much (or merely) the future *per se*, but is more precisely a multi-dimensional phase space perception of the "predator-prey" dynamics of his and his descendants' possible interactions with humanity.

Dune contains numerous predator-prey metaphors that reinforce its ecological theme while also, like its things-within-things and turbulence metaphors, associating that theme with chaos theory. Reverend Mother Gaius Helen Mohiam has "a predatory look" as she tests Paul with "the box" (7). Duke Leto's "face was predatory," and he feels he "*must rule with eye and claw—as the hawk among lesser birds*" (49, 101). Paul knows that "what the Great Houses … fear most" is to be "cut out of the herd and killed," like Duke Leto, by the Emperor; and at their last encounter "the Emperor … reminded the Baron of the Duke Leto long dead. There was that same look of the predatory bird" (223–24, 456). Baron Harkonnen sees others as "rabbits" and himself as "the carnivore," advises Rabban that he "must be the carnivore …

always hungry and thirsty ... like me," and revels in Feyd's "ferocity" (175, 182, 239–40, 235). The Harkonnens abandon their search for Paul and Jessica because "the hunter does not seek dead game" (283). And a "predatory bird" teaches Paul that predation is "the way of this desert," of Arrakis (269). While Leto II sees himself as a "good" predator whose actions benefit his prey, the Bene Gesserit see the Honored Matres as "bad" predators. Odrade argues that, "like voracious predators, they never consider how they exterminate their prey.... Reduce the numbers of those upon whom you feed and you bring your own structure crashing down"; she predicts that they will bring about their own ruin through the operation of another feedback-loop dynamic analogous to another ecological model: "We remember the relationship between a food animal called a snowshoe rabbit and a predatory cat called a lynx. The cat population always grew to follow the population of the rabbits, and then overfeeding dumped the predators into famine times and severe die-back ... what we intend for the Honored Matres" (*Chapterhouse*, 92–93).

"Odrade was astonished that the Honored Matres did not see" the feedback loop that dooms them, see that "violence builds more violence and the pendulum swings until the violent ones are shattered," that "the oppressed *will* have their day and heaven help the oppressor when that day comes" (6, 128, 147). Like their use of "feedback keyed to the sexual response" that makes it possible (290), the Honored Matre's oppression through sexual enslavement involves another such feedback loop to which they seem oblivious, as they are unconcerned about "what counterforces ... they call forth" (*Heretics*, 442). And, like the Honored Matre's sexual amplification technique or the catastrophic "feedback from a ... lasgun-shield explosion" (*Dune*, 146), the methods used to restore a ghola's persona also employ feedback. Gholas are conditioned to perform an act that is fundamentally intolerable to the original personality, and when that conditioning is triggered, the resulting conflict forces the original persona to reassert itself. Hayt regains Duncan Idaho's persona when his conditioning to kill Paul, to whom he is completely loyal, is activated by Bijaz and triggered at the absolutely extraordinary climax of *Messiah* (259)—the most masterfully crafted moment in the Dune series. Subsequent Idaho gholas repeatedly regain their original's persona when their conditioning to kill a Face Dancer who appears to be Paul, whom Duncan "had served and adored," is triggered (*Emperor*, 45). And the young Miles Teg clone's persona is similarly but innovatively restored when Sheeana Brugh's attempt to use Honored Matre sexual amplification techniques on him conflicts with his persona's conditioning to resist sexual imprinting (*Chapterhouse*, 290–92).

The life cycle of Dune's sandworms constitutes yet another explicitly ecological feedback system: Young Leto II conjectures that "the sandtrout ... was introduced here from some other place. This was a wet planet then.... Sandtrout encysted the available free water, made this a desert planet.... In a planet sufficiently dry, they could move to their sandworm phase" (*Children*, 32). The sandtrout had initially transformed Dune from a wet to a dry planet, and in the thirty-five centuries between *Children* and *God Emperor*, Leto II's implementation of Kynes' plan "to transform the water cycle" on Arrakis reverses this process and transforms Dune from desert to garden planet. But, as Leto II's death returns sandtrout to Dune, Rakis is reverting back to its desert-planet state again fifteen centuries later, in *Heretics*, prior to its destruction by the Honored Matres in *Chapterhouse*.

This is but one example of another frequently repeated theme closely associated both with the series' ecological motif and with the operation of feedback loops in dynamical systems that informs it—the highly ironic theme of things becoming or engendering their opposites, of metamorphosis into the Other. The doom that stalks the Honored Matres and the passion for liberty aroused by Leto II's 3,508 years of oppression are further examples. Herbert "suggests that ... any tendency carried to an extreme will eventually lead to its opposite" (McLean, 145), and things become or engender their opposites repeatedly in the Dune series, often through some easily identifiable feedback mechanism, just as "order falls apart into chaos ... [and] chaos makes order" within dynamical systems (Briggs and Peat, 14). For "feedback, like nonlinearity, embodies an essential tension between order and chaos," and "the sudden appearance of order out of chaos is the rule rather than the exception"—as well as the archetype of transformation into one's opposite (26, 43). This is why "dynamical things are generally counterintuitive" (Gleick, 292), why "living in [a nonlinear world] involves living with paradox" (Briggs and Peat, 181). Thus, while the frequent repetition of this theme of metamorphosis into the Other is an element of the Dune series' fractal plot structure, one instance of duplication across the same scale, the very occurrence of this theme as a prominent motif in the series is in itself yet another manifestation of the series' use of chaos-theory concepts to reinforce its ecological theme.

Echoing the planet's own repeated transformations into its opposite, many things become their opposites on Dune. On joining the Fremen, Jessica realizes "that the use of time was turned around here: night was the day of activity and day was the time of rest" (*Dune*, 297). The Fremen see their exchange of day for night, to adapt to desert conditions, as exchanging "the time of order" and "the time of chaos" (*Children*, 245). Jessica's "other memories" from Reverend Mother Ramallo reveal that these hardened survivors and peerless warriors, the Fremen, had been "a people grown soft with an easy planet" prior to their relocation to Dune (*Dune*, 358); and they grow soft again when Dune becomes a garden planet during Leto II's reign. As Schmitt-v. Muhlenfels points out, "the statement about consequences by the two Kyneses becomes unintentionally ironic: these ecologists overlooked crucial consequences of the ecological transformation of Arrakis" (29). Like the transformations of Dune, Giedi Prime, "gutted long ago by the Harkonnens," is "restored" from ecological disaster to forest planet by the Caladanians, who come to rule their ancestral enemies' world (*Heretics*, 111).

The Atreides' relocation from Caladan to Arrakis, from water planet to desert planet, echoes Dune's transformations; and the Atreides are themselves radically transformed many times there. The "apparent victory" of the Atreides replacing the Harkonnens on Arrakis is itself a "trap" that leads to defeat through Harkonnen treachery (*Dune*, 4, 14), and this involves several feedback loops through which acts and aspirations produce the opposite of what is intended. For example, to avenge his wife's torture and probable death at the hands of the Harkonnens, Yueh betrays Duke Leto, his patron and the Harkonnen's arch enemy, in order to place Leto in a position to kill the Baron; but the Baron lives, and his plot to destroy the Atreides succeeds, in the short term, primarily due to Yueh's treachery. Yet the Baron's scheme to have Rabban so oppress the Fremen that they will welcome Feyd as "their savior" backfires as well; it merely makes the Fremen more receptive to Paul's religious leadership, for "*repression makes a religion flourish*" (379). And the Baron plots not only to destroy the Atreides, but also to place a Harkonnen on throne, while the Emperor aids him out of fear of the Atreides' growing military and political power, yet the end result of all their intrigues is that Paul becomes Emperor. Thus, the Atreides go from being planetary governors to exiles to rebel terrorists to Emperors of the known universe. However, Paul perceives that this apparent final victory over the Harkonnens and the Emperor is a tragedy, not only for the Fremen, but also for his family, himself, and humanity: Its cost is the jihad his prescience predicts but that he lacks the will to prevent, for it is the direct result of his attempts to avenge his father's death and reclaim the Dukedome, and all the other "paths" he foresees are even less acceptable.

Herbert's careful development of characters as foils, shadows, and doubles in the Dune series is a recurring aspect of this theme of metamorphosis into the Other. While the fair, fleshy, reckless and grossly sensualistic Harkonnens are meticulously presented as foils to the dark, lean, restrained and perceptive Atreides, Paul learns that he *is* Harkonnen, his opposite and his enemy, when he perceives that his mother is the Baron's unacknowledged daughter.

And Gurney Halleck sees that another price of the victory on Dune is Paul's Harkonnen-like ruthlessness, the loss of that paramount concern "for the men" that had been one of his father's defining traits (414). Although Emperor, Paul sees himself as "the Ultimate Servant" (*Messiah*, 169) because he has accepted his tragic role. And, while still a prescient seer, he is literally blinded through the treachery of conspirators in *Messiah*. This again forces him into exile in the desert, the traditional fate of any blind Fremen; from there, as The Prophet, he preaches against his own legacy, the religion established in his name. Yet Leto II redeems Paul's tragic victory on Dune by accepting one of those "paths" Paul had rejected and thereby ensuring humanity's survival through becoming The Worm.

Leto II, who predicts that Dune will one day be "desert again" (*Emperor*, 121), asserts as well, not only that oppression engenders freedom, but also that humans "seek ... peace. Even as they ... create the seeds of turmoil and violence" (*Chapterhouse*, 9), and that "the outcome of ... peace [is] its opposite" (*Children*, 407). He further suggests, shortly after merging with the sand trout to begin his metamorphosis into The Worm, that everything becomes its opposite: "The beginning and the end are one.... A phase has closed. Out of that closing grows the beginning of its opposite.... Everything returns later in changed form" (403). Scytale, the Tleilaxu conspirator in *Messiah*, believes Paul will "destroy himself before changing into the opposite of that pattern [he has become—because] that had been the way with the Tleilaxu kwisatz haderach" (174; *see also* 22), implying that any kwisatz haderach is destined to become his opposite. Yet Leto II survives becoming his father's as well as his own opposite.

He, like his sister Ghanima and his aunt Alia, is born possessing all the memories and personae of his ancestors; somewhat like a Reverend Mother, he possesses minds within minds, "lives within lives." Yet this condition is the antithesis of Paul's prescience: Paul knows the future, whereas Leto II knows the past. Still, Leto II's "genetic memory" contains all the prescient visions his father had had up to the point of his son's conception; and while he too is prescient, Leto II rarely uses this ability, preferring instead to go on extended "memory safaris." An embodiment of humanity due to his genetic memory—he tells Moneo, "if there's any true crypt of *my* ancestors, *I* am that crypt"—he must surrender his humanity in becoming The Worm to save humanity (*Emperor*, 37). Ghanima tells Prince Farad'n, not only that Leto II is "no longer human" after merging with the sand trout, but also that his lost humanity is especially painful "because the memory of being human is so rich in him. Think of all those lives" (*Children*, 396). While this idea that one mind can contain the memories and personalities of literally millions of other

people may be the Dune series' most outrageous hypothesis, it too is supported by chaos theory—by that fractal shape of these "lives within lives"
itself—because, like "holograms, ... fractals ... suggest that each part or phenomenon in the physical world represents a microcosm of the whole" (Briggs
and Peat, 112).

Yet, while Leto II martyrs himself for humanity over a period of thirty-
five centuries, he must still be a cruel despot to teach humanity his lesson of
freedom; while he vows, "I will be known for kindliness" (*Children*, 55), he
is reviled as The Worm while alive and remembered as The Tyrant for millennia after his death. Idaho ghola number 3 asserts that Leto II is "more
gross and evil that any Baron Harkonnen ever dreamed of being" (*Emperor*,
339). Indeed, with his "gross" bulk held aloft in an Ixian cart by "suspensors"
(15), Leto II has evolved into a monstrous parody of the prototypical Atreides
foil, the Baron Harkonnen, who also uses suspensors to support his obese
form. And this ironic reversal suggested by Leto II's physical transformation
is foreshadowed by Alia's psychological transformation. Although Alia kills
the Baron, her grandfather, in *Dune*, his persona is among the multitude
inhabiting *her* genetic memory. The Baron's persona eventually supplants
Alia's and usurps her body during her adolescence, in *Children*, and then
uses the "possessed" Alia to execute his revenge from the grave: while his
attempt to destroy the Atreides dynasty is thwarted by Leto II, the Baron's
persona succeeds in destroying his killer, Alia herself, who is finally driven
to commit suicide.

The parodoxical dynamic of things becoming their opposites is imbed-
ded in the Bene Gesserit maxim "that which submits rules" (*Dune*, 26), and
the Honored Matres are the Bene Gesserit's shadows. The Bene Gesserit consider the Honored Matres to be "a terrible distortion" and "*a nasty echo*," and
Honored-Matre-turned-Reverend-Mother Murbella asserts that the two
groups are "Almost Sisters," that in their "coldness" the Bene Gesserit are
"just like Honored Matres" (*Chapterhouse*, 49, 155, 205, 207). The Bene
Gesserit addiction to melange is mirrored in the Honored Matre addiction
to an adrenaline-based substitute, and Bene Gesserit sexual imprinting
evolves into Honored Matre sexual amplification techniques. Bene Gesserit
Sisters and Fish Speaker soldiers sent out in the Scattering had returned 1,500
years later as their opposites, the Honored Matres. Yet the two groups' similarity is emphasized in the very event that reconciles this opposition:
Murbella becomes the leader of both sisterhoods at the conclusion of *Chapterhouse*.

Hayt (the first Duncan Idaho ghola) and his successors experience a
more subtle evolution into Idaho's opposite. In *Messiah* this ghola of "Idaho,

the Atreides lieutenant who perished saving the life of young Paul" (9), freely admits that he has been created by the Tleilaxu to be the instrument of Paul's death. Still, Hayt is unaware that he has been conditioned to murder Paul in his moment of grief on learning that Chani has died while giving birth to Leto II and Ghanima—the "trigger" in effect once Bijaz activates Hayt's Theilaxu conditioning—but this assassination attempt fails when the conflict it creates within the ghola revives his original's persona. (The *real* Tleilaxu plot had been to co-opt Paul, not to kill him, by demonstrating through restoring Idaho's persona at the moment of Paul's grief over Chani's death that the Tleilaxu can likewise replace Chani with a perfect replica.) Ironically, while a nearly identical staged conflict restores the original's persona, which always refuses to kill "Paul," to the hundreds of Idaho gholas subsequently delivered to Leto II, all but a few eventually turn against The Worm, Paul's son, and attempt to assassinate *him*. Idaho ghola number 3 finally succeeds by assisting Siona, another Atreides, in killing Leto II at the climax of *God Emperor*.

Idaho ghola number 3's and Siona's rebellion is nurtured by Leto II's millennia of tyranny, just as he intends. And Leto II had himself rebelled, with Ghanima, against Alia. His dictum that oppression generates freedom has its corollary in the Bene Gesserit maxim that "laws to suppress tend to strengthen what they would prohibit" (*Chapterhouse*, 119). Ironically, this paradox is also demonstrated on a smaller scale in the unanticipated results of Reverend Mother Schwangyu's oppressive treatment of Idaho ghola number 4, an attempt to control him that "had planted something wildly independent in the ghola" (*Heretics*, 198). Not only are Paul, Leto II, Ghanima, Siona, and the vast majority of Idaho gholas rebels, but so too are Jessica, the "rebel" Sheeana, and "rebellious Murbella" (*Chapterhouse*, 46–47), the Honored Matres (*see* 154–55), and Odrade. Paul's rebellion precipitates his jihad, which echoes the Butlerian Jihad or "Great Revolt" that had occurred 10,000 years earlier. And Odrade, who rebels against Reverend Mother Superior Taraza, sees rebellion as "a Bene Gesserit pattern"; like Leto II, she also wants her subordinates, the acolyte Streggi as well as Murbella, to "disobey" and "*defy*" her (7, 294, 283). As with the theme of metamorphosis into the Other, this *repetition* of the rebellion theme is another element of the Dune series' fractal structure, another instance of duplication across the same scale.

Addiction and disguise are among the many other themes and motifs that are similarly reiterated. In the initial Dune series characters exhibit addictions to sexual practices, power, control, myths or ideologies or religions, patterns and habits, and self-concept, as well as to various fantastic drugs.

The Baron articulates this theme in *Dune* when he points out to guard captain Nefud that "the absence of a thing ... can be as deadly as the *presence*.... The absence of anything ... we're addicted to" (234). And Nefud is addicted to semuta (*see* 184), as is Otheym's daughter Lichna in *Messiah*. Other drugs mentioned in *Dune* alone include the stimulant rachag, the truth-drug verite, the Mentat's sapho juice, the elacca drug administered to gladiators, the Water of Life as used in the sietch tau orgies, and the Bene Gesserit's truthtrance drug. Even the "antidote" to the "residual poison" the Harkonnens administer daily to Hawat is an addictive drug, the point the Baron is making to Nefud, as its absence will cause Hawat's death (*Dune*, 233). Of course, melange is "severely addictive when imbibed in [large] quantities" (523); the Fremen, Guild Navigators, and most of the nobility are addicted to it. The Baron is also addicted to food, power, and sex with young boys. And creating sexual addiction is the primary means through which Honored Matres, who are themselves addicted to their adrenaline-based melange substitute, maintain control over their male minions.

As their interest in manupulating politics and religion, their use of "voice" and "sexual imprinting," their breeding scheme, their expertise in nerve and muscle control, and their definition of "a human" as someone "who can override any nerve in the body" (10) all indicate, the Bene Gesserit (like Kynes and Leto II) are addicted to control and manipulation as well as to melange. Schmitt-v. Muhlenfels not only notes that "the Bene Gesserit ... held a profoundly manipulative attitude towards all things religious ... manipulated everyone and everything," but also points out the "obvious connection between the special theme of ecology and the other themes in the Dune novels, especially ... manipulation," that the Dune series is "a general criticism of manipulation ... not only with reference to ecology but also and above all with reference to the fields of religion and politics" (32, 31). The Fremen are addicted to traditions, such as their rule that leadership is determined by a fight to the death, and are reluctant to abandon them even when they are counterproductive. They are also addicted to their religious beliefs and legends, including their faith in a "Mahdi" or savior, Paul, which is so powerful that by the end of *Dune* even "Stilgar had been transformed from the Fremen Naib to a *creature* of the Lisan al-Gaib, a receptacle for awe and obedience" (469). And Paul, like all the nobility, is addicted to power and position; even though he sees it will bring the Jihad, he cannot abandon his compulsion to reclaim his father's Dukedom. McLean argues that, "like melange addiction, prescience can be a trap to those who try to use it to avoid risk" (146); and in attempting to avoid his Jihad Paul, like the Guild Navigators, becomes addicted to prescience as well as to melange.

Like the theme of metamorphosis into the Other, the disguise motif is not only another element of the Dune series' fractal plot structure due to its frequent reiteration—another instance of duplication across the same scale—but is also symbolically related to chaos theory because chaos is "order *masquerading* as randomness" (Gleick, 22). Yueh, the traitor who "thought that he might be part of a pattern more involuted and complicated than his mind could grasp," is a secret Harkonnen agent in *Dune* (60). In *Messiah* Scytale is first disguised as Otheym's daughter Lichna and later, when Paul encounters Bijaz, as Otheym himself. Paul assumes the guise of The Prophet throughout *Children*. Leto II writes "pseudonymous histories" and claims in other ways as well to practice "*Taquiyya*," the Fremen art of "concealing the identity when revealing it might be harmful" (*Emperor*, 215). And Idaho ghola number 4, Reverend Mother Lucilla, and Bene Gesserit Bashar Alef Burzmali adopt a variety of disguises on Gammu (formerly Geidi Prime), where knowing "how to change your identity" is a necessity (*Heretics*, 374).

However, the principle artists of disguise in the Dune series are the Tleilaxu Face Dancers, whose genetically-engineered musculature enables them to mimic the appearance of any humanoid. Slaves of the Tleilaxu Masters, Face Dancers eventually develop the ability to absorb a victim's persona as well, via touch, and the disguise then becomes so perfect that even the Face Dancer does not know it is not the individual it is imitating. Face Dancers mimic Paul repeatedly in the process of restoring to the Idaho gholas Idaho's persona; ironically, a horde of Face Dancers all disguised as Idaho attacks Leto II in *Emperor* (133), and Face Dancers also impersonate Miles Teg and Rakian priest Tuek, among many others, in *Heretics* (159–61, 406–08). Through their Face Dancers, the Tleilaxu have infiltrated everywhere; and, while the Tleilaxu Masters (with Leto II) are the master schemers in the Dune series, *Chapterhouse* suggests that Face Dancers in the Scattering have broken free of their Tleilaxu Masters, have gained control of the universe beyond the Old Empire (431–33), and are the dominant power from which the Honored Matres are fleeing in returning to the "million worlds" of the known universe.

A "feint within a feint" is a disguise within a disguise, after all; and this is an apt description of the Tleilaxu, whose fractal, "plan within a plan" pattern of scheming merely echoes the similarly nested, fractal patterns of their concept of identity, the personae they display to others, and their genetic structure—as well as their Face Dancers' preeminence in mimicry. Miles Teg remembers his mother's warning that "Tleilaxu strategy is always woven within a web of strategies, any one of which may be the real strategy," a trait she erroneously believes they "learned from" the Bene Gesserit (*Heretics*, 65).

And Taraza recollects that "you broke the Tleilaxu egg only to find another egg inside—ad infinitum" (408), a fractal image reminiscent of the Tleilaxu's description of themselves encrypted (appropriately) in their maxim, "Corruption wears infinite disguises" (*Chapterhouse*, 83). The "Report on Bene Gesserit Motives and Purposes" prepared for Jessica "immediately after the Arrakis Affair" (the events of *Dune*) comes to "the inescapable conclusion that the inefficient Bene Gesserit behavior in this affair was a product of an even higher plan of which they were completely unaware" (*Dune*, 510), and the subsequent novels suggest that the plotters of this "higher plan" are the Tleilaxu.

The Tleilaxu name for themselves could be translated as 'the unnameable'" (*Heretics*, 408). Scytale sees both himself and his people as presenting an outward face that is nothing but a mask covering still deeper layers of "masks" (*Chapterhouse*, 86), and the Bene Gesserit suspect "the Tleilaxu had deliberately created a masking-image of themselves … a mask of obscenity" (*Heretics*, 170–71) fashioned through "eons of Tleilaxu deception, creating an image of inept stupidities" (*Chapterhouse*, 90). "Bene Gesserit Analysis" concludes that "the Tleilaxu secret must be in their sperm. Our tests prove that their sperm does not carry forward in a straight genetic fashion.... Secrecy at the deepest levels," and that "it must also be in the eggs that the Tleilaxu Masters conceal their most essential secrets" (*Heretics*, 97, 167).

The last surviving Tleilaxu, Scytale, finally becomes an objective correlative of this fractal Tleilaxu pattern of hidden things within hidden things. With the Idaho ghola number 4, the Teg clone, and Sheeana, he escapes the known universe in a stolen, undetectable no-ship at the conclusion of *Chapterhouse*; but he carries within him, in an undetectable "nullentropy tube in his chest," the "ghola cells" of the entire Tleilaxu race, including his own cells (432–33). Thus, given the proper technology, he has literally within him the capacity to replicate his people. As might be expected in a series concerned as much as anything else with the Bene Gesserit scheme to "breed" a kwisatz haderach and all its repercussions, replication—the defining characteristic of the fractal image—is itself a repetitive theme in the Dune series: The Idaho gholas and the Tleilaxu (who genetically engineer themselves, as well as their Face Dancers and gholas, rather than mate) are the products of artificial genetic replication; the Bene Gesserit replicate their "other memories," already a replication of others' personae, by sharing them among themselves to assure their preservation when their lives are threatened; and Alia's, Leto II's, and Ghanima's "genetic memories" are, similarly, molecular or sub-molecular replications of the lives and recollections of their ancestors.

The Monomyth as Fractal Pattern in Frank Herbert's Dune *Novels*

Frank Herbert's initial Dune series' remaining reiterated elements include such motifs and themes as certain characters having special births and exceptional gifts, being orphaned and exiled, receiving calls to adventures in unknown worlds where they undergo symbolic deaths and rebirths, enduring tests and trials, encountering mother and father figures, and experiencing apotheoses or moments of enlightenment. All are among the many characteristic elements of the monomyth, and the series most clearly exhibits an overall fractal structure—and thus best accomplishes the impressive aesthetic achievement of mirroring its ecological theme in its structure—by reiterating the monomyth (albeit with variations, innovations, and inversions) in each of its component volumes. The artistry of this aesthetic achievement is compounded by the fact that the monomyth itself is intrinsically and thoroughly fractal as well as by the fact that mirroring is an essential characteristic of the fractal image (its self-similarity across the same and on descending scales). That the monomyth and its component elements recur in each novel in the initial series demonstrates that series' fractal self-similarity across the same scale (volume after volume). That the monomyth and the process that it symbolizes, attaining spiritual enlightenment, both exhibit thoroughly fractal structures in themselves—while also constituting the fractal structure of each volume—demonstrates the series' fractal self-similarity on descending scales (structure-within-structure).

Moreover, examining the monomyth as it appears in the Dune series also reveals an unusual, oblique use of this fundamental plot structure: the monomyth supplies tremendous narrative power not only when it provides the structure and content of the main plot—that is, when the protagonist is the monomythic hero—but also when it is incorporated into the structure of a subsidiary plot intersecting the main plot, when the monomythic hero is a secondary character. Paul Atreides and his son Leto II as a child, the series' two most prescient characters, are monomythic heroes as well as protagonists in *Dune* and *Children*, respectively; yet the monomythic hero is himself a reiteration, a revenant replica, in each novel in the series in which he is not the main character. The remaining monomythic heroes are the three most prominent Idaho gholas—Hayt in *Messiah,* Idaho, ghola number 3 in *God Emperor,* and Idaho ghola number 4 in *Heretics*—and the clone of the deceased Miles Teg in *Chapterhouse.* The climax to *Messiah* provides such a powerful narrative impact because it is at this moment in the novel that the climax of the monomythic subplot involving Hayt—in which the ghola's symbolic death and rebirth, crucial trial, atonement with the father, and apotheosis all occur simultaneously—intersects (both precipitates and is precipitated by) the climax of the main plot involving Paul, in which Chani dies and the Tleilaxu's true plan to co-opt Paul with the promise of a perfect ghola duplicate is revealed.

In *The Hero with a Thousand Faces*, Joseph Campbell defines the monomyth as that single "consciously controlled" pattern most widely exhibited in the world's folk tales, myths, and religious fables (255–56). Its morphology is, in broad outline, that of the quest. The hero is called to an adventure, crosses the threshold to an unknown world to endure tests and trials, and usually returns with a boon that benefits his fellows (36–38). Although agreeing with Carl Jung that "the changes rung on the simple scale of the monomyth defy description" (246), Campbell's analysis fills in this outline with an anatomy of the archetypal hero and descriptions of those specific incidents likely to occur at each stage of his adventure. The product of a virgin or special birth (297–314), the hero may have been exiled or orphaned as a child, may be seeking his father, and may triumph over pretenders as the true son (318–34). He possesses exceptional gifts, and the world that he inhabits suffers symbolic deficiencies (37). He does not fear death and is destined to make the world spiritually significant and humankind comprehensible to itself (388). If a warrior, he will change the status quo (334–41). If a lover, his triumph may be symbolized by a woman, and accomplishing the impossible task may lead him to the bridal bed (342–45). If a tyrant or ruler, his search for the father will lead to the invisible unknown from which he will return as a lawgiver (345–49). If a world-redeemer, he will learn that he and the father are one (349–54). If a saint or mystic, he will transcend life and myth to enter an inexpressible realm beyond forms (354–55).

The adventure's departure stage entails up to five incidents: receiving a call to adventure in the guise of a blunder that reveals an unknown world or the appearance of a terrifying herald character; refusing the call; receiving supernatural aid; crossing a magical threshold that leads to a sphere of rebirth; and being swallowed in "The Belly of the Whale," a descent into the unknown symbolizing death and resurrection that may involve an underground journey symbolic of a descent into hell (36). The initiation stage includes up to six incidents: numerous tests and trials, including the hero's assimilation of his opposite, shadow, or unsuspected self; meeting, and perhaps marrying, a mother-goddess; encountering a temptress; atonement with the father; apotheosis; and acquiring a boon (36). The return stage also contains up to six incidents: refusing to return; magical flight from the unknown world; rescue from outside the unknown world; recrossing the threshold; attaining the power to cross the threshold freely; and the hero's realization that he is the vehicle of the cosmic cycle of change (37).

Norman Spinrad discusses the appearance of the monomyth in the Dune series, yet he recognizes the monomythic hero in Paul and Leto II only, in the series' protagonists, but not in the Idaho gholas and the Teg clone as well. Spinrad observes that *Dune* is among those "novels of real literary worth" that retell the "cross-cultural archetypal tale" explicated in *The Hero with a Thousand Faces* but that the monomyth often becomes a "formula for crud" in stories in which the hero fails to "attain ... spiritual transcendence" (151–52). Accurately noting that Paul "ultimately fails" to perform the "final task of the true hero ... for the modern world," which is to return "to the world of men not as an avatar of the godhead, but as Everyman reborn, as the *democratic* avatar of the godhead within us all," Spinrad excuses Herbert in recognizing that Paul is tragically aware of his failure to "transcend his transcendence" and that such tragic irony "makes the first three books in the Dune series ... a mordant commentary on the story of the Hero with a Thousand Faces ... instead of a masturbatory power fantasy" (153–55). However, Spinrad inaccurately indicts the "latter Dune novels" for retelling the monomyth without retaining its spiritual significance or providing any saving, compensatory irony—and suggests that Leto II in *God Emperor* is nothing more than a "degenerate" monomythic hero, "the Emperor of Everything" as "Der Fuhrer" (156–58 passim).

While *Heretics* and *Chapterhouse* are clearly weaker in many respects than the earlier Dune novels (but cannot be faulted for lacking irony), Leto II does finally transcend his transcendence by engineering his own death in *God Emperor* and thus returning freedom to the humanity from whom he has systematically stripped it—thus becoming, in Spinrad's own terms, yet another "*democratic* avatar of the godhead within us all." Leto II transcends his transcendence in the very act of attaining it. The only reason that he becomes "an avatar of the godhead" by merging with the sand trout in *Children* is to pursue his explicit plan to correct Paul's vision of the future (redeem Paul's failure to transcend his transcendence), a goal that takes him 3,508 years, the initial sacrifice of his humanity, and the final sacrifice of his extended life to accomplish and that compels him—in an epic irony equal to any in the first three Dune novels—to oppress humanity for three millennia in order finally to liberate it. Moreover, the monomythic heroes in the final three Dune novels are Idaho ghola number 3, Idaho ghola number 4, and the Teg clone—not Leto II, who is instead recast in *God Emperor* as a herald of the unknown world, the hermit/teacher/guide who provides a talisman, and the ogre-father with whom the hero must be atoned—and all three of these oblique monomythic heroes are literal examples of "everyman reborn, as the *democratic* avatar of the godhead within us all."

That the Dune novels *are* an ironic commentary on the monomyth, however, is but one of the many innovations that Herbert introduces in utilizing this plot structure in each volume in the series. Far from indicating a want of creative imagination, this recycling of the monomyth entails an inventive investigation of this archetypal plot that reveals its intrinsic fractal character while reinforcing the series' ecological theme by mirroring theme in structure. While Herbert's specific inversions, variations, and ironic manipulations of the monomyth are discussed in detail below, several broader reinterpretations are worth noting at this point. Chief among these is the decision to make the monomythic hero a secondary character and the monomyth a subplot in *Messiah, God Emperor, Heretics,* and *Chapterhouse.* This further undercuts the status of the hero, which Herbert has already undercut by dramatizing in *Dune* the tragedy that can ensue when a "planet was afflicted by a hero," a facet of his ecological theme of "understanding consequences" (500, 498). While Paul and Leto II, as protagonists as monomythic heroes in *Dune* and *Children,* are consummate plotters and schemers, the Idaho gholas and Teg clone are merely agents, pawns in the schemes of others, as secondary characters as monomythic heroes in the remaining novels. Also, while Paul's and Leto II's apotheoses entail the acquisition of supreme power, the Idaho gholas' and Teg clone's apotheoses are always essentially revelations of self—and as such are intrinsically more conducive to the retention of that spiritual center of the monomyth Spinrad values; indeed, Campbell argues that the monomyth is the "adventure of the discovery of the self" (8). While Paul and Leto II are very similar in most respects as monomythic heroes, Leto II seizes even greater personal power than his father had, in accepting the path leading to The Worm that Paul had rejected, yet he finally relinquishes that power to attain the complete self-effacement that Paul cannot bear but that the hero must exhibit if the monomyth's spiritual dimension is to be retained.

Herbert also achieves remarkable ironies by assigning to the same character (or his reiterations) different, often diametrically opposed roles from the monomyth in different volumes of the series. Leto II evolves from hero to Tyrant because "the hero of yesterday becomes the tyrant of tomorrow"; when "no longer the mediator between the two worlds ... the Emperor becomes the tyrant-ogre ... the usurper from whom the world is now to be saved," and thus "the deeds of the [fully human hero] frequently include the slaying of the [earlier semi-animal titan-hero]" (Campbell, 353, 349, 338). That Leto II literally becomes The Worm who holds humanity firmly in check strongly reinforces this idea that he evolves from hero to tyrant. The Worm is a type of dragon, and the "tyrant-ogre" as "the dragon to be slain by [the hero] is precisely the monster of the status quo" who "exists only to be broken, cut into chunks, and scattered abroad" (337), much as Leto II is when he dissolves in the Idaho River. Not only does Leto II, *Children's* monomythic hero, become herald of the unknown world, hermit/teacher/guide, and a literal semi-animal titan-hero as dragon/ogre-father to Idaho ghola number 3 as monomythic hero in *God Emperor*, but so, too, does Paul, *Dune's* monomythic hero, become a herald and father figure to Hayt as monomythic hero in *Messiah* as well as herald, hermit/wizard/guide who provides supernatural aid and personifies the hero's destiny, and father to Leto II as monomythic hero in *Children*. Conversely, Idaho, is both teacher and guardian to Paul in *Dune*, prior to becoming the monomythic hero himself as Hayt in *Messiah*; and, while Teg is teacher and father figure to Idaho ghola number 4 as monomythic hero in *Heretics*, Idaho, ghola number 4 becomes herald and father figure to the Teg clone as monomythic hero in *Chapterhouse*. Such role inversions involve female characters as well. For example, Jessica and Alia—who assume the role of "goddess" as the "universal mother" who combines all opposites in *Dune* and *Messiah*, respectively—are both incarnations of the "goddess" as the "bad mother" in *Children*.

Finally, while Campbell's monomyth is a structure that shapes the adventure of a male hero only—and relegates to women only such roles as "crone," "goddess," or "temptress"—another of Herbert's innovations is to have female characters frequently share in the hero's role (in addition to assuming those roles normally taken by women) either by participating in crucial incidents in the hero's stead or by partaking in much of the adventure with the hero. Thus, more than Idaho ghola number 3, it is Siona who possesses an exceptional gift, invisibility to prescience, and experiences the apotheosis and receives its revelation in *God Emperor*. While both bring about Leto II's death, Siona, not Idaho ghola number 3, "must be tested" with "spice-essence" in the unknown world of Leto II's Sareer (15, 347), just as she alone survives the D-wolf attack at the novel's beginning. Similarly, in *Heretics*, the desert waif Sheeana, "a new Siona" (87), is as much an orphan who possesses exceptional gifts (she controls the sandworms after one devours her parents and village), crosses a threshold to an unknown world to be tested (in Keen, where she is tested by its priests), and participates in an underground journey (to the remains of Sietch Tabr) as is Idaho ghola number 4; and she, not Idaho ghola number 4, acts as the "initiating priest" who restores the Teg clone's persona in *Chapterhouse* (290–91). Likewise, Murbella, as much as the Teg clone, is an orphan (Honored Matres kill her parents) who experiences in the spice agony an apotheosis that is also a death and rebirth experience in

Chapterhouse (327–30). To a lesser extent, Jessica shares much of Paul's adventure in *Dune*, while Ghanima shares the beginning of Leto II's adventure in *Children*.

Each of the Dune series' monomythic heroes is the product of a special or virgin birth and possesses exceptional gifts. Royal-born Paul is "*a freak*"; the unanticipated culmination of the Bene Gesserit breeding scheme who appears one generation too soon, he is a genetic mutation who possesses the unique abilities of a kwisatz haderach, "a male Bene Gesserit whose organic mental powers would bridge space and time" (*Dune*, 195, 522). Leto II's birth and abilities are even more exceptional. "An aware, thinking entity before birth" (*Messiah*, 244), Leto II gestates in a monstrously accelerated pregnancy that kills his mother in childbirth and is then "born with a totality of genetic memory" (*Children*, 4)—with full access to the memories of all his ancestors—as well as with the potential to develop all of Paul's prescient abilities and to merge with Dune's sand trout. Reproduced in axlotl tanks from cell scrapings, the three Idaho gholas and the Teg clone are literally virgin births, as "axlotl tanks" are Tleilaxu females "linked" by "a maze of dark tubes ... to giant metal containers" (*Heretics*, 426). Each also exhibits exceptional abilities. Every Idaho ghola shares with the original the distinction of being the greatest swordsman in history; Hayt is also a Zensunni philosopher and a Mentat; Idaho ghola number 3 is "more reckless than any of the others" (*Emperor*, 297); and Idaho ghola number 4, who had "long ... known he was something special" (*Heretics*, 22), has accelerated reflexes and the ability not only to recover his original's persona but also to regain the memories of his scores of past ghola lives, to amplify female sexual response, and to perceive the Face Dancer "masters" in the Scattering and their "net" (*Chapterhouse*, 75). Another "special child" (12), the Teg clone, in recovering his original's persona, acquires Mentat Bashar Miles Teg's "military genius" (3) as well as the extraordinary powers that Teg had developed before his death—super-human speed and the ability to sense imminent danger and to perceive no-ships (spacecraft that are invisible to prescience).

Moreover, each of these monomythic heroes is an exile or an orphan, most are seeking a father in some way, and several triumph over pretenders as the true son. Already exiled from Caladan to Arrakis, Paul is partially orphaned by Leto's assassination and must flee Arrakeen, the Imperial city, to live in a desert exile among the Fremen while seeking vengeance against those who killed his father; he defeats Feyd-Rautha, the deceased Baron Harkonnen's designated heir and thus a pretender to Paul's ducal fief, at *Dune*'s conclusion. Leto II is orphaned at *Messiah*'s conclusion by Chani's death in childbirth and Paul's disappearance into, and apparent death in, the desert.

In *Children*, Leto II echoes his father's flight from Arrakeen when he exiles himself from Sietch Tabr to the deep desert in pretending to fall victim to House Corrino's attempt to assassinate him, and he eventually abandons his humanity (another mode of exile) in merging with the sand trout. Suspecting that a wandering desert "Preacher" may be his "father" in disguise (34), Leto II seeks and finally confronts The Preacher, recognizes him as his "father" (340), Paul, and then triumphs over three pretenders: Assan Tariq (The Preacher's guide and surrogate son), Alia (Leto II's aunt, who rules as Regent), and Farad'n (the former Emperor's grandson and scion of House Corrino). The three Idaho gholas and the Teg clone share two uniquely different forms of exile: being separated from one's persona until it is restored via a psychic conflict that forces it to reassert itself and being dissociated from one's own time, as each is reborn after his death (thousands of years after, for Idaho ghola number 3 and Idaho ghola number 4) into a world radically different from the one that he had known. Schwangyu tells Idaho ghola number 4 that he is "an orphan" to keep him from guessing that he is a ghola (*Heretics*, 29); and this is literally true, of course, as his parents have been dead for five millennia. Thus, the Idaho gholas and the Teg clone each sublimates the monomythic hero's search for the father into a desperate quest for knowledge of a more immediate predecessor, an obsession with recovering his original persona, the driving desire to *"know myself as once I was"* (*Messiah*, 131).

Each of these monomythic heroes also demonstrates that he has no fear of death. For example, one expressed purpose of Paul's initiation as a sandrider is to show "Shai-hulud" that he has "no fear" (*Dune*, 384), and Paul freely offers his life to a dying Hawat at *Dune's* conclusion (474), while Leto II clearly orchestrates his own death throughout *God Emperor*. Each also inhabits a world that suffers symbolic deficiencies and acts either to make the world spiritually significant or, in some way, to make humankind more comprehensible to itself. Water, of course, is what is lacking on Arrakis, and this absence is symbolic of the Fremen's lack of freedom at the hands of their Harkonnen oppressors. On a deeper level, however, this lack of water is also symbolic of a spiritual emptiness—a divorce from the unconscious and from the divinity that dwells within one's humanity—for there are no wells on Dune, and Campbell notes that "the well is symbolical of the unconscious" (74) and that the hero becomes an incarnation of the divine to reveal to all that everyone is an incarnation of the divine. Paul—whom the Fremen accept as their "Lisan al-Gaib" or "Mahdi," the "messiah" of "prophecy" who will "lead them to true freedom"—teaches the Fremen that "they're a people" as well as "how to escape their bondage" (*Dune*, 101, 451); only reluctantly does he found the new religion of Muad'Dib that sweeps across the universe with his Jihad and that diminishes the Fremen by making many of them religious bureaucrats preoccupied with political infighting.

Stilgar laments that the Dune of *Children* lacks the "cleaner values" of his old Fremen days (3). While another sign of spiritual emptiness, this loss of those values that had enabled the Fremen to survive Dune's harsh environment foreshadows that threat to the survival of the human species that Leto II foresees—and that his "Golden Path" is designed to counter. Leto II "could ... see himself as the potentially deified figure to lead mankind into a rebirth" (78). He claims that he is "here to give purpose to evolution and, therefore, to give purpose to our lives," that he will "create a new consciousness in all men" (346, 406). The monomythic hero's role in making the world spiritually significant and humankind comprehensible to itself is also personified in that struggle for self-knowledge with which the Idaho gholas and the Teg clone in *Messiah*, *God Emperor*, *Heretics*, and *Chapterhouse* are all obsessed.

Another deficiency of these worlds, and most explicitly in *God Emperor*, is lack of freedom—the boon that Paul had won for the Fremen, that Leto II strips from all humanity during his 3,508-year reign as The Tyrant, and that Idaho ghola number 3 and Siona must regain for humankind through Leto II's death. However, the greatest symbolic deficiency in the last three initial Dune novels—which focus on Leto II and then on the Bene Gesserit—is love. Although Leto II is saved from nearly losing touch with all human emotions by falling in love with Hwi Noree in *God Emperor*, his metamorphosis has deprived him of the possibility of physical love. Conversely, the Bene Gesserit, while adept at physical love, "are taught to reject love" as an emotion and "to protect themselves against it" (*Heretics*, 130, 345). They view "damnable love, weakening love" (117) as a "dangerous" (152, 344, 345, 368) and "suspect" (*Chapterhouse*, 24) "aberration ... a sign of rot" (58), as a "failure" to be "distrusted" and "avoided" (*Heretics*, 21, 16, 118), and as "ancient detritus" that must be rooted out of their sisterhood (*Chapterhouse*, 50). However, the conclusion of *Chapterhouse* suggests that through the influence of Idaho ghola number 4 and his lover, Murbella, the Bene Gesserit will "relearn emotions" and in that way, like Leto II before them, "cling to" their nearly lost "humanity" (296, 316).

While each of the Dune series' monomythic heroes exhibits at least two of the five archetypal qualities of the hero, Paul embodies all five. He is "warrior," "lover," "ruler," "world-redeemer," and "mystic." Leto II encompasses all of these aspects except "lover." Each Idaho ghola is a "warrior" and a "lover," while Hayt and Idaho ghola number 4 are "mystics" as well, and the Teg clone is a "warrior" and a "mystic." Within an acceptable degree of latitude, each also fulfills that specific destiny associated with each aspect of the hero that he embodies. For example, consider Paul's correspondence to each quality of the hero and the ways in which most of these others are also heroes as "mystics." Irulan writes that Paul "*was warrior and mystic, ogre and saint*" (*Dune*, 466). As a warrior, he changes the status quo by driving the Harkonnens from Dune and toppling the Corrino dynasty. He is a lover in his relationship with Chani, yet his triumph is ironically symbolized by another woman, Irulan, whom he claims as "bride" because she is his "key to the throne, and that's all she'll ever be" (471). Born and bred "to rule" (31), Paul initially becomes a ruler as military and spiritual leader of the Fremen, then as Emperor of the known universe; while he does not literally seek his father, who is dead, he does flee Arrakeen into the unknown regions of the desert "to avenge my father" (226), and he returns as the lawgiver who establishes a new political and spiritual order, decreeing that "we live by Atreides law now" (*Messiah*, 205). Claiming Dune as his "ducal fief" because "it comes to me through my father," Paul takes his father's place when he finally puts his "father's ducal signet" ring on his finger immediately before launching the assault on Arrakeen (*Dune*, 428); in becoming a world-redeemer by then freeing Dune from Harkonnen oppression, to avenge his father, he learns that he and the father are one.

A mystic by virtue of his prescient abilities, Paul transcends life and myth to enter an inexpressible realm beyond forms on at least two occasions. He falls into the deathlike trance in which he experiences "the vision of pure time" after he transmutes the Water of Life, the act that fully awakens his prescience (360), and he disappears again "into the desert—like a Fremen" after he is blinded at the conclusion of *Messiah* (272). This act of fealty to their customs makes Paul a "saint" (253, 279) to the Fremen, some of whom believe "that he had entered the ruh-world where all possible futures existed, that he would be present henceforth in the *alam al-mythal*" (273), "the mystical world of similitudes" (*Dune*, 513). Indeed, Leto II believes that "Paul Atreides had passed from the universe of reality into the *alam al-mythal* while still alive" (*Children*, 339). Paul had previously explained that, due to his prescience, "I am in the world beyond this world here. For me, they are the same…. I live in the cycle of being where the war of good and evil has its arena"; his priesthood teaches that "*he has gone on a journey into that land where we walk without footprints*" (*Messiah*, 205, 271).

Although it is a quality inherent in his prescient abilities, Hwi Noree specifically notes that Leto II is also a "mystic" (*Emperor*, 392). His ancestral "other memories" constitute the inexpressible realm beyond forms that he enters, in his frequent memory "*safaris*," during his protracted lifetime; and after his death this realm beyond forms is the "endless dream" in which he lives on as "pearls of awareness" within the sandworms (and their progeny) to which his death gives birth—and in which he attains the "formless" realm of "immortality" by becoming an undying myth (36, 423, 420). As Zensunni philosophers and Mentats, Hayt and Idaho ghola number 4 are mystics as well—as is the Teg clone, who is also a Mentat—and at the conclusion of *Chapterhouse* both the Teg clone and Idaho ghola number 4 use their no-ship prison to escape the universe of the Dune series for an unknown destination in an unknown universe. Like Paul (another Mentat) at the conclusion of *Messiah*, they, too, finally enter an inexpressible realm beyond forms, as mystics, in disappearing from the universe known to humanity.

The hero receives a "call to adventure" in the form of a "blunder" that "reveals an unsuspected world" or the appearance of a "herald"—usually "a beast," some shadowy, veiled, mysterious figure, or someone "dark, loathly, or terrifying, judged evil by the world"—who may literally call the hero "to live … or … to die" (Campbell, 51, 53), and the Dune novels feature many such blunders and heralds. Typical "regions of the unknown" include the "desert" or "alien land" (79). As Arrakeen, Dune's Imperial city, is an outpost of the Empire, the "unknown world" of *Dune* is not so much the entire planet Arrakis as it is specifically its mysterious and literally unknown deep desert, home of the Fremen, to which Paul and Jessica flee in escaping the Harkonnens. Thus, while "Arrakis is an unknown," it is only in its desert that Paul "passed … into the deep unknown" (152, 227). As Yueh's treachery precipitates Paul's and Jessica's flight, the blunder that reveals this unknown world is their failure to recognize that Yueh is the traitor about whom they have been warned. The six heralds in *Dune* are Reverend Mother Gaius Helen Mohiam, "an old crone … a witch shadow—hair like matted spiderwebs, hooded 'round darkness of features," who appears at Castle Caladan to administer a test that will determine immediately if Paul will live or die (3); the evil Baron Harkonnen, a "*beast*" with loathly habits who first appears "half-hidden in shadows" and "a shadow among shadows" as he reveals the plot that is meant to encompass Paul's death as well as Duke Leto's (181, 14, 17); the Shadout Mapes, a Fremen servant who is almost killed by a hunter-seeker meant for Paul; Stilgar, the Fremen Naib from the desert who appears "in hood and black veil" at the Atreides war council (92); the mysterious Kynes, who first takes Paul into the desert; and the terrifying "monster" worm that Paul sees there devouring the spice harvester (124), an especially appropriate herald in that it is literally "the underworld serpent … who represents the life-progenitive, demiurgic powers of the abyss" (Campbell, 52).

The two conspirators most responsible for resurrecting Hayt as a ghola and employing him in their scheme—Edric, the "monstrous" and "repellant" Guild Navigator, and Scytale, the shape-shifting Tleilaxu—are the loathly and evil heralds in *Messiah* (15). Rather than reveal the unknown world to the hero, however, these heralds introduce this novel's monomythic hero, Hayt (who is actually its most significant "unknown"), into what is an unknown world only to him, Paul's court in Arrakeen; this initial inversion is appropriate because the monomyth itself is inverted in this and the last three novels, wherein the monomyth is not the primary plot and the main character is not the monomythic hero. Paul himself, in the guise of The Preacher, is the veiled and mysterious herald of the unknown world in *Children*; emerging from the desert, he wears a "mask" while interviewing Farad'n on Salusa Secundus, and it is his very existence that lures Leto II from the safety of Sietch Tabr to seek his father in the "unknown" world of Jacurutu, the legendary lost sietch of the water-stealers and The Preacher's secret, deep-desert base (85, 277). (In a further ironic reversal, The Preacher also serves as Leto II's herald on their return to the known world, Alia's court at Arrakeen, at the novel's conclusion.) Early in *Children*, Farad'n's mother, Princess Wensicia, dispatches two Laza tigers from Salusa Secundus to Arrakis to assassinate Leto II and Ghanima; as their attack is the immediate cause of Leto's flight from Sietch Tabr into the unknown regions of the desert, these terrifying predatory beasts also serve as this novel's heralds of the unknown world.

Idaho ghola number 3's predecessor in Leto II's service, Idaho ghola number 2, botches his attempt to assassinate The Worm, and this is the blunder that necessitates the introduction of Idaho ghola number 3 into the unknown world, to him, of Leto II's Citadel in *God Emperor*. In yet another inversion, Leto II, *Children*'s monomythic hero, then becomes the herald in *God Emperor*—just as Paul, *Dune*'s monomythic hero, becomes a herald in *Children*. The most monstrous and terrifying herald in the Dune series—literally a beast and believed by Idaho ghola number 3 to be "more gross and evil than any Baron Harkonnen ever dreamed of being"—Emperor Leto II first "interviews" the ghola "in a darkened room" and from the obscurity of "shadows among shadows and blackness where not even the source of the voice could be fixed" (*Emperor*, 339, 86, 87). As he is raised exclusively within the Bene Gesserit's Gammu Keep, the world outside the Keep (a world that had been his native planet Giedi Prime some 5,000 years earlier)—and, most specifically, the ancient Harkonnen no-globe in which he finally seeks refuge from prescient searchers—is the unknown world for Idaho ghola number 4 in *Heretics*. Thus, the blunder that thrusts him into this unknown world is Schwangyu's complicity in the failed Tleilaxu raid on the Keep—which forces Idaho ghola number 4, Miles Teg, and Reverend Mother Lucilla to flee into

Gammu's forests—and the *"old and wizened"* Schwangyu is the herald (1). Similarly, the unknown world in *Chapterhouse* is the no-ship in which Idaho ghola number 4 is imprisoned and in relation to which he now serves as herald to the Teg clone.

A narrative that adheres to the monomyth's overall pattern need not contain each, or even most, of its incidents, nor must it arrange them in precisely the order described by Campbell. There is only one slim suggestion in the Dune novels that the hero ever refuses the initial call to adventure, for instance: When Hayt asks Bijaz about axlotl tanks in *Messiah*, the dwarf responds, "We had a terrific struggle with you. The flesh did not want to come back." (226) After receiving the call to adventure, the hero acquires supernatural aid from a figure who may personify his destiny. This might be a protective old man or crone who provides a talisman in a setting suggesting a womblike sense of peace; or it might be a guide, teacher, wizard, ferryman, hermit, or smith who offers aid in a context of danger or temptation (Campbell, 69–73). Campbell points out that today the role of "the doctor ... is precisely that of the Wise Old Man of the myths and fairy tales" and that "not infrequently the dangerous aspect of the 'mercurial' figure is stressed; for he is the lurer of the innocent soul into realms of trial" (9, 73). In *Dune*, ironically, it is Dr. Yueh, Paul's "teacher" (4), whose treachery propels Paul toward his destiny but who nonetheless also provides Paul with talismans and aid in contexts that suggest both the safety of the womb and mortal danger. Yueh impulsively gives his dead wife's miniature Orange Catholic Bible to Paul (who later quotes its verses to the Fremen) while they are secure in Castle Caladan, and he subsequently hides Leto's ducal signet ring and a fremkit, which enables Paul and Jessica to survive the desert, in the ornithopter that is meant to take them to their deaths. Still, Paul has about as many "supernatural" helpers as his adventure in the unknown world has heralds, but these other *"companion-teachers"*—Thufir Hawat, Jessica, Idaho, Weapons-Master Gurney Halleck, and Duke Leto—all offer aid solely in the context of the dangers awaiting them on Arrakis (28).

Paul—who, as The Preacher, is both a "hermit" and a "wizard" in *Children*—leaves to his son, Leto II, "that most powerful of all mystic talismans: the divine authenticity of Muad'Dib's religious bequest" (2). Paul is most specifically Leto II's "guide" to his "Golden Path," his destiny, as the "Golden Path" is the content of Paul's "last vision," which is revealed to Leto II when Paul's persona temporarily possesses him (72). Edric, who is a type of "ferryman" as a Guild Navigator, conveys Hayt to Paul's court in *Messiah*. Hayt's Tleilaxu eyes are a talisman intended to remind Paul of the ghola's origins; and the Tleilaxu also provide Hayt with a "guide," Bijaz, an older "brother ...

from the same tank" whose task is to activate the subliminal compulsion that, when triggered at Chani's death, will be the catalyst that awakens the ghola's original persona (229). Leto II, who sees himself as humanity's "teacher" and also plays the role of "hermit" in *God Emperor*, displays to Idaho ghola number 3 *"the crysknife of Muad'Dib … the talisman of our lives"* during the ghola's initiation into Leto II's Feast of Siaynoq (208). Idaho ghola number 3's other "supernatural" helpers are Leto II's loyal agent Nayla and major domo Moneo, who serve as Idaho ghola number 3's "guides" in the Citadel. The twelfth ghola to be used in the Bene Gesserit's *"dangerous* project," as the previous eleven had all been murdered, Idaho ghola number 4, like Paul, is provided with numerous "teachers" in a context of impending danger: In addition to the Reverend Mothers Schwangyu, Geasa, Tamalane, and Lucilla, another of these teachers is Teg, who is told that "desperate attempts will be made to kill or capture our ghola" and who reawakens Idaho ghola number 4's original Duncan Idaho persona in the ancient Harkonnen no-globe, a secure womb "cut out of Time" (*Heretics*, 8, 110, 224). Similarly, Idaho, ghola number 4 and Sheeana act as "supernatural" helpers in awakening the Teg clone's original persona in the equally womblike no-ship of *Chapterhouse*.

After receiving supernatural aid, the hero crosses a threshold to the unknown world, which leads to a sphere of rebirth and may be defended by a protective guardian and/or a destructive watchman (Campbell, 77–89). Dune's deep desert is the unknown world to Paul and Leto II in *Dune* and *Children*, and the desert is a sphere of rebirth for Paul in several ways. As Yueh had planned, both their enemies and allies alike presume that Paul and Jessica have died there, killed by the "sandblast storm" through which they make their escape; and, much as Jessica "felt reborn" on emerging unscathed from the storm, Paul "was like one come back from the dead" on recovering from his first prescient vision soon after they encounter Stilgar's troop (*Dune*, 234, 242, 297). Moreover, Paul's newfound *"sense* of the future" gives him "the look … *of someone forced to the knowledge of his own mortality*," a premonition of death that is followed almost immediately by a symbol of rebirth, his foreseeing that the Fremen will rechristen him "Muad'Dib" (197, 199). Paul and Jessica encounter both destructive watchmen and protective guardians in crossing the threshold to the unknown world. The destructive watchmen are the two Harkonnen guards ordered to take them to the desert to die, Kinet and Czigo; *"the ones the Baron set to watch this pair*," whom Jessica sees following them; and those *"watchers for the watchers"* that she assumes also exist (169). The protective guardians include Idaho, who is killed in an underground Ecological Testing Station while covering Paul and Jessica's escape; Kynes, who offers them temporary shelter in the station and shields them after Idaho is killed; and Stilgar, who finds them in the desert and obeys Kynes' order to "*protect*" and "*save*" Paul (276).

The threshold to the unknown crossed by Leto II and Ghanima in *Children* is Sietch Tabr's "qanat," the water-barrier that separates Stilgar's sietch from the desert proper (167), and the desert is a sphere of death and rebirth for Leto II in much the same way that it is for Paul. After the twins kill the Laza Tigers, Ghanima returns to the sietch under the influence of a self-induced hypnotic suggestion to believe that Leto II has been slain and forestalls any pursuit by convincing everyone (including herself) that he is dead, while Leto II sets off for Jacurutu, "a perfect place for the dead to hide—among ... the dead of another age" (213). After sacrificing his humanity by merging with the sandtrout, yet another symbolic death, Leto II is known as the "Desert Demon," another rechristening that symbolizes rebirth (364). Stilgar, the official "guardian of the orphaned twins," is the threshold's protective guardian, while its destructive watchmen are Palimbasha—the Fremen traitor whom Ghanima kills after she discovers him standing in a "hidden entrance" to the sietch with "the transmitter which had released the Tigers"— and his "watching" accomplices (2, 198).

Paul's court in Arrakeen is the unknown world to Hayt in *Messiah*. Its protective guardian is Stilgar, who—in yet another inversion of the monomyth—seeks to protect the court from the ghola, rather than to protect the monomythic hero from the unknown world. Hayt's complete rebirth does not occur until his original persona is reawakened at the novel's climax and "he knew himself as Duncan Idaho" (259). In a similar inversion in *God Emperor*, Nayla is the guardian who seeks to protect the Citadel from Idaho ghola number 3, to whom it is an unknown world, while its destructive watchmen are the D-wolves who attack Siona and her companions as they flee the Citadel in the novel's first scene. Literally a sphere, the Harkonnen no-globe hidden in Gammu's forests is most specifically the unknown world that is a sphere of rebirth for Idaho ghola number 4, who regains his original persona there. In *Heretics*, Idaho, ghola number 4 traverses "a shallow cave musky with the odors of a native bear" to enter the no-globe through a "portal ... decorated with Harkonnen griffins" (221). The absent bear and decorative griffins are this unknown world's ineffectual watchmen. Similarly, the unknown world that is the Teg clone's sphere of rebirth in *Chapterhouse* is, most specifically, the no-ship in which he regains his original Miles Teg persona. In an inversion similar to those involving Stilgar in *Messiah* and Nayla in *God Emperor*, the "comeyes built into the glittering surface of a doorway" are this threshold's guardians, but they keep constant watch over both Idaho ghola number 4 and the Teg clone to protect the Bene Gesserit from any threat that they might pose; and the "watchers" who observe as Sheeana restores the Teg clone's persona include several potentially destructive watchmen, as three of them are Bene Gesserit Proctors "prepared to kill" the clone should he exhibit any sign that he may be another kwisatz haderach (*Chapterhouse*, 70, 291, 296).

In the departure stage's final incident the hero is "swallowed" in "the belly of the whale," a journey to the World Womb or World Navel in which "the hero goes inward, to be born again" (Campbell, 90–91). This is often either a literal or a symbolic underground journey that depicts a literal or figurative descent into hades, and *memento mori* in the form of bones or skeletons are sometimes in evidence. The hero may be literally or symbolically mutilated, dismembered, or killed; or he may merely enter a temple or similar structure that is guarded by gargoyles (92). The Idaho gholas and Teg clone must each "go inward, to be born again," of course, in that each must be brought to a point of internal crisis that will reawaken the original persona; thus, the journey to the World Womb is implicit in each of their stories, even if the narrative does not depict the moment of reawakening (as in Idaho ghola number 3's case). Of particular interest in connection with the remaining monomythic heroes, Paul and Leto II, is Campbell's assertion that "the hero as the incarnation of God is himself the navel of the world, the umbilical point through which the energies of eternity break into time" (41), for both are worshiped as gods, and the Bene Gesserit ultimately conclude that they did not so much predict the future as create its specific path or shape with their prescient powers.

Arrakis in general and its desert in particular—the unknown worlds of the first four Dune novels—are repeatedly compared to "hell" in *Dune* (44–45, 124, 196, 209, 263, 284); and Gammu, the location of *Heretics'* unknown world, is referred to as a "hell hole" several times in *Heretics* (235, 375) and *Chapterhouse* (256). The worms, which literally threaten to "swallow" Paul and Jessica in the desert, also reinforce this reading of Dune as hell in that the biblical Satan is cast into hades in the form of a serpent. The Fremen word "Shaitan" means "Satan" as well as sandworm (*Dune*, 529), and—like Milton's Satan, only more literally—the worms carry their hell within them, another interesting inversion. Due to its peculiar metabolic chemistry, a worm's "burning mouth" resembles a "cave of mysterious fire" in which Odrade sees "reflections of lambent orange flames" (*Heretics*, 249). Worms are successfully relocated to the planet Chapterhouse, which is *Chapterhouse's* unknown world.

In a series of literal underground journeys, Paul and Jessica are buried alive by a sandstorm in their first night in a stilltent in the open desert; are subsequently taken "down rock steps into darkness" to an underground desert "cave chamber," the Ecological Testing Station in which Idaho dies defending them; find temporary sanctuary from the worms in the subterranean Cave of the Ridges to which Stilgar leads them; and finally find refuge in Sietch Tabr, a larger series of underground caverns (*Dune*, 220, 288). After his duel with Jamis in the Cave of the Ridges, Paul receives his Fremen "troop name.... Usul" from Stilgar and chooses Paul-Muad'Dib as his public "name of manhood," a dual rechristening that signifies his rebirth as a member of Stilgar's troop; he later declares, "I am a Fremen born this day" when he subsequently performs the "rite to initiate a sandrider"and mounts a sandworm without assistance (306–7, 404, 338). Paul's most crucial death and rebirth experience occurs later still, when he transmutes the Water of Life in the Cave of Birds and *"lay as one dead"* for three weeks before reviving (437). His symbolic mutilation is displaced, however, as it occurs when Mohiam tests him with "the box" in the first chapter, and "he thought he could feel ... the flesh crisping and dropping away" from his hand (9).

In an initial inversion of an underground journey, Leto II emerges from Sietch Tabr, an underworld, into the open desert to fake his death at the claws of the Laza tigers in *Children*; yet he avoids being slain by the tigers only by going underground again, diving several meters into a "narrow cut in the rocks ... until darkness enfolded him" (183). Like Paul, he also spends a night in a stilltent beneath the sand, to avoid detection after killing the tigers. His destination—Jacurutu, "the perfect place for the dead to hide" (213)—is yet another underground sietch, one in which he is first bludgeoned unconscious and then repeatedly threatened with death before being quizzed by Assan Tariq's father, Namri, who "saw himself as Mirzabah, the Iron Hammer with which the dead are beaten who cannot reply satisfactorily to the questions they must answer before entry into paradise" (247). Moreover, Jacurutu is guarded by a type of gargoyle—"a sinuous rock outcropping" that "lay like an immense worm atop the sand, flat and threatening" (234). After escaping Jacurutu, Leto II again buries himself alive beneath the sand in a stilltent, this time to escape a sandstorm; too deep beneath the surface to get air, he "sent himself into a dormancy trance where his lungs would move only once an hour" (302)—a deathlike state similar to the trance in which Paul lay for three weeks after drinking the Water of Life. Already symbolically killed, "dead to her" as a consequence of the hypnotic suggestion that Ghanima employs to convince herself that he has been slain by the tigers, Leto II is also mutilated in the desert when he allows the sand trout to penetrate his body: "He was no longer human. Cilia had crept into his flesh, forming a new creature" (338–39).

Idaho ghola number 3 endures several underground journeys that are clearly symbolic descents into hell in *God Emperor*. The ghola's first and many subsequent interviews with Leto II occur in an underground "crypt … which Idaho found so repellant—the dust of centuries there and the odors of ancient decay" (209). Leto II's "crypt" is literally a "mausoleum," and its sepulchral contents constitute a particularly pointed *memento mori* for the ghola, as "mostly the Duncans," his identical predecessors in Leto II's service, are interred there (37). The no-globe to which Idaho ghola number 4 initially flees in *Heretics* is hidden underground, inside a "cave," and the "Harkonnen griffins" decorating its "access tube" are its gargoyles (221). As much a mausoleum as Leto II's "crypt," the no-globe also contains explicit *memento mori* in the form of "twenty-one skeletons preserved in transparent plaz along a wall … the artisans who had built the place, all slain by the Harkonnens to preserve the secret" (224). While Teg reawakens Idaho ghola number 4's original persona within the no-globe, through a process that might be considered a symbolic dismemberment in that it creates "mental and physical agony in an almost helpless victim," the Bene Gesserit pretend that Teg, Lucilla, and the ghola are dead by staging a "dramatic and believable" show of "mourning" as a diversion while attempting to find the missing trio (233, 270). Leaving the no-globe, Idaho ghola number 4 and Lucilla descend into "the stygian outlet of the tunnel" leading to a command center inside a live tree, but they soon find a more secure subterranean haven in a "room apparently cut into rock" in a "cave complex"—to which the ghola is led in darkness by a "cord" clipped to his belt, a metaphorical umbilical cord, and where he is symbolically reborn when disguised as a Tleilaxu Master (325, 327, 372). Similarly, the Teg clone is symbolically reborn in a metaphorical underground location when Teg's persona is reawakened, for Idaho ghola number 4's "no-ship prison … was a cave of wonders," and the specific room in which Teg's persona is restored to his clone reminds Odrade of "an animal's cave" (*Chapterhouse*, 70, 288).

The first incident in the monomyth's initiation stage is the road of trials, a series of tests in which the hero is aided by the supernatural helpers' advice or agents, by the talismans given him, or by a "benign power everywhere supporting him"; it may also require that the hero "assimilates his opposite," which may be his own "unsuspected self" or shadow (Campbell, 97, 108). Paul's prescience is the "benign power everywhere supporting him," and his three most critical trials are all explicit initiation rituals. The first is Mohiam's "test" involving the box, a Bene-Gesserit rite intended "to determine if you're human"; the second is "the deadly test" of mounting and riding a sandworm, the Fremen "rite to initiate a sandrider"; the third is "*the test that the Reverend Mothers have survived,"* transmuting the poisonous Water of Life (*Dune*, 9, 386, 388, 437). Paul's duel with Jamis is a similar trial. Jamis invokes "the amtal rule," the "test to destruction," in challenging Paul; Stilgar affirms that "death is the test of it"; and immediately afterwards Paul is accepted as a member of Stilgar's troop and twice rechristened (299, 513, 303).

Paul assimilates his opposite—who is also his unsuspected self, his shadow—in his final trial in *Dune*, his duel with Feyd. Not only are the Atreides presented as foils to the Harkonnens, *"the Light"* to their *"Darkness,"* throughout the novel—while Paul realizes in the desert that *"he is Harkonnen"* through Jessica—but Paul and Feyd, cousins who are almost the same age, are also meticulously developed as shadows (13, 205). Had Jessica obeyed and given birth to a daughter, instead of to Paul, the Bene Gesserit would have mated her to Feyd to produce their Kwisatz Haderach in the next generation. The Baron's observation that Feyd "aspires to rule my Barony, yet he cannot rule himself" immediately follows Paul's test with the box, which demonstrates his self-control (17). Similarly, Paul's duel with Jamis, a fair fight in which Paul is reluctant to kill his opponent, is juxtaposed to Feyd's hundredth gladiatorial match, a fixed fight in which Feyd demonstrates his bloodthirsty ruthlessness; afterward, Count Fenring compares the two youths in wondering what Feyd "could've been with some other upbringing—with the Atreides code to guide him, for example" (339). Paul loves his father and strives to avenge his death, while Feyd despises the Baron and attempts to assassinate him. Moreover, while the Baron plots to have Feyd "go to Arrakis as their savior" and eventually *"gain the throne,"* Paul becomes both the Fremen "messiah" and, immediately after killing Feyd, the emperor (379, 235, 101).

Early in *Children*, Leto II predicts that he and Ghanima will "be tested … in the spice … in the desert and in the Trial of Possession," and Jessica believes that "Leto had to be tested" to assure that he is not possessed by any of the personae inhabiting his "other memories" (80–81, 205). Following his ordeal with the Laza tigers, his spice ordeal that is the test for possession conducted at Jacurutu, and his subsequently surviving a sandstorm in the desert, Leto II's final test is to accept the "Golden Path"—"this trial he and Ghanima had chosen"—and thus submit to losing his humanity by merging with the sand trout (237). Leto II must then assimilate his opposite twice— in his final confrontations with his shadow, Alia, and his double, Farad'n. Alia is Leto II's shadow, not only as the "Regent" ruling in his and Ghanima's name but also in that she, too, is "born with a totality of genetic memory, a terrifying awareness that set their Aunt Alia and themselves apart from all other living humans"; possessed by the Baron's persona, she is the "abomi-nation" that either twin may yet become (10, 4, 51). While Leto II is raised on Arrakis, Farad'n is raised on Salusa Secundus, which is "much like Arrakis" (*Dune*, 32). Both have "doubts" about wanting "to become Emperor" (*Children*, 82, 92); both have prescient dreams (*see* 34, 86, 113); and Jessica, who becomes Farad'n's teacher and surrogate mother, discovers that "he … was consciously copying the Atreides" and that "he reminded her with heart-tugging abruptness of her own lost son," Leto II's father Paul (211, 252). Leto II's return to Arrakeen forces Alia to reveal that "she was possessed" and to commit suicide; he then takes control of Farad'n's troops, makes Farad'n his "Scribe" and (as Ghanima's husband) the "secret father of [his] royal line," and renames him Harq al-Ada (393, 407).

Hayt's crucial trial in *Messiah* is to overcome the Tleilaxu compulsion to kill Paul, once it is triggered, by recovering his original's persona. Ironically, his "supernatural" helpers are the Tleilaxu themselves, who had implaned the compulsion as a mechanism for reviving the persona; Bijaz, who activates the compulsion at the appropriate time, is their agent. Hayt's unsuspected self is not only his original's persona, which he literally assimilates by inte-grating it into his personality once it is resurrected, but also Bijaz, his shadow in that they "are like brothers" who "grew in the same tank"; the ghola is the dwarf's "target … the instrument [he] was taught to play," and Hayt finally kills Bijaz at Paul's command (228–29). The remaining Idaho gholas and the Teg clone each endure a similar trial, among others, that results in the assim-ilation of his unsuspected self in that each likewise experiences a trauma that reawakens his original's persona, which each then integrates into his person-ality.

The hero might also encounter a goddess, a temptress, or both. The god-dess may be "the Lady of the House of Sleep," who is bliss and perfection, or the "universal mother," who is the combination of all opposites; and this meeting sometimes culminates in a mystical marriage at a special location; however, the goddess may be the "bad mother"—who is absent, unattainable, forbidding, punishing, or the locus of forbidden desire and who may threaten castration (Campbell, 109–10, 113–14, 120–25, 111). Three women in *Dune* rep-resent various aspects of the goddess. Chani, who appears repeatedly to Paul in his earliest prescient dreams, is the "Lady of the House of Sleep." The com-plex and rebellious Jessica is the "universal mother" who combines all oppo-sites. Reverend Mother Mohiam is the "bad mother," as the test with the box that she administers to Paul on Caladan is a symbolic castration. Paul also encounters temptresses in Harah, Jamis' widow, whom he must accept for one year as either wife or servant, and in Irulan, a statuesque beauty whom he takes as his wife to secure the throne but whom he steadfastly refuses to take as his lover.

The Fremen view Alia as a "*demi-goddess*," a "goddess," and "*the womb of heaven*" in *Messiah* (91, 109, 209), where she assumes the roles of the "Lady of the House of Sleep" and the terrifying "universal mother" who combines all opposites. In "telling the story of the Far Places visited by the Priestess in her holy trance," Alia's acolytes chant that "she guards our dreaming souls," and "The Irulan Report" on "St. Alia of the Knife" notes that "*she represents ultimate tension*"; Bijaz expands on this in telling Hayt that "she is the virgin-harlot.... She is vulgar, witty, knowledgeable to a depth that terrifies, cruel when she is most kind, unthinking when she thinks, and when she seeks to build she is as destructive as a coriolis storm" (180, 91, 227). Sabiha, Namri's daughter, is "the Lady of the House of Sleep" and the temptress in *Children*. She guards Leto II while he endures the spice ordeal at Jacurutu, and his visions of the two of them "entwined in love" (281) tempt him to renounce his "Golden Path," whose necessary metamorphosis dictates celibacy. Jessica becomes the "bad mother" in *Children*. Much like Mohiam vis-à-vis Paul on Caladan, she arrives on Arrakis after a twenty-three-year absence prepared to kill Leto II and Ghanima with a "poisoned needle ... the gom jabbar" (99) should they prove to be possessed. Alia and Farad'n's mother, Wensicia, who plot independently to murder the twins, also assume the role of the "goddess" as "bad mother" in *Children*.

Siona is the "goddess" to Idaho ghola number 3, although both rebel against Leto II's plan to mate them throughout *God Emperor*, and Hwi Noree is Idaho ghola number 3's temptress; even though their love is forbidden because she is Leto II's fiancée, Hwi and the ghola yield to their mutual temptation during one night of passion in the Citadel. Reverend Mother Lucilla, a professional seductress who has been ordered to sexually imprint Idaho ghola number 4, is the temptress in *Heretics*, but Idaho ghola number 4 is able to resist her advances after Teg restores his original persona. Reverend Mother Schwangyu, who plots with the Tleilaxu to have Idaho ghola number 4 killed, is his "bad mother." So is Murbella, the Honored Matre whose plan to use her sexual amplification techniques to enslave the ghola goes awry when Idaho ghola number 4's Tleilaxu conditioning compels him to use those same techniques on her simultaneously, but their consequent mutual bonding ultimately makes Murbella Idaho ghola number 4's "goddess." Sheeana is the temptress who seduces the pubescent Teg clone in a successful attempt to restore his original's persona in a more humane way in *Chapterhouse*. Ironically, the clone perceives her as a "bad mother," for he has been conditioned to resist sexual imprinting and mistakes her actions as an attempt to imprint him. The true "bad mothers" in *Chapterhouse* are Great Honored Matre Logno, who captures the Teg clone and Odrade, and the predecessor whom she had assassinated, Great Honored Matre Dama, who murders Lucilla and is responsible for the Bene Gesserit's near-extermination, Dune's incineration, and the original Teg's death. In another irony, Odrade, Teg's daughter and the Mother Superior who wants her subordinates to rebel, is the "universal mother" who combines all opposites vis-à-vis the Teg clone, who calls her "mother" throughout *Chapterhouse* (14, 293, 307).

After encountering the goddess and temptress, the monomythic hero may experience atonement with the father or a father figure, who is "the initiating priest through whom the young being passes on into the larger world," but this "requires an abandonment of the attachment to ego itself"; and the "initiation rites" that enact atonement with the father may contain both "a dramatized expression of the Oedipal aggression of the older generation; and the ... patricidal impulse of the younger," as "there is a new element of rivalry in the picture: the son against the father for mastery of the universe" (Campbell, 136, 130, 139, 136). The father can be, and often appears to be, a tyrant or ogre, and the son cannot achieve atonement until he sees beyond this manifestation of the father. The hero "must have faith that the father is merciful, and then a reliance on that mercy. Therewith ... the dreadful ogres dissolve," the hero "beholds the face of the father, understands—and the two are atoned" (130, 147). Paul vows to avenge his father by overcoming the tyrant-ogre father figures personified in the Baron Harkonnen (his maternal grandfather) and the Emperor. As Emperor, Paul is himself a father figure to Hayt; he is "the initiating priest" through whom the hero "passes into the world" in that he is the recipient of their gift as well as the catalyst that the Tleilaxu use to reawaken the ghola's original persona. Hayt is conditioned to murder Paul when he speaks the words "she is gone" on learning of Chani's death, but the resulting conflict between this compulsion and the original persona's loyalty to the Atreides forces that original persona to emerge. This staged psychic drama, which compels the Idaho-ego to supplant the ghola-ego, combines wonderfully the idea that atonement with the father "requires an abandonment of the attachment to ego" with the notion that it also may contain "a dramatized expression of the ... patricidal impulse."

Paul is also "the initiating priest" through whom Leto II "passes into the world" in two quite different ways. First, Paul prevents Leto II from being assassinated moments after his birth by killing Scytale at the conclusion of *Messiah*. Subsequently, in *Children*, the Paul-persona within Leto II promises, "I will protect you in the trance. The others within will not take you" (255) when Leto II undergoes the spice ordeal at Jacurutu, an initiation ritual in which he must abandon attachment to his ego to establish a harmony with his "other memories," any one of which might otherwise possess him. Thus, Leto II "let go of himself and became himself, his own person compassing the entirety of his past" (279). After escaping Jacurutu and merging with the sand trout, Leto II finds Paul in the desert and "beholds the face of the father": "Leto studied this face, seeing the lines of likeness as though they had been outlined in light. The lines formed an indefinable reconciliation" (341). Then Leto II forces Paul into a "battle of the visions" from which he knows "*only one vision will emerge*" (343, 334)—an atonement that is also a contest "for mastery of the universe," for when Leto II's vision prevails, Paul acknowledges, "This is your universe now" and agrees to "do his bidding" (346, 372).

Much as Paul as Emperor is a benign father figure to Hayt in *Messiah*, so, too, in *God Emperor* is Leto II as the Tyrant an ogre-father to Idaho ghola number 3. Leto II is "the initiating priest" through whom Idaho ghola number 3 passes into the world in that the ghola is created solely for his service, and his conflict with Leto II is "oedipal" as well as "patricidal," for his proximate emotional motivation for killing Leto II is to prevent him from marrying Hwi Noree. This is also a contest for mastery of the universe, which must be wrested from Leto II through his death so that it can revert back to humanity, for "the hero is to slay the tenacious aspect of the father (dragon, tester, ogre king) and release from its ban the vital energies that feed the universe ... in accordance with the father's will or against it" (Campbell, 352). As The Worm, Leto II is the tyrant-ogre as "dragon," and his Worm's-body—literally his "tenacious aspect" because it is responsible for his longevity—literally "dissolves" when it is plunged into the Idaho River. It is Leto II's "will" that Idaho ghola number 3 and Siona slay him, and atonement is achieved when he tells the ghola, "I think of all my Duncans I approve of you the most" (419). Much as Paul is "the initiating priest" through whom Hayt "passes into the world"— the catalyst through whom Hayt's original Duncan Idaho persona is resurrected—so, too, is Teg, already a father figure to Idaho ghola number 4, the "initiating priest" through whom Idaho ghola number 4 regains his original persona in *Heretics*. Reciprocally, in *Chapterhouse*, Idaho, ghola number 4 is the "initiating priest" to the Teg clone in that the more humane method used to awaken the Teg persona had been his "idea" (293). The atonement of resurrected "son" and father figure as "initiating priest" in both *Heretics* and *Chapterhouse* occurs when the "son" in each instance forgives the father figure for the pain involved in the reawakening.

The penultimate incident in the initiation stage is the hero's apotheosis. This is symbolized by an annihilation of consciousness that entails the merging of time and eternity and is characterized by a symbolic transcendence of duality—representing a return to the lost unity that preceded creation—signaled by the unification of such opposites as time and eternity, good and evil, male and female, birth and death, truth and illusion, or friend and enemy. Paul's apotheosis occurs when he finally transmutes the Water of Life and enters the plane of apotheosis for the three weeks in which he lies in a death-like trance, his consciousness annihilated, while exploring his visions. His prescience is itself essentially a conflation of time and eternity, but in transmuting the Water of Life he also unites within himself the male/female polarity through becoming a male Bene Gesserit Reverend Mother.

Leto II as monomythic hero experiences a similar apotheosis in *Children* when he endures the spice ordeal at Jacurutu; he literally transcends his humanity soon afterward when he merges with the sand trout, a metamorphosis that makes him "*a living god*" (400) to his Fremen followers but that is also a unification of the man/beast polarity. As the Tyrant who must deprive humanity of freedom for over three millennia to ensure its salvation, he also unites the good/evil, cruelty/kindness, friend/enemy polarities. Moreover, as the phallic "Worm" who has lost his male reproductive organs to his gradual metamorphosis but can nourish Siona in the desert by having her "tease … moisture" from "flaps" near his face while she lies in the marsupial-like pouch formed by his front segment (*Emperor*, 347), he is also "the image of the bisexual god" of myth—"that father" who is "the womb, the mother, of a second birth … so that death was not the end" (Campbell, 162 passim), in that his death by immersion in water is also the rebirth of the sandworms. The Teg clone and Idaho gholas all experience apotheosis in the annihilation of consciousness that accompanies the reawakening of their originals' personae. Idaho ghola number 4 experiences a second and greater apotheosis when Murbella reawakens all of his past ghola selves, and both Idaho ghola number 4 and the Teg clone emulate the archetypal final apotheosis of the Buddha when they symbolically "shatter … the bounds of the last threshold" (Campbell, 150) in escaping from their universe into another, "unidentifiable universe" at the conclusion of *Chapterhouse* (427).

Receiving the ultimate boon, which represents "the means for the regeneration of [the hero's] society as a whole" (Campbell, 38), is the final incident in the initiation stage. The ultimate boon in its highest form is transcendent revelation, but the hero usually seeks such lesser gifts as immortality or extended life, power, or wealth (189). The transcendent revelation bestowed by their prescient visions at the moment of apotheosis is the greatest boon acquired by both Paul and Leto II, and in both instances this boon represents the regeneration of their societies. Paul uses his prescience to free the Fremen from Harkonnen bondage, and Leto II uses his to ensure the survival of humanity through the establishment of his "Golden Path," which leads to humankind's regeneration in the Scattering. Paul's and Leto II's boons also entail the acquisition of supreme power and wealth, and Leto's metamorphosis greatly extends his life span. The Teg clone and Idaho gholas achieve a more limited revelation in the apotheoses that accompany the resurrections of their originals' personae, and Idaho ghola number 4's second apotheosis leads to a series of further revelations. This rebirth of personality that completes the resurrection of their bodies from the axlotl tanks is also a form of serial "immortality" (*Chapterhouse*, 80), however, and Leto II bestows the lesser boons of power and wealth on Idaho ghola number 3 in predicting that the Fish Speaker army will choose him as their leader and in revealing to him the location of the vast spice hoard at Sietch Tabr.

Several incidents may occur in the return stage; but some are mutually exclusive, and only several—rather than most or all, as in the earlier stages—are likely to appear in any given narrative. The hero could refuse to return or give the boon to humanity, his return could be opposed or furthered by "magic" means, his attempt to return could end in failure, or he could be rescued from outside the unknown world; in crossing the return threshold, the hero might convey new wisdom to the known world, reject the unknown world to embrace the known world, experience a dilation of time, encounter danger that requires him to insulate himself from the known world, or return with a talisman of his quest; and on returning, the hero may become the "master of the two worlds," which involves acquiring the ability to pass freely between them, or achieve the "freedom to live," to work in the known world without anxiety as a conscious vehicle of the cosmic cycle of change (Campbell, 193–243). While Leto II is tempted to "*just walk away into that desert*" (*Children*, 381) rather than return to the known world, only Idaho ghola number 4 and, to a lesser extent, the Teg clone refuse to return and share their boons. Idaho ghola number 4 hides the reawakening of all his past ghola personae and those talents that he acquires in his second apotheosis from the Bene Gesserit because he fears that "they would suspect he was a latent Kwisatz Haderach," and the Teg clone likewise feels that "they must not learn the full extent of my abilities" for the same reason (*Chapterhouse*, 71, 305) At the conclusion of *Chapterhouse*, Idaho, ghola number 4 and the Teg clone escape from the known universe in their no-ship prison and choose to cross the threshold to a new unknown world rather than return to their known worlds (the Gammu Keep and Chapterhouse, respectively).

The only example of a rescue from outside the unknown world in these novels is Teg's liberation, prior his death on Rakis, of Idaho ghola number 4 (and his companions) from Honored-Matre captivity on Gammu, which occurs between chapters in *Heretics*. In *Dune*, Paul's return to Arrakeen is both opposed by "magic" means, the Guild fleet orbiting Arrakis and five legions of Sardaukar camped on the Arrakeen plain, and furthered by "magic" means—Paul's prescience, his willingness to use the "Water of Death" to destroy the spice, the great sandstorm through which the Fremen attack astride giant worms, and the use of "atomics" to blast a way for storm and worms through the Shield Wall. Leto II's return from the desert to Arrakeen in *Children* is also furthered by "magic" means, the super-human speed and strength that he acquires through his metamorphosis; his invulnerable sand trout skin is the "insulation" that protects him from the "danger" of returning, Alia's treachery. Each monomythic hero experiences a dilation of time in the unknown world, but this always occurs during his apotheosis, not during the return-threshold crossing. The three-week trance that Paul experiences after transmuting the Water of Life, while occupying an eternity of subjective time, seems to him to have occupied only a "few minutes" of real time (*Dune*, 443). Leto II experiences similar time dilations during his spice ordeal in *Children*. The Teg clone and Idaho gholas each experience each original persona's entire lifetime in the instant in which each is awakened, and in his second apotheosis Idaho ghola number 4 also acquires in a moment the "memories" of all his previous lives as a ghola, "until he wondered how he could hold them all" (*Heretics*, 426).

Each monomythic hero likewise leaves the unknown world with a human talisman and with an awareness that he is the vehicle of the cosmic cycle of change. Leto II brings back Paul, in the guise of The Preacher, in *Children*; and Paul, the Idaho gholas, and the Teg clone each acquires his "goddess" in the unknown world and usually takes her from it. Paul returns from the desert with Chani in *Dune*; Hayt falls in love with Alia in Paul's court in *Messiah*; Idaho number 3 leaves Leto II's Citadel for Tuono with Siona in *God Emperor*; Idaho number 4 leaves Gammu with Murbella in *Heretics*; and the Teg clone escapes from both Chapterhouse and the known universe with Sheeana in *Chapterhouse*. Leto II, who calls himself "the first truly long-range planner in human history," vows "to create a new conscious-ness in all men" as he anticipates a 4,000-year reign as Emperor in *Children* (396, 406); and Paul tells Chani, "We are at a turning point in the succession of ages and we have our parts to play" in *Messiah* (205). Hayt—who imme-diately echoes Paul's last words in *Messiah*, "Now I am free" (272)—had achieved his "freedom to live" in acquiring his original Duncan Idaho per-sona. Idaho ghola number 3 becomes the "master of the two worlds" upon Leto II's death, which anticipates his assuming temporal power in the empire; and he becomes a vehicle of cosmic change both through participating in

Leto II's assassination and through becoming Siona's mate and thus the father of the "new Atreides" who are invisible to prescience (*Emperor*, 420). Both Idaho ghola number 4 and the Teg clone gain the ability to pass freely between the known and unknown worlds only when they finally escape their Bene Gesserit captivity in their stolen no-ship—but use that freedom to cross a new threshold to a greater unknown.

The mutations, inversions, and variations on the monomyth that occur as the Dune series progresses underscore a crucial insight common to both chaos theory and the Dune series—that everything changes—yet, like chaos theory, the monomyth, too, indicates that even perpetual change occurs within the dynamics of a still larger pattern that governs transition on the border of chaos and order. The central death-and-resurrection motif that resonates throughout the monomyth, being "swallowed in the belly of the whale," the hero's "passing and returning[,] demonstrate that through all the contraries of phenomenality the Uncreate-Imperishable remains" (Campbell, 93). Herbert's aesthetic achievement in mirroring the Dune series' ecological (chaos theory) theme in a fractal structure through recycling the monomyth is marvelously compounded, not only in that mirroring is the essence of any fractal structure, but also in that the monomyth is already thoroughly fractal—in its derivation, its own structure, and its symbolic significance as a vehicle for conveying the concept of spiritual enlightenment.

The Monomyth and Chaos Theory

Not only does Frank Herbert's original Dune series replicate the monomyth's theme, transcendence, as well as its plot structure, but it also echoes the fractal pattern incorporated into both this plot structure and the thought process involved in transcending dualities to attain enlightenment that this plot structure not only represents but also embodies—in its "Meeting with the Goddess," "Atonement with the Father," and "Apotheosis" episodes, which collectively recapitulate the Bodhisattva myth as a way to enlightenment (*See* Campbell, 149–71). "A visual representation of chaotic behavior," a fractal is an image "with an infinite amount of self-similarity" generated in "the realm of dynamical systems" by the "repeated application of an algorithm" or the reiteration of recursive geometric procedures (Laplante, 20, 3–4, 14–15). "Above all, fractal [means] self-similar" (Gleick, 103), and "'self-similarity' … means a repetition of detail at descending scales" (Briggs and Peat, 90)— "pattern inside of pattern" (Gleick, 103)—as well as duplication across the same scale. Thus, in a fractal image "the structure of the whole is often

reflected in every part," and any part might appear to be both "a small reproduction of the larger image" and a near-clone of innumerable like structures
on the same scale (Laplante, 3). "As … incorporation of the separate epipha-
nies of the Mother Goddess and the Father into the encompassing revelation
of the bisexual god [the Bodhisattva] suggests … the very process of transcendence through which one is to achieve enlightenment has a familiar
shape—the fractal structure of self-similarity on descending scales. This
process is the attainment of revelation-within-revelation or of revelation-
beyond-revelation, depending on how one looks at it; and both ways of looking at it are ultimately the same, just as both describe the same structure, the
pattern of self-similarity on descending scales also exhibited in the temporal
structure of the cosmogonic cycle [revealed to the hero in Apotheosis], with
its progressively lesser cycles nested within each great round, and the analogous shells-within-shells physical structure of the cosmic egg," both of which
Campbell discusses extensively (Palumbo, 200; see also 200–216 and Campbell, 255–378).

As the thought process through which one attains enlightenment exhibits
a fractal structure—a complex fractal matrix of thought—it is not too surprising that the monomyth itself, which represents and embodies this process,
also exhibits a fractal structure. One can discern this structure by keeping in
mind, first, that the Bodhisattva myth is a way to enlightenment that also
reveals the monomyth's symbolic meaning, attaining enlightenment and conveying it to others, and, second, that the monomyth "is a magnification of the
formula represented in the rites of passage: *separation—initiation—return*,"
yet—as "separation" here is "some sort of dying to the world" followed by "the
interval of the hero's nonentity, so that he comes back as one reborn"—the
reenactment of this formula in these rites symbolizes death-and-rebirth as a
metaphor for the initiate's transcendence of one "stage" of life to the next, so
that each repetition of the death-and-rebirth motif within the monomyth is
a reiteration of its overall "*separation—initiation—return*" structure on a
smaller scale (Campbell, 30, 35–36). Then, by relying solely on Campbell's
explications of the monomyth's seventeen episode, one can deduce that each
episode "mirrors the monomyth as a whole in at least one of three ways: by
echoing its 'separation—initiation—return' structure symbolically in one or
more death-and-rebirth incidents, symbols, or metaphors; by representing
this structure literally in containing one or more initiation rituals per se; or
by reflecting the symbolic action of the whole, which is attaining enlightenment and conveying it to others, through recapitulating in a relevant context
one or more aspects of the Bodhisattva myth" (Palumbo, *Chaos*, 218; see 216–
23 for a thorough analysis of each episode).

Like the monomyth itself, Hayles' analysis of chaos theory as a paradigm shift related to the larger paradigm shift of "cultural postmodernism" entails a death-and-rebirth metaphor as a symbol of transcendence, for she defines "cultural postmodernism as the realization that what has always been thought of as the essential, unvarying components of human experience are not natural facts of life but social constructions[,] ... a denaturing process," and argues that "when the essential components of human experience are denatured ... the human subject ... is also deconstructed and then reconstructed in ways that fundamentally alter what it means to be human. The postmodern anticipates and implies the posthuman" (265–66). She argues that this chaos theory paradigm also involves a "denaturing of time"—in which we no longer perceive time as a "continuous orderly progression" but have instead a "growing sense that the future is already used up before it arrives"—and that "the denaturing of time" leads to "the denaturing of the human," which entails abolishing "at least three distinct oppositions ... human/animal ... human/machine ... and physical/nonphysical" (279, 282, 284). As a consequence of their prescience, both Paul and Leto II are tormented by this sense "that the future, like the past, has already happened" (279); and while Paul's prescience more clearly exhibits "the denaturing of time," Leto II's transformation into The Worm embodies that loss of distinction between human and animal that signifies "the denaturing of the human." Likewise, Hayt embodies the loss of distinction between human and machine, in that his Tleilaxu eyes make him a cyborg; and Idaho ghola number 4 (with the Bene Gesserit, Paul, Alia, Ghanima, and Leto II) embodies the loss of distinction between physical and nonphysical, in that the locus of his memories of all his past ghola lives (like the loci of "other memories" and ancestral memories) is entirely problematical.

It is certainly possible that both Campbell's monomyth and chaos theory are accurate hypotheses, in which case the fact that the monomyth is so relentlessly consistent with chaos theory can be explained merely by observing that humanity intuited and inscribed in myths, as well as in prehistoric scroll loops and Celtic handicrafts, those same fractal structures underlying phenomenal reality that have only recently been perceived and investigated by scientists. However, an alternative and more logically persuasive explanation that does not depend on accepting either of these theories as "true" is that Campbell and the chaos theory scientists (and Herbert as well) are all pioneers anticipating or participating in the same comprehensive, emerging paradigm that has manifested itself at numerous sites within the same integrated culture at least since the early 1940s. That is, perhaps Campbell and the chaos theory scientists, in devising totalizing structures of myth and reality, respectively, are more immediately reflecting the same new paradigm that was just beginning to emerge during World War II and that is also mirrored in the relationship between content and structure in Herbert's fiction.

In any case, it is remarkable that Frank Herbert should develop this convoluted aesthetic of content echoing form echoing concept in a series in which the core concept's key premise is that content echoes form—the self-similarity of fractal geometry, which is indispensable to chaos theory, their mutual core concept—and even more remarkable that he began to do so before that concept was articulated by the scientific community. It is astonishing that the monomyth, the self-similar structure of myth reiterated in each Dune novel as the fractal structure that echoes the series' chaos theory concept, ecology, should in itself exhibit such a thorough fractal structure—and that the cosmogonic cycle, which the monomyth mirrors and symbolically contains, should also exhibit such a variety of temporal and physical fractal structures. But it is truly amazing that attaining enlightenment, part of the monomyth's symbolic action, involves the contemplation of a complex fractal matrix of thought. Analogously, in studying fractal basin boundaries in magnetization-and-nonmagnetization-in-materials phase transitions, mathematician Heinz-Otto Peitgen and physicist Peter Richter found fractal images that "seemed more and more random, until suddenly, unexpectedly, deep in the heart of a bewildering region, appeared a familiar oblate form, studded with buds: the Mandelbrot set, every tendril and every atom in place. It was another signpost of universality. 'Perhaps we should believe in magic,' they wrote" (Gleick, 236, citing *The Beauty of Fractals*). To find that the chaos theory concept informing the Dune series is mirrored in its fractal structures, that its recurring fractal structure is the monomyth, that the monomyth itself exhibits a thorough fractal structure and also mirrors the cosmogonic cycle and symbolizes the process of attaining enlightenment, and then to find that both the cosmogonic cycle and the process of attaining enlightenment exhibit their own fractal structures is to encounter a similar, dizzying phenomenon. In one way or another, this, too, indicates "universality"—or perhaps we should believe in magic!

Bibliography

Briggs, John, and F. David Peat. *Turbulent Mirror*. New York: Harper and Row, 1989; Perennial Library, 1990.

Campbell, Joseph. *The Hero with a Thousand Faces*. 2nd ed. Bollingen Series XVIII. Princeton: Princeton University Press, 1968.

DiTommaso, Lorenzo. "History and Historical Effect in Frank Herbert's *Dune*." *Science-Fiction Studies* 19 (1992), 311–25.

Gleick, James. *Chaos: Making a New Science*. New York: Penguin, 1987.

Hayles, N. Katherine. *Chaos Bound: Orderly Disorder in Contemporary Literature and Science*. Ithaca: Cornell University Press, 1990.

Herbert, Brian, and Kevin J. Anderson. *Dune: The Battle of Corrin*. New York: Tor, 2004.

———. *Dune: The Butlerian Jihad*. New York: Tor, 2002.

———. *Dune: House Atreides*. New York: Bantam, 1999.

———. *Dune: House Corrino*. New York: Bantam, 2001.

———. *Dune: House Harkonnen*. New York: Bantam, 2000.

———. *Dune: The Machine Crusade*. New York: Tor, 2003.

———. *Hunters of Dune*. New York: Tor, 2006.

———. *Mentats of Dune*. New York: Tor, 2014.

———. *Navigators of Dune*. New York: Tor, 2016.

———. *Paul of Dune*. New York: Tor, 2008.

———. *Sandworms of Dune*. New York: Tor, 2007.

———. *Sisterhood of Dune*. New York: Tor, 2011.

———. *The Winds of Dune*. New York: Tor, 2009.

Herbert, Frank. *Chapterhouse: Dune*. New York: G. P. Putnam's Sons, 1985; Ace Books, 1987.

———. *Children of Dune*. New York: Berkley Books, 1981.

———. *Dune*. New York: Chilton Book Co., 1965; Berkley Books, 1977; Ace Books, 1987.

———. *Dune Messiah*. New York: Berkley Books, 1975.

———. *God Emperor of Dune*. New York: G. P. Putnam's Sons, 1981; Berkley Books, 1983; Ace Books, 1987.

———. *Heretics of Dune*. New York: G. P. Putnam's Sons, 1984; Berkley Books, 1986.

Laplante, Phil. *Fractal Mania*. New York: Windcrest/McGraw Hill, 1994.

McLean, Susan. "A Question of Balance: Death and Immortality in Frank Herbert's Dune Series." In *Death and the Serpent*. Carl Yoke, ed. Westport, Connecticut: Greenwood Press, 1985.

McNelly, Willis E. *The Dune Encyclopedia*. New York: Berkley Books, 1984.

Palumbo, Donald E. *Chaos Theory, Asimov's Foundations and Robot's, and Herbert's Dune: The Fractal Aesthetic of Epic Science Fiction*. Contributions to the Study of Science Fiction and Fantasy, Number 100. Westport, Connecticut: Greenwood Press, 2002.

Prigogine, Ilya, and Isabelle Stengers. *Order Out of Chaos: Man's New Dialogue with Nature*. New York: Bantam, 1984.

Schmitt-v. Muhlenfels, Astrid. "The Theme of Ecology in Frank Herbert's *Dune* Novels." In *The Role of Geography in a Post-Industrial Society*. Hans W. Windhorst, ed. Vechta: Vechtaer Druckerei und Verlag GmbH, 1987.

Spinrad, Norman. "Emperor of Everything." In *Science Fiction in the Real World*. Carbondale: Southern Illinois University Press, 1990.

The Companion

Abad, Yakup (10,170–10,233)—Yakup Abad was a friend of Namri who, with Namri, saw Thatta's vision of the City of Tombs in the Arrakeen desert. [*Children of Dune*]

Abomination—Abomination is a Bene Gesserit term for someone pre-born—born with with all the powers and awareness of a Bene Gesserit Reverend Mother—who might become possessed by the persona of one of his or her ancestors as a consequence of repeatedly ingesting an overdose of spice. [*Dune, Children of Dune*]

Abumojandis (10,154–10,207)—An aide to Bannerjee, Abumojandis was a Fremen Naib and a traitor to Paul Muad'Dib who was identified as such by Bijaz in 10,207. [*Dune Messiah*]

Acline—Acline was a planet at which Bene Gesserit Supreme Bashar Miles Teg directed a major military engagement involving the sixty-seventh Gammu that saved many lives. [*Heretics of Dune*]

Agamemnon (prehistoric)—King of Mycenae, husband to Clytemnestra, and father to Orestes, Electra, and Iphigenia, Agamemnon was a distant ancestor of the Atreides and one of the personae inhabiting Alia Atreides' consciousness. [*Children of Dune*]

Agarves, Buer (10,199–10,218)—Small, round-faced Buer Agarves was a former citizen of Sietch Tabr who became Ziarenka Valefor's aide. In 10,216 the persona of Baron Vladimir Harkonnen possessing her urged Alia Atreides to have sexual relations with Agarves; Alia successfully resisted the Baron at first, but she subsequently capitulated. In 10,217 Agarves brought to Alia the news that her lover Ziarenko Javid and her husband Hayt (who had by then acquired Duncan Idaho's persona) were dead. Alia then ordered Agarves to seek and kill Stilgar, promising him that he would be the new Naib of Sietch Tabr once he brought her Stilgar's head, and Agarves led an unsuccessful search and destroy force that sought Stilgar and his companions, who had fled from Sietch Tabr into the desert. In 10,218 Argaves arranged a secret meeting with Stilgar in the Tanzerouf to bring him the false message that Alia would forgive him and his followers, including Ghanima and Irulan, if he would return Ghanima to Arrakeen. Stilgar murdered Agarves at that meeting, but a transmitter that Alia had secretly hidden in

Argaves' boot led to Stilgar's desert location kidnappers sent by Alia who abducted Stilgar, Ghanima, and Irulan. [*Children of Dune*]

Ahl as-sunna wal-jamas—Ahl as-sunna wal-jamas was a Fremen term that referred to the real world of the senses. [*Children of Dune*]

akarso—Akarso is a plant with yellow berries and oblong, green and white striped leaves that is native to the planet Sikun. The stimulant rachag is made from the akarso's yellow berries. [*Dune*]

Akeli, Reverend Mother (13,664–13,762)—Bene Gesserit Reverend Mother Akeli was an author of the Welbeck Abridgement, a 13,726 report to the Bene Gesserit. [*God Emperor of Dune*]

alam al-mithra—In Fremen mythology the alam al-mithra is the mystical world of similitudes in which all physical limitations are removed. [*Dune*]

Albans, Gilbertus (41–119)—Gilbertus Albans founded the Order of Mentats. [*Chapterhouse: Dune*]

Albe (10,096–10,169)—Albe was the famed artist who had painted the portrait of Duke Leto Atreides' father, Duke Paulus Atreides, that Lady Jessica had hung in the Great Hall of the Ducal Palace in Arrakeen in 10,191. [*Dune*]

Albertus (14,984–15,232)—Weak, poorly-educated Albertus was in 15,232 the senior Rakian priest at Dar-es-Balat. He was killed in the destruction of Ralkis. [*Heretics of Dune*]

Al Dhanab—One of the original Bene Gesserit safe planets, Al Dhanab was an inhospitable artificial world, much like Salusa Secundus, that the Bene Gesserit had once considered making into a planetary no-chamber, but the energy requirements made such a plan untenable. Senior Security Mother Darwi Odrade was sent to Al Dhanab to prepare her for her mission to Arrakis shortly after she had survived the Spice Agony. [*Heretics of Dune*]

al-Fali, Ghadhean (10,142–10,221)—Short, wiry, stately, beak-nosed, narrow-faced Ghadhean al-Fali was a Fremen Naib and one of Paul Muad'Dib's death commandos. In 10,216 he signed a petition addressed to Alia Atreides demanding that Jessica be placed on the Imperial Council. Subsequently, during one of Alia's morning audiences, he disabled a priest who had attempted to kill Jessica with a maula pistol in the mistaken belief that he was the intended target. He then stood back to back with Jessica, to shield her from harm, and later publicly complained to her that the sandworms were disappearing from Arrakis. Afterwards he helped Jessica escape Arrakeen to his own Sietch, Red Chasm Sietch, and was subsequently ordered by Jessica to go to Sietch Tabr. [*Children of Dune*]

Alhosa (15,128–15,232)—Puffy, fat, heavy-featured, blonde-haired Alhosa was a female Rakian priest who served as Sheeana's day attendant after she was adopted by the Rakian priests in 15,223. Alhosa was killed in the destruction of Rakis. [*Heretics of Dune*]

Ali, Shakir—Shakir Ali was a character from Fremen mythology who, with Thatta, had a vision of the City of Tombs. [*Children of Dune*]

Alia—*See* **Atreides, Lady Alia**.

Alia's Fane—A temple built for Alia Atreides against the wall of Emperor Paul Muad'Dib's keep, Alia's Fane contained Alia's Hall of Oracles. [*Dune Messiah*]

Aline (13,701–13,726)—One of Siona's ten companions in the theft in 13,726 of The Stolen Journals from Emperor Leto II's Citadel fortress in the Sareer, Aline was killed by a pack of D-wolves in Arrakis' Forbidden Forest following the raid on the Citadel. [*God Emperor of Dune*]

Alpha Centauri B—Alpha Centauri B is the star, part of a binary star system, about which the planet Ecaz orbits. [*Dune*]

Alyama—The word "Alyama" means "Blessed One" in Islamiyat, the ancient language of the Tleilaxu. Waff, the Tleilaxu Master of Masters, referred to Sheeana Brugh as "Alyama" when he encountered her on Rakis. [*Heretics of Dune*]

Ambitorm (14,920–15,232)—Old, wrinkled, dish-faced, flat-nosed, brown-eyed, springy, tireless Ambitorm, who was also known as Tormsa, was a Gammu native, disguised as a Face Dancer, who served as Duncan Idaho ghola number 4's guide after he and Reverend Mother Lucilla had escaped from the Harkonnen no-globe on Gammu and the ghola had disguised himself as a Tleilaxu Master. Ambitorm was ambushed and killed by Honored Matre Murbella in an abandoned factory on the outskirts of Ysai. [*Heretics of Dune*]

Ampoliros—The *Ampoliros*, a pre-Guild starship, is the legendary "Flying Dutchman" of space. [*Dune*]

Ampre (13,226–13,299)—Ampre was Director of Ix's Outfederation Affairs in 13,276. [*God Emperor of Dune*]

amtal rule—The amtal rule was the Freman practice of testing something to its destruction. On Arrakis the amtal rule involved a fight to the death to test the truth of a proposition. Jamis invoked the Amtal Rule in the Cave of Ridges in 10,191 to test if Paul Atreides was the Fremen Lisan Al-Gaib, and he was slain by Paul. [*Dune*]

"Analysis: The Arrakeen Crisis"—"Analysis: The Arrakkeen Crisis" is one of the many volumes authored by Princess Irulan. [*Dune*]

Analysis of History: Muad'Dib—A history of Muad'Dib thought to be heresy by the Qizarate (the priests of the Religion of Muad'Dib) and the Bene Gesserit, *Analysis of History: Muad'Dib* was written by Bronso of IX, who was subsequently condemned to death. [*Dune Messiah*]

Ancient Teachings—The Ancient Teachings are, collectively, one of the several factors that shaped the religious beliefs of the Imperium in the 102nd century, the time of Muad'Dib. The Ancient Teachings include the writings of the Zensunni Wanderers, the Navachristianity of Chusuk, the Buddislamic Variants of the types dominant at Lankiveil and Sikun, the Blend Books of the Mahayana Lankavatara, the Zen Hekiganshu of III Delta Pavonis, the Tawrah and Talmudic Zabur surviving on Salusa Secundus, the Obeah Ritual, the Muadh Quran of Caladan, the teachings of the universe's many Hindu outcroppings, and the lessons of the Butlerian Jihad. [*Dune*]

Andaud, Gaus (23,458–23,814)— Gaus Andaud was a noted 237th- and 238th-century historian who delivered a preoration on the metamorphosis of Emperor Leto II in 23,726, on the 10,000th anniversary of Leto II's death. [*Heretics of Dune*]

Andidyu—Andidyu was a planet on which a battle did not occur because Bene Gesserit Supreme Bashar Miles Teg's diplomacy had prevailed. [*Heretics of Dune*]

Angelika, Honored Matre (15,209–15,538)—Honored Matre Angelika unsuccessfully attacked Great Honored Matre Murbella on Junction immediately after Murbella had killed Great Honored Matre Longo and Senior Dame Elpek in 15,245. Murbella then spared Angelika, after she formally recognized that Murbella was the new Great Honored Matre, and named her to be the first member of Murbella's Honored Matre Council. [*Chapterhouse: Dune*]

Anirul (10,141–10,176)—A Bene Gesserit of Hidden Rank, Anirul was the wife of Emperor Shaddam IV. She bore him five daughters: Irulan, Chalice, Wensicia, Josifa, and Rugi. [*Dune*]

Anouk (13,701–13,739)—Anouk was an aide to Nayla who witnessed Siona's interview with Ixian Ambassador to Arrakis Iyo Kobat in Onn, on Arrakis, in 13,726. [*God Emperor of Dune*]

Anteac, Reverend Mother Tertius Eileen (13,666–13,726)—One of Reverend Mother Bellonda's ancestors, Bene Gesserit Reverend Mother Tertius Eileen Anteac—who had a mysterious scar on her forehead, a frightening manner, and the ability to detect Tlielaxu Face Dancer mimics—was a Truthsayer and a Mentat who attended the 13,726 festival in Onn, on Arrakis, with Reverend Mother Marcus Claire Luyseyal. The two Reverend Mothers were informed by Othwi Yake that Tleilaxu Face Dancers had infiltrated Arrakis' Ixian Embassy and would attempt to assassinate Emperor Leto II during his peregrination to Onn for the festival, and they conveyed this intelligence to Leto II via his Fish Speakers. Anteac and Luyseyal subsequently conversed with Leto II when he met with the Bene Gesserit delegation to the festival in False Sietch, and Anteac later summoned Hwi Noree to meet with Leto II. Leto II then sent Anteac to locate Malky and the Ixian no-globe after Hwi Noree had given Anteac details about the device in which she had been conceived, born, and raised. Anteac once spoke to a Duncan Idaho ghola, probably Duncan Idaho Ghola number 2, on Wallach IX. She was killed during the Fish Speaker raid on Ix that captured Malky. [*God Emperor of Dune, Chapterhouse: Dune*]

Aql—Aql was the Fremen test of reason that was administered at Minah to those youths who wished to be accepted as adults. [*Dune*]

Arafel—"Arafel" was a Fremen term that signified the cloud-darkness of holy judgement at the end of the universe. [*God Emperor of Dune, Heretics of Dune*]

Aramsham, Captain (10,151–10,195)—A tall, flat-featured, scarred Sardaukar commander, Captain Aramsham was captured by Paul Atreides and his Fedaykin in the Cave of Birds in 10,193. Paul allowed Aramsham and another Sardaukar captive to escape so that they could bring word to Emperor Shaddam IV that Paul still lived and was the alter ego of the Fremen leader Muad'Dib. [*Dune*]

Arbelough—At the battle for the planet Arbelough, which had been infiltrated and perverted by Face Dancers, Bene Gesserit Supreme Bashar Miles Teg joined his troops at the front to bolster their morale. [*Heretics of Dune*]

arifa—Arifa is a Fremen term for "judge." [*Children of Dune*]

Arkie (10,168–10,191)—Arkie was an Atreides soldier who died shortly after the fall of Arrakeen to the Harkonnens. Thufir Hawat permitted the Fremen to take Arkie's body and to extract the water from his corpse, as the Fremen do with their own dead, as a sign that the remaining Atreides troopers under his command had joined the Fremen. [*Dune*]

Arkwright, Noah—Noah Arkwright was a pseudonym under which Emperor Leto II wrote several reknowned histories. [*God Emperor of Dune*]

Arrakeen—The first settlement on Arrakis and the planetary capital in the days of the Old Empire, Arrakeen was 200 kilometers southwest of Carthag. Duke Leto Atreides chose Arrakeen as his seat of government when he relocated the Atreides to Arrakis in 10,191. The city was taken by the Harkonnens that same year and retaken by Paul Muad'Dib in 10,193. By the 153rd century the city's name had been shortened to Keen. [*Dune, Heretics of Dune*]

Arrakis—The third planet in the Canopus system, popularly known as

"Dune," Arrakis was a desert planet with small polar ice caps to which the Atreides relocated from Caladan in 10,191. It has two small moons, and its gravity is 90% of Earth's gravity. It was ruled by the Harkonnens from 10,111 to 10,191, then briefly by the Atreides, and then briefly by the Harkonnens again from 10,191 to 10,193. It was in the 102nd century the universe's sole source of mélange. The dominant natives on the planet were the Fremen, who lived in Sietch communities in the deep desert. The more-civilized, non–Fremen natives lived in grabens and sinks that protected them from the planet's fierce coriolis storms. In the 102nd century one had to wear a stillsuit, as did the Fremen, to preserve the body's moisture when traversing the surface of Arrakis. At Emperor Paul Muad'Dib's command, Arrakis was being transformed from a desert planet into a water-rich paradise by 10,207. Due to this ecological transformation, by 10,216 forested hills were beginning to appear on Arrakis and the sandworms were retreating into the deep desert, and by 10,218 melange production had fallen to 10% of what it had been at its peak under the Harkonnens in the 102nd century. By the 138th century the only desert remaining on Arrakis was Emperor Leto II's Sareer, and the weather on Arrakis was controlled by Ixian satellites. Arrakis had come to be known as Rakis by the 143rd century. By the 153rd century the sand trout spawned by Emperor Leto II's death had turned most of Rakis back into a desert; while there were green belts and watered oases in Rakis' higher latitudes, a meridian belt of desert girdled the entire planet. Rakis was totally destroyed by the Honored Matres in 15,232—in their failed attempt to kill Duncan Idaho ghola number 4, who had already left the planet for Chapterhouse in the no-ship from the Scattering that Bene Gesserit Supreme Bashar Miles Teg had captured on Gammu—as a consequence of Reverend Mother Superior Alma Mavis Taraza's scheme to manipulate the Honored Matres into eliminating Rakis' sandworms. [*Dune, Children of Dune, God Emperor of Dune, Heretics of Dune*]

"Arrakis Awakening"—"Arrakis Awakening" is one of the many volumes authored by Princess Irulan. [*Dune*]

The Arrakis Workbook—*The Arrakis Workbook* was a volume authored by Dr. Liet-Kynes. [*Children of Dune*]

Ar-Razzaq—In Zensunni legend and Fremen mythology, Ar-Razzaq is the resident of the City of Tombs who provides food for all who ask. [*Children of Dune*]

Ashkoko, Yanshuph (9,011–9,089)—Yanshuph Ashkoko, Royal Chemist during the reign of Shakkad the Wise, first discovered the geriatric properties of mélange. [*Children of Dune*]

Assur-nasir-apli (prehistoric)—Known as the cruelest of the cruel,

Assur-nasir-apli was an ancient Terran ancestor of Emperor Leto II who had slain his own father to establish his reign. [*God Emperor of Dune*]

atomics—Most great houses in the Landsraad in the 102nd century, like the Atreides, possessed a hoard of nuclear weapons, known as atomics, even though the Great Convention mandated that the use of atomics against humans shall be a cause for planetary obliteration. The Atreides used their family atomics to blast a hole in the Shield Wall protecting the basin in which Arrakeen was located during their 10,193 battle to retake Arrakeen, thus allowing a huge coriolis storm to hit Arrakeen during the Fremen attack. All stockpiles of atomics possessed by the Great and Minor Houses were discovered and confiscated during the reign of Emperor Leto II (10,218–13,726). [*Dune, God Emperor of Dune*]

Atreides, Duke Leto (10,140–10,191)—The son of Duke Paulus Atreides and the father of Paul Atreides and Lady Alia Atreides, Duke Leto Atreides relocated the Atreides from Caladan to Arrakis in 10,191 on orders from Emperor Shaddam IV. Tall, olive-skinned, thin, gray-eyed, and dark-haired, Leto was at the time of this relocation the unofficial spokesman for the Landsraad's noble houses. Often charming, witty, compassionate, and tender, he could at times be cold, demanding, selfish, harsh, and cruel—characteristics he had in common with his

father. During the Harkonnen's successful 10,191 assault on Arrakeen, Leto was drugged by Dr. Wellington Yueh, a traitor who placed a poisoned false tooth in Leto's mouth in the hope that Leto could use it to kill Baron Vladimir Harkonnen. Leto died in trying to kill the Baron with the poison in the false tooth, committing suicide in the process, but the Baron narrowly survived this assassination attempt. Leto's skull was subsequently enshrined at El Kuds, a promontory above Harg Pass. [*Dune, Dune Messiah*]

Atreides, Duke Paulus (10,119–10,168)—The father of Duke Leto Atreides and the grandfather of Paul Atreides, Duke Paulus Atreides was killed in a bullfight. He was brave, cold, demanding, selfish, harsh, and cruel, characteristics he passed along to his son Leto. [*Dune*]

Atreides, Ghanima—*See* **Ghanima Atreides**.

Atreides, Lady Alia (10,191–10,218)—The daughter of Duke Leto Atreides and Lady Jessica, Lady Alia Atreides was a fetus when Jessica transmuted the Water of Life to become a Bene Gesserit Reverend Mother in 10,191. Thus Alia, too, became a Reverend Mother, before her birth, and shared in Reverend Mother Romallo's outpouring of her memories to Jessica at the moment of Romallo's death. Also known as Alia-the-Strange-One, Alia was taken captive by Sardaukar during a raid on Sietch Tabr in 10,193 and was transported to Arrakeen, where she was interrogated by Emperor Shaddam IV and where she killed Baron Vladimir Harokennen with a gom jabbar during the Fremen assault on the city. Oval-faced, bronze-haired, wide-mouthed Alia had become a beautiful, passionate, reckless woman by 10,207, by which time she was venerated as a demi-goddess by the Fremen but was known as Hawt, the Fish Monster, on the out-worlds conquered by Paul Muad'Dib's Jihad. Following the blinding of Emperor Paul Muad'Dib by a stone burner in Arrakeen in 10,207, Alia presided over the trial of Korba for conspiracy against Muad'Dib. Soon thereafter she consumed a massive overdose of spice in an unsuccessful attempt to penetrate with her prescience the murkiness created by the Dune Tarot, but she was saved by Hayt, who had her stomach pumped and who subsequently admitted that he was in love with her. With Hayt, Bijaz, Paul, Edric, Reverened Mother Gaius Helen Mohiam, Scytale disguised as Lichna, Stilgar, Harah, and Princess Irulan, Alia accompanied Chani when she returned to the desert, to Sietch Tabr, to give birth. After Chani's death in childbirth Alia ordered Korba and the other Fremen traitors to Muad'Dib, Edric, and Mohiam executed. While still at Sietch Tabr she realized that she loved Hayt (who had by then recovered Duncan Idaho's persona) just as Hayt loved her, and they were married shortly thereafter. Alia ruled the

Empire as Regent after Paul disappeared into the desert, from 10,207 to 10,218, but during that time she succumbed to abomination—became possessed by the personae of her ancestors. She was present when her mother Jessica arrived in Arrakeen in 10,216, after a 23-year absence from Arrakis, but by that year she had become so beset by the ancestors inhabiting her consciousness that she made a bargain with one of them, her maternal grandfather Baron Vladimir Harkonnen: She agreed to allow the Baron contact with her senses during the moments when she was intimate with her lovers in return for his protection against all the other personae within her who threatened to overwhelm her consciousness and her ego. The Baron then advised her to take Ziarenko Javid as her lover and to kill him in her bed should he subsequently reveal that he had betrayed her. She had used her Bene Gesserit training in the manipulation of body chemistry to keep herself from physically aging beyond the age of 16, but under the influence of the Baron she eventually gained weight. Shortly after Jessica's arrival on Arrakis, Alia ordered Hayt (now with Duncan Idaho's persona) to abduct Jessica in such a way as to make it look like an act of House Corrino's, but she really hoped that Hayt would murder Jessica to eliminate at least one individual who knew that Alia was an abomination. She subsequently conspired with Javid to have one of her priests assassinate Jessica with a maula pistol during one of Alia's morning audiences, but the assassination attempt failed and Jessica publicly accused Alia of having instigated it. Several months later the Preacher revealed to Alia that he was her brother, Paul Atreides, while preaching in Arrakeen against the religion of Muad'Dib. Subsequently—after Ghanima had returned to Sietch Tabr believing that Leto Atreides II had been slain by the Laza tigers—she tried to get Ghanima to accept bethrothal to Prince Farad'n Corrino, and Ghanima finally did accept on the condition that she be permitted to kill Farad'n once she was bethrothed to him. When Hayt returned to Arrakis, after having taken Jessica to Salusa Secundus, Alia decided that she must have him killed. She was then forced by rebellious Fremen to send Ghanima to Sietch Tabr, and she afterwards ordered Hayt to go to Sietch Tabr—ostensibly to spy on Ghanima and Irulan—and had planned to have him killed en route by her chief amazon, Ziarenka Valefor. However, suspecting this plot, Hayt did not wait for Valefor but flew to Sietch Tabr alone. After learning from her lover Buer Agarves that her lover Javid had been killed by her husband Hayt and that Hayt had been killed by Stilgar, she ordered Argaves to seek and slay Stilgar, promising him that he would become Naib of Sietch Tabr once he brought her Stilgar's head. Stilgar then slew Argaves instead, but a transmitter that

Alia had secretly hidden in Argaves' boot led Alia's agents to Stilgar's desert location, and he, Ghanima, and Irulan were abducted and returned to Arrakeen, where Alia had Stilgar and Irulan imprisoned. Subsequently Alia was confronted by Leto Atreides II and Ghanima, and Leto II used his super-strength to overcome her and her guards and then gave her the choice of submitting to a trial of possession or committing suicide. Alia chose suicide and in 10,218 leapt through a window of her temple to her death. [*Dune, Dune Messiah, Children of Dune*]

Atreides, Leto (10,192–10,193)—The son of Paul Atreides and Chani, Leto Atreides was killed in his infancy during a Sardaukar raid on a relocated Sietch Tabr in 10,193. [*Dune*]

Atreides II, Leto—*See* **Leto Atreides II.**

"The Atreides Manifesto"—"The Atreides Manifesto" was written in the 153rd century by Senior Security Mother Darwi Odrade, an Atreides, on the orders of Bene Gesserit Reverend Mother Superior Alma Mavis Taraza. It maintains both that the universe is magical and cannot be understood through words and that God and all his works are no more than human creations. [*Heretics of Dune*]

Atreides, Paul (10,176–10,218)—Son of Duke Leto Atreides and Lady Jessica, and the grandson on his mother's side of Baron Vladimir Harkonnen and Tanidia Nerus, a Bene Gesserit, Paul Atreides spent the first fifteen years of his life on Caladan. Oval-faced, green-eyed, and dark-haired, during his childhood he had prescient dreams and exhibited the ability to know when someone was telling the truth or lying. In his youth on Caladan he was instructed by Dr. Wellington Yueh, Gurney Hallek, Duncan Idaho, Thufir Hawat, Lady Jessica, and Duke Leto. He was tested with the gom jabbar by Mohiam, who declared him "human," immediately prior to the Atreides' relocation to Arrakis. Paul exhibited mentat capabilities in his youth and agreed to continue his training as a mentat in 10,191. Shortly after arriving on Arrakis he saved the Shadout Mapes' life when she was nearly struck by a hunter-seeker that was targeting him. Drugged by Dr. Yueh and captured by the Harkonnens during their 10,191 assault on Arrakeen, he escaped into the desert with Lady Jessica due to Dr. Yueh's intervention. While in the desert, after the fall of Arrakeen and the death of Duke Leto, his prescient powers began to manifest themselves. These powers included the limited ability to forsee the future and to know what was happening elsewhere in the present moment. Rescued from the desert by Duncan Idaho and Dr. Liet Kynes, Paul and Jessica were taken to an underground Imperial Ecological Testing Station where Idaho was killed and where Kynes directed them to a

hidden Fremen ornithopter, which Paul flew into a sandstorm to escape the Harkonnens, who then assumed that he had perished in the storm. Paul and Jessica were subsequently found in the desert, at Tuono Basin, by Stilgar and his band of forty Fremen, who took them to Cave of Ridges, where Paul killed Jamis in a knife fight that was to determine whether or not he was the Fremen Lisan-al-Gaib, an off-world prophet. In Cave of Ridges Paul then assumed his secret Fremen name, Usul, and his public Fremen name, Paul Muad'Dib. In 10,193, at the age of eighteen, he first mounted and rode a sandworm without assistance, a Fremen rite of initiation into adulthood, at Habbanya Erg. Shortly thereafter he was reunited with Gurney Hallek at Habbanya Ridge. He subsequently transmuted the Water of Life, to become a male Bene Gesserit Reverend Mother, in Cave of Birds. In 10,193 he also led the Fremen assault on Arrakeen and defeated the Harkonnens and Emperor Shaddam IV. As a condition of the Emperor's surrender, Paul was betrothed to Princess Irulan, the Emperor's eldest daughter, and assumed the throne as Emperor of the Known Universe. In 10,207 Paul welcomed Edric as a Guild Ambassador to his court in Arrakeen and accepted Edric's gift of the ghola Hayt. By this time the Dune Tarot had so muddied the currents of time that only a huge dose of spice essence could enable Paul to exercise his prescience, but he nevertheless had a vision of a falling moon that he interpreted as a sign that he must disengage himself from his empire and his Jihad. Other prescient visions revealed to Paul that Chani would die in childbirth. For this reason he attempted unsuccessfully to bargain with Mohiam, offering to impregnate Irulan via artificial insemination (to preserve his genes for the Bene Gesserit) in return for Chani's life. He was subsequently visited by Scytale, disguised as Otheyem's daughter Lichna, who asked him to go to Otheym with Chani to learn of a conspiracy against them being hatched by the Fremen. However, Paul—seeing through Scytale's disguise—decided to visit Otheym alone. As was his custom, Paul then travelled through the streets of Arrakeen disguised as a Fremen from the inner desert and was guided to Otheym's house by Rasir, an old Fremen who had known Paul from his days in Sietch Tabr. There, Otheym gave Paul Bijaz, a dwarf whom Otheym claimed was a human distrans who had recorded the names of the Fremen traitors. On leaving Otheym's dwelling Paul remanded Bijaz into Stilgar's custody immediately before Otheym's house was consumed by a stone burner that blinded Paul, just as his prescience had forseen. However, Paul's memories of his prophetic visions enabled him to act as a sighted man even though he was blind, much to the amazement of all witnesses. Paul ordered that the many others blinded by the stone burner should be given Tlielaxu eyes at his expense and that the fate of a blind Fremen—to be taken to the desert to die—would not be his fate because his oracular visions gave him the ability to see even though blinded. He subsequently accompanied Chani—with Bijaz, Hayt, Alia, Edric, Mohiam, Scytale disgiuised as Lichna, Stilgar, Harah, and Irulan—when she returned to the desert, to Sietch Tabr, to give birth. After Chani died in childbirth, Paul uttering the words "She is gone" triggered Hayt's Tleilaxu-born compulsion to kill him. However, this compulsion created such a conflict with Hayt's submerged, loyal Duncan Idaho persona that that persona emerged and Hayt was restored to his original self, as the Tleilaxu had intended. Yet Paul was surprised to learn that Chani had given birth to both a boy and a girl, as his prescience had revealed to him only the birth of a daughter. Almost immediately after Chani's death and the birth of the twins, Scytale (still disguised as Lichna) revealed his true identity to Paul and offered him a bargain—the dead Chani fully restored to him, as Idaho had been restored, in return for his empire—while simultaneously threatening to kill the newborn twins should Paul refuse. However, Paul then perceived the entire scene from the perspective of his infant son, Leto II, and killed Scytale with a hurled crysknife. When Bijaz then reiterated Scytale's bargain, Paul ordered Hayt (who now had the persona of Duncan Idaho) to kill him. Bereft of his prescient visions and thus now truly blind, Paul finally walked into the desert to die, as would any blind Fremen. In the guise of The Preacher, he was slain by a crysknife-wielding priest in the streets of Arrakeen in 10,218. Paul is the author of "A Time of Reflection" and, as Muad'Dib, of "The Pillars of the Universe." *See* **The Preacher**. [*Dune, Dune Messiah, Children of Dune*]

Atreides, Siona Ibn Faud al-Seyefa— *See* **Siona Ibn Faud al-Seyefa Atreides**.

The Attendant—The Attendant was a rock outcropping near Sietch Tabr that resembled a dark, sinuous sandworm. In 10,216 Leto Atreides II and Ghanima often met at a secret hiding place near the Attendant. [*Children of Dune*]

aumas—Also known as "chaumas," aumas is poison administered in one's food. [*Dune*]

Auqaf—Auqaf was the military arm of the religion of Muad'Dib. [*Children of Dune*]

awareness spectrum narcotics—Frequently fatal, except to desensitized individuals who are able to transform their poison configuration within their own bodies, awareness spectrum narcotics can be used to induce truthtrance or to transform a Bene Gesserit into a Reverend Mother. The Water of Life is an awareness spectrum narcotic. [*Dune*]

axlotl tanks—Secretly the bodies of Tleilaxu females connected to mechanisms that precisely controlled chemical balances and limited variables, axlotl tanks were used by the Bene Tleilax in the 103rd century to grow gholas, living human beings cloned from the cells of cadavers. Once the Tleilaxu discovered how to revive a ghola's memories of its past life in 10,207, they used the axlotl tanks to produce gholas of deceased Tleilaxu Masters, thus insuring the Masters of a kind of serial immortality. By the 153rd century the Tleilaxu had learned how to produce mélange in axlotl tanks, and the bulk of the mélange in the known universe was by then manufactured in them. Shortly after the destriuction of Rakis in 15,232, the Bene Gesserit acquired axlotl tank technology from the Bene Tleilax and used volunteers to serve as axlotl tanks. The Miles Teg clone, born in 15,234, was the first product of the Bene Gesserit axlotl tanks. [*Dune Messiah, Heretics of Dune, Chapterhouse: Dune*]

Ayil—Ayil was the Day of the Kwisatz Hadderach, the first Holy Day of those who followed the religion of Muad'Dib. It recognized the deified Paul Atreides as that person who was everywhere simultaneously and commemorated his supposed death, which made his presence "real in all places." Most pilgrims on Hajj tried to time their stay on Arrakis to coincide with Ayil. [*Children of Dune*]

bahr bela ma—Fremen for "the ocean without water," the phrase "bahr bela ma" refers to the open desert of Arrakis. [*God Emperor of Dune*]

Bakka—In Fremen legend, Bakka is the weeper who morns for all mankind. [*Dune*]

Baldik (15,198–15,232)—Baldik was a young Rakian priest in High Priest Hedley Tuek's service. He was killed in the destruction of Rakis. [*Heretics of Dune*]

baliset—A nine-stringed musical instrument strummed with a multipick, the baliset is related to the zithra and is tuned to the Chusuk scale. It was the favorite instrument of Imperial troubadors. Famed baliset players of history include Paul Atreides, Gurney Hallek, Jamis, Chatt the Leaper, and Tagir Mohandis. [*Dune*]

"Ballet Master"—"Ballet Master" was a sculpture in Great Honored Matre Dama's quarters on Junction. [*Chapterhouse: Dune*]

Bandalong—Bandalong was the capital city on Tleilax. [*Heretics of Dune*]

Bannerjee (10,173–10,241)—Heavy, dark-haired, intelligent, and loyal, Bannerjee was descended from a line of smugglers and by 10,207 had become the chief of Emperor Paul Muad'Dib's security detail. [*Dune Messiah*]

barachans—Barachans were high, crescent-shaped dunes that moved like waves across Arrakis. [*Children of Dune*]

Baraka—A Baraka is a living holy man who possesses magical powers. [*Dune*]

Baram, Sister (15,128–15,176)—Short, fat Sister Baram was a failed Reverend Mother, a Bene Gesserit who had never been permitted to attempt the Spice Agony. She had been the Night Proctor at the Bene Gesserit school on Chapterhouse when Alma Mavis Taraza and Darwi Odrade had been students there. She died relatively young of the nervous system defect that had prevented her from becoming a Reverend Mother. [*Heretics of Dune*]

Barandiko Incident—Bene Gesserit Supreme Bashar Miles Teg and Reverend Mother Superior Alma Mavis Taraza pooled all of their combined energies to prevent a bloody confrontation during the Barandiko Incident. [*Heretics of Dune*]

Barony—Barony was the capital city on Geidi Prime in which Duncan Idaho had been tortured by the Harkonnens in the 102nd century prior to his having been recruited by the Atreides. The city had been renamed Yasi by the 153rd century, at which time it was a repellant, sprawling mass of warrens surrounding the ancient, massive Keep—which was 45 kilometers long, 30 kilometers wide,

950 stories tall, and composed entirely of plasteel and armor-plaz. [*Heretics of Dune*]

Bashar—Often Colonel Bashar, a Bashar was an officer of the Sardaukar with a rank just above that of Colonel. The rank was created for military rulers of planetary subdistricts. [*Dune*]

batigh—A batigh was a little melon on the desert's edge that offered its water to anyone who found it. [*Children of Dune*]

Bator—Bator was a Sardaukar rank between Levenbrech and Burseg. [*Children of Dune*]

Behaleth (10,188–10,235)—Behaleth was a Fremen smuggler and a citizen of Shuloch, the secret desert sietch of the Cast Out, who accompanied Leto Atreides II and Muriz from the deep desert south of Jacurutu to Shuloch. [*Children of Dune*]

Bela Tegeuse—The fifth planet orbiting Kuentsing, Bela Tegeuse was the third stopping place of the Zensunni Wanderers (the Fremen) during their migration. By then a Bene Gesserit planet, it was captured by the Honored Matres in the 153rd century [*Dune, Chapterhouse: Dune*]

Bellonda, Reverend Mother (14,882–15,266)—A Mentat who was in charge of the Bene Gesserit Archives in the early 153rd century, old, fat, florid, viscious, hypocritical, cold-eyed, blunt-toothed Reverend Mother Bellonda was one of the few to know Senior Security Mother Darwi Odrade's genetic history as well as one of the very few, with Reverend Mother Superior Alma Mavis Taraza and Sister Hesterion of Archives, to possess all the memories of the unbroken line of Bene Gesserit Reverend Mother Superiors. Opposed to the Bene Gesserit ghola project, she had nevertheless briefed Bene Gesserit Supreme Bashar Miles Teg prior to his travelling to Gammu to guard Duncan Idaho ghola number 4. She wanted Odrade killed when she learned that Odrade had proposed that the Bene Gesserit serve as missionaries for the Bene Tleilax. She also wanted Idaho ghola number 4 killed, but a 15,244 discussion with him in his no-ship on Chapterhouse convinced her that he was more valuable to the Bene Gesserit alive than she had realized. She lost weight in 15,245 at Sheeana's urging and as a consequence of the pressures of being a member of Reverend Mother Superior Odrade's Council. As a Mentat she eventually deduced Odrade's plot against the Honored Matres but did not reveal what she had discovered. She subsequently received Odrade's and Reverend Mother Dortujla's other memories prior to to Odrade's, Dortujla's, and Reverend Mother Tamalane's trip to Junction to parlay with the Honored Matres. In 15,245 she also observed Honored Matre Murbella undergo the Spice Agony in the Chapterhouse no-ship. She wore glasses and preferred chairdogs to chairs. [*Heretics of Dune, Chapterhouse: Dune*]

Bene Gesserit—An ancient school of mental and physical training, the Bene Gesserit order was established primarily for female students after the Butlerian Jihad. Bene Gesserit adepts have keen powers of observation and memory, can control any muscle in their bodies, are skilled in hand-to-hand combat, are students of Galactic politics, and can control others through voice manipulation. A Bene Gesserit can attain the rank of Reverend Mother by undergoing the Spice Agony and successfully transmuting the Water of Life. The Bene Gesserit bury their dead quickly and without ceremony. They organize themselves with a minimum of bureaucracy because they believe that bureaucracy engenders aristocracy. By the 138th century the Bene Gesserit order was in constrained circumstances due to Emperor Leto II's tight control over their supply of mélange. During this century the Bene Gesserit attempted unsuccessfully to ally themselves with Leto II's Fish Speakers and also attempted unsuccessfully to participate as a partner in some of Leto II's ventures. They believed that both Malky and Hwi Noree had been genetically bred to serve as Ixian Ambassadors to Leto II's court on Arrakis. In 13,726 Bene Gesserit Reverend Mothers Tertius Eileen Anteac and Marcus Claire Luyseyal warned Leto II that the Tleilaxu would attempt to assassinate him during his peregrination to the festival city of Onn. By the 153rd century the Bene Gesserit had become one of the most powerful forces in the universe—equal to the Guild, the Bene Tleilax, and Ix, and superior to the Fish Speakers and to CHOAM—and had fallen into the role of arbiters for the complex galactic society of that era. But by this time they had come to distrust the emotion of love, which they tried to avoid in themselves and to manipulate in others, and also avoided music. The Bene Gesserit acquired axlotl tank technology from the Bene Tleilax shortly after the destruction of Rakis in 15,232. In 15,243, to avoid extermination by the Honored Matres, the Bene Gesserit sent numerous cells out into a second Scattering to unknown planets on no-ships that also carried a cargo of sand trout. In 15,244 only twelve planets remained under Bene Gesserit control, including Chapterhouse and Buzzell, as all the others had been obliterated or captured by the Honored Matres. The Bene Gesserit successfully co-opted the Honored Matres in 15,245, when Honored Matre/Reverend Mother Murbella killed Great Honored Matre Longo to become the Great Honored Matre herself and shortly thereafter received deceased Reverend Mother Superior Darwi Odrade's most recent memories to become the Bene Gesserit Reverend Mother Superior as well. [*Dune, God Emperor of Dune, Heretics of Dune, Chapterhouse: Dune*]

Bene Sherk—In 10,216 Bene Sherk was a scattering of new settlements on Arrakis that encroached on the open bled east of Jacurutu. [*Children of Dune*]

Bene Tleilax—*See* **Tleilaxu**.

Benotto, Hadi (14,220–14,298)—In the 143rd century Hadi Benotto and his research team discovered Emperor Leto II's original journals, inscribed by an Ixian dictatel on ridulian crystal paper, in one of the first Ixian no-globes, which was buried at Dar-es-Balat on Rakis (Arrakis). [*God Emperor of Dune*]

Bewt, Lingar (10,140–10,203)—Round-faced, thick-lipped, large-eyed, darkly-tanned Lingar Bewt was a water-shipper on Arrakis who was used but never controlled by the Harkonnens. He attended the formal banquet in Arrakeen hosted by Duke Leto Atreides and Lady Jessica in 10,191. [*Dune*]

B. G.—An abbreviation for Bene Gesserit, B. G. also means "Before Guild"—signifying a time period prior to the Spacing Guild's monopoly on interstellar travel—when used with a date. [*Dune*]

Bhotani—Bhotani is the ancient language from which the hunting language Chakobsa is derived. The Bhotani were also the hired assassins in the first Wars of Assassins. [*Dune*]

Biarek—Biarek is a planet in the Imperium whose Central Temple was attacked in the aftermath of Alia Atreides' suicide in 10,218. [*Children of Dune*]

Bijaz (10,190–10,207)—Possessing some powers of prescience and talented in manipulating language, Bijaz was a Tleilaxu ghola and the dwarf who welcomed Emperor Paul Muad'Dib to Otheym's house in Arrakeen's suburbs in 10,207. Otheym told Paul that Bijaz was a human distrans, created by the Tleilaxu, who had recorded the names of all the Fremen traitors who were plotting against Paul. Hidden from Paul's prescience by Edric, as he was a part of the 10,206–07 Bene Gesserit/Tleilaxu/Guild conspiracy against Paul, Bijaz left Otheym's house with Paul and was soon remanded into Stilgar's custody. On being questioned by Hayt after Paul was subsequently blinded by a stone burner, Bijaz claimed to have been present when Hayt had been removed from his Tleilaxu axlotl tank and that he had been created in the same tank in which Hayt had been created. He then activated Hayt's Tleilaxu-born compulsion to attempt to assassinate Paul when he uttered the words "She is gone" and gave to Hayt, as a hypnotic suggestion, a message to deliver to Paul at that moment—that the Tleilaxu would create a precise duplicate of Chani in return for Paul's empire and his renunciation of the Religion of Muad'Dib and its Qizarate. Bijaz then accompanied Chani—with Paul, Hayt, Alia, Edric,

Reverend Mother Helen Gaius Mohiam, Scytale disgiuised as Lichna, Stilgar, Harah, and Princess Irulan—when she returned to the desert, to Sietch Tabr, to give birth. After Chani died in childbirth and Paul had killed Scytale, Bijaz reiterated Scytale's offer to restore to Paul the dead Chani in return for his empire and was then killed, on Paul's orders, by Hayt (who now possessed the persona of Duncan Idaho). [*Dune Messiah*]

Bikouros (10,155–10,207)—Bikouros was a Fremen Naib who was identified by Bijaz in 10,207 as being one of the Fremen traitors conspiring against Emperor Paul Muad'Dib. [*Dune Messiah*]

bindu suspension—Bindu suspension is the self-induced, drastic slowing of one's metabolism through control of one's nervous system. Lady Jessica used bindu suspension to survive being inadvertently but briefly buried in sand after she and Paul had escaped into the desert following the fall of Arrakeen in 10,191. [*Dune*]

Blend Books—The Blend Books of the Mahayana Lankavatara are among the Ancient Teachings that shaped the dominant religious beliefs of the Imperium of the 102nd century, the time of Muad-Dib. [*Dune*]

Bodal—The first thing reaffirmed at ghufran and khel, Bodal is the ultimate revenge sought by the Tleilaxu. [*Heretics of Dune*]

Bomoko, Toure (13th millennium AD)—One of the Ulema of the Zensunnis and one of the "Fourteen Sages" who never recanted the teachings of the Orange Catholic Bible, Toure Bomoko was the Chairman of the Commission of Ecumenical Translators (C. E. T.). He was forced to flee into exile and is reported to have died on Tupile. [*Dune*]

The Book of Leto—The Book of Leto is a volume authored by Harq al-Ada. [*Children of Dune*]

Bordanos—Bordanos, who have no sense of smell, are tall, heavy-bodied, thick-armed Gammu natives bred and trained to operate the compression machinery that harnesses Gammu's sewer gasses. [*Heretics of Dune*]

Bramlis, Lon (14,233–14,286)—Lon Bramlis was a noted 143rd-century poet. [*God Emperor of Dune*]

Broken Lands—Fremen raiders from the Broken Lands destroyed the qanats in Arrakis' Kagga Basin in 10,216. [*Children of Dune*]

Bronso of Ix (10,155–10,205)—Denounced as a heretic by both the Bene Gesserit and the Qizarate (the priests of the Religion of Muad'Dib), Bronso of Ix was a historian who was condemned to death for writing in his *Analysis of History: MuadDdib* that Paul Atreides had lost something essential to his human nature in becoming Muad'Dib and that he was a product of his Bene Gesserit training and their kwisatz hadderach. [*Dune Messiah*]

Broom, Jacob (prehistoric)—Jacob Broom was one of Emperor Leto II's ancestors. [*God Emperor of Dune*]

Brugh, Sheeana—*See* **Sheeana Brugh**.

Buddislamic Variants—The Buddislamic Variants of the types prevalent on Lankiveil and Sikun are among the Ancient Teachings that shaped the dominant religious beliefs of the Imperium of the 102nd century, the time of Muad'Dib. [*Dune*]

Burseg—Burseg was a Sardaukar rank between Bator and Colonel, with duties equivalent to those of a commanding general. [*Dune, Children of Dune*]

Burzmali, Bashar Alef (15,043–15,243)—Supreme Bene Gesserit Bashar Miles Teg's favorite student, short, blond, slender, green-eyed, triangle-faced Bashar Alef Burzmali was trained by Teg and became Supreme Bashar for the Bene Gesserit following Teg's retirement. In 15,232 he was sent to Gammu to assist Teg, who had come out of retirement for this mission, in guarding and preserving the life of Duncan Idaho ghola number 4. He subsequently returned to Chapterhouse and deduced with Reverend Mother Superior Alma Mavis Taraza that Teg, Reverend Mother Lucilla, and the Idaho ghola must be hiding in a Harkonnen no-globe on Gammu. Under the pretext of placing a funeral marker for Teg at the last place Teg was known to have been, Burzmali returned to Gammu to search for the no-globe, found it, and left a message near it for Teg that arranged for Teg, Lucilla, and the ghola to escape from the no-globe to a safe haven on Gammu. He then set up a command post in a pilingitam tree near the no-globe and rescued Teg, Lucilla, and the ghola as they escaped, while under heavy attack, from it. Burzmali subsequently entered Ysai, with Lucilla, while disguised as a Gammu field worker named Skar, Lucilla's client, while Lucilla was disguised as an Honored Matre postulant, Pira, who was working on Gammu as a playfem. After traversing Ysai, the two encountered in an abandoned factory on the city's outskirts Honored Matre Murbella, who had previously captured the ghola. Burzmali, Lucilla, the ghola, and Murbella were then taken to Rakis in a no-ship from the Scattering that had been captured by Teg. Burzmali was killed, with four million Bene Gesserit soldiers, while defending the planet Lampadas, which was destroyed by the Honored Matres in 15,243. [*Heretics of Dune, Chapterhouse: Dune*]

Butlerian Jihad—Also known as the Great Revolt, the Butlerian Jihad was the century-long (201–108 B.G.) revolt against the rule of humanity by artificial intelligences that occurred in the 13th millennium AD. It greatly shaped the dominant religious beliefs of the 102nd century, the time of Muad'Dib. [*Dune*]

The Buterlian Jihad—The Butlerian

Jihad is a volume authored by Harq al-Ada. [*Children of Dune*]

Buzzell—A very cold ocean planet with small, scattered islands, in the 153rd century Buzzell was a Bene Gesserit punishment planet on which banished Reverend Mother Dortujla was posted. It was desired by the Honored Matres as a planet on which they could breed amphibious slaves to gather soostones and so was not destroyed when the Honored Matres destroyed Rakis in 15,232 and the Tleilaxu planets shortly thereafter. In 15,244 strangers commanded by women came to Buzzell and removed all the Reverend Mothers from the planet. Soostones are found on Buzzell. [*Chapterhouse: Dune*]

Cadelam family—The Cadelam family was a Fremen clan that had once ruled Sietch Abbir. [*Children of Dune*]

Cahueit (10,162–10,207)—Cahueit was a Fremen Naib who was identified by Bijaz in 10,207 as being one of the Fremen traitors conspiring against Emperor Paul Muad'Dib. [*Dune Messiah*]

Caid—A Caid was an officer of the Sardaukar whose rank was between that of a Bashar and a Burseg. It was the rank of the military governor of a full planetary district whose duties mostly involved dealing with civilians. [*Dune*]

Caladan—The third planet orbiting Delta Pavonis and an idyllic water planet, Caladan is the birthworld of Paul Atreides, also known as Muad'Dib, and the ancestral home-world of the Atreides, who ruled it for 26 generations prior to their relocation to Arrakis in 10,191. Count Hasimir Fenring governed Caladan in abstentia from 10,191 to 10,193, when Gurney Hallek became the planet's governor. Jessica returned to Caladan with Hallek in 10,193 and remained there with him until 10,216. The people of Caladan rebuilt Gammu after the Famine Times and the Scattering of the 138th century. By the 153rd century Caladan had come to be known as Dan. [*Dune, Children of Dune, Heretics of Dune*]

Cania (15,148–15,232)—Old, blue-eyed, stub-nosed, gray-haired, narrow-mouthed Cania was a female Rakian priest who had been Sheeana's night attendand when she was adopted by the Rakian priests at eight years of age. Cania was killed in the destruction of Rakis. [*Heretics of Dune*]

Canopus—Canopus is the white star about which Arrakis orbits. [*Dune*]

Caprock—Caprock was a month in the Fremen calendar that occurred in mid–Autumn. [*Dune*]

Carlana (14,909–15,185)—Tiny, doll-faced, red-blonde-haired Carlana was a Bene Gesserit acolyte who had unsuccessfully attempted to pry information from Miles Teg when he was an eleven-year-old boy on Lernaeus. [*Heretics of Dune*]

carryall—Essentially a large or-nithopter, a carryall was a flying wing used on Arrakis to transport mélange hunting, mining, and refining equipment. A carryall was especially useful for rapidly moving a harvester out of the path of an attacking sandworm. [*Dune*]

Carthag—A megalopolis about 200 kilometers northeast of Arrakeen, Carthag was the cheap and brassy Harkonnen capital on Arrakis. [*Dune*]

casmine—A stimulant, casmine is a genetically modified blood strength-ener from the Gammu pharma-copoeia. [*Chapterhouse: Dune*]

Cast Out—In the 103rd century the Cast Out were renegade Fremen smugglers who inhabited Shuloch, a secret desert Sietch. [*Children of Dune*]

Castle Caladan—By the time of the Atreides relocation to Arrakis in 10,191, Castle Caladan had been the home of the Atreides for 26 genera-tions. [*Dune*]

Castle Corrino—Castle Corrino was the royal palace on Salusa Secundus to which Emperor Shaddam IV and four of his daughters were exiled fol-lowing Paul Muad'Dib's victory on Arrakis in 10,193. [*Children of Dune*]

Cave of Birds—Cave of Birds was a cave in Habbanya Ridge where Paul Atreides held Gurney Hallek's smug-gler crew after he was reunited with Gurney in the desert of Arrakis in

10,193. Paul and his Fedyakin discov-ered ten Sardaukar among Gurney's men and captured three of them, killing the rest. Subsequently, Paul made Cave of Birds his command post for an attack against the Harkon-nens, and he later transmuted the Water of Life in Cave of Birds. [*Dune*]

Cave of the Ridges—Cave of the Ridges was a cave complex, about ten to twelve kilometers from Sietch Tabr, in which Stilgar's band of forty Fre-men took refuge after they found Paul Atreides and Lady Jessica in the desert while en route to Sietch Tabr. Paul defeated Jamis in a knife fight in Cave of the Ridges, and it is there that he assumed his Fremen names, Usul and Paul Muad'Dib. The water cache in Cave of the Ridges, one of the thousands of water caches the Freman had hidden in the desert, contained 38 million decaliters of water. [*Dune*]

Cedon—Cedon is a planet famed for its fire jewels. [*Dune Messiah*]

Central—Central was the adminis-trative capital of Chapterhouse in the 153rd century. [*Chapterhouse: Dune*]

Cenva, Norma (98–20 B.G.)—A fe-male intellectual, Aurelius Venport's mistress, and one of Emperor Leto II's ancestors, Norma Cevna designed the first Guild ship. [*God Emperor of Dune*]

Cerbol Revolt—In 14,973, when he was 50, Bene Gesserit Supreme Bashar Miles Teg blunted the Cerbol Revolt of Bene Gesserit troops against the Bene Gesserit. [*Heretics of Dune*]

chairdog—In the 153rd century and subsequently, the chairdog is a species of living, animated furniture that fits itself to and cuddles the user. [*Heretics of Dune*]

Chakobsa—Chakobsa is an ancient human hunting language derived from the ancient Bhotani dialect. [*Dune*]

Chalice, Princess (10,178–10,270)— One of Emperor Shaddam IV's and Anirul's five daughters, Princess Chalice accompanied Shaddam IV into retirement on Salusa Secundus in 10,193. [*Dune*]

Chani (10,175–10,207)—Stilgar's niece, Dr. Liet-Kynes' and Faroula's daughter, and Paul Atreides' lover, elfin-faced Chani was among Stilgar's band of forty Fremen who found Paul and Lady Jessica in the desert after the fall of Arrakeen in 10,191. The woman who had appeared in Paul's prescient dreams, she was charged by Stilgar with looking after Paul's welfare during the Fremen band's subsequent trek to Sietch Tabr. She was named a sayyadina by Reverend Mother Romallo immediately before Lady Jessica transmuted the Water of Life to become a Reverend Mother herself, and she then presided over the ceremony that consecrated Jessica as a Reverend Mother. She gave birth to Paul's first son, Leto, in 10,192. She also served as sayyadina of the rite of riding a sandworm when Paul first mounted a sandworm without assistance in 10,193. Subsequently sent with the infant Leto into the southern desert, she returned north to Cave of Birds, on Jessica's summons, to revive Paul after he had transmuted the Water of Life. Between 10,193 and 10,207 she was secretly dosed by Princess Irulan with a contraceptive drug in her food to prevent her from having any children by Paul, who had become Emperor. As a consequence, she suggested to Paul in 10,207 that he impregnate his wife Irulan so that he would have an heir. However, by then Chani had adopted a Fremen diet intended to promote fertility, and this diet prevented Irulan from having any further opportunity to administer the contraceptive. Thus, Chani became pregnant with Paul's twins, but the pregnancy was complicated and accelerated by the contraceptive. Chani subsequently returned to the desert, to Sietch Tabr, to give birth accompanied by Paul, Bijaz, Hayt, Edric, Reverend Mother Gaius Helen Mohiam, Scytale disguised as Lichna, Stilgar, Alia, Irulan, and Harah. She died there giving birth to Paul's twins, Leto II and Ghanima. [*Dune, Dune Messiah, God Emperor of Dune*]

Chapterhouse—A moonless planet Settled by the Bene Gesserit in the 138th century, Chapterhouse served as the administrative headquarters of the Bene Gesserit well into the 153rd

century, when its location was un-
recorded and it was concealed behind
a moat of no-ships. In 15,232 a sandworm was transported from Ralkis to
Chapterhouse in the no-ship from
the Scattering that had been captured
on Gammu by Bene Gesserit Supreme
Bashar Miles Teg. The worm was
there induced to metamorphose into
sand trout, which eventually transformed Chapterhouse into a desert
planet on which the mature sandworm could exist. The first, small
(one meter long) sandworm appeared
on Chapterhouse in 15,245. [*Heretics
of Dune, Chapterhouse: Dune*]

Chatt the Leaper (10,163–10,197)—A
baliset player and the captain of Paul
Muad'Dib's Fedaykin guard in 10,193,
Chatt the Leaper joined Paul, Stilgar,
Korba, and Otheym in making battle
plans against the Harkennens in Cave
of Birds. [*Dune*]

chaumas—Also known as "aumas,"
chaumas is poison administered in
one's food. [*Dune*]

chaumurky—Also known as "murky"
or "musky," chaumurky is poison administered in one's drink. [*Dune*]

Chenoeh, Sister Quintinius Violet
(13,660–13,734)—Bene Gesserits, Sisters Quintinius Violet Chenoeh and
Tawsuoko reported to the Sisterhood
in 13,726 that Emperor Leto II had
executed nine historians in 12,334
for their pretentious lies. Later in
13,726 Chenoeh accompanied and
conversed with Leto II during his

peregrination to the festival city of
Onn; she afterwards reported some
of Leto II's words accurately and immediately to the Bene Gesserit, but at
his command she preserved some of
Leto II's message to be communicated
to the Bene Gesserit only after her
death. She died of mélange incompat-
ibility, in the 53rd year of her sisterhood, during her attempt to become
a Reverend Mother. In the 153rd
century a bust of Sister Chenoeh sat
in Reverend Mother Superior Alva
Mavis Taraza's private chambers
on Chapterhouse. [*God Emperor of
Dune*]

cheops—Cheops is a nine-level game
of pyramid chess whose object is to
place one's opponent's king in check
while placing one's queen at the apex
simultaneously. [*Dune*]

"A Child's History of Muad'Dib"—
"A Child's History of Muad'Dib" is
one of the many volumes authored by
Princess Irulan. [*Dune*]

CHOAM—An acronym for Combine
Honnete Ober Advancer Mercantiles,
CHOAM was in the 102nd century the
universal economic development cor-
poration controlled by the Emperor
and the Great Houses, with the Bene
Gesserit and the Spacing Guild as
silent partners. In 10,191 Emperor
Shaddam IV and his allies controlled
59.65% of the CHOAM directorship's
votes. In 10,216 House Atreides
owned 51% of CHOAM's shares, and
the priesthood of Muad'Dib owned
another 5%. By the 153rd century

CHOAM had degenerated into a trading network held together by the loosest of ties. The CHOAM company flag is a yellow field with a black and red circle in the center. [*Dune, Children of Dune, Chapterhouse: Dune*]

Choda (1,117–1,156)—Choda was a Zensunni prophet. [*Children of Dune*]

cholister—A monoped sea creature found on the very cold Bene Gesserit punishment planet Buzzell, the cholister produces soostones, one of the most highly-valued jewels in the universe, in its abraided carapace. [*Chapterhouse: Dune*]

The Church of Shai-Hulud, The Divided God—Held in contempt by the Bene Gesserit and their Supreme Bashar, Miles Teg, The Church of Shai-Hulud, The Divided God, was a religion that flourished on Rakis in the 153rd century. [*Heretics of Dune*]

Chusuk—The fourth planet in the Theta Shalish system, Chusuk is known for the quality of its musical instruments. Gurney Hallek owned a baliset—which is tuned to the Chusuk scale—that was made by Varota on Chusuk. [*Dune*]

cibus hood—A cibus hood was a mask of Ixian design that could conceal the identity of its wearer from even the most subtle instruments of detection. [*God Emperor of Dune*]

cielago—A cielago is a modified bat of Arrakis that had been adapted to carry distrans messages. [*Dune*]

Citadel—The Citadel was the location of Great Honored Matre Dama's headquarters on Junction. The Miles Teg clone's successful 15,245 attack on Junction centered on the Citadel. [*Chapterhouse: Dune*]

Citadel Fortress—Emperor Leto II's Citadel Fortress was located in the Sareer, the sole remaining desert on Arrakis in the 138th century. It was bordered by the Forbidden Forest and guarded by D-wolves. It was torn down during the Famine Times that followed Leto II's death in 13,726. [*God Emperor of Dune, Heretics of Dune*]

City of Tombs—In Zensunni legend and Fremen mythology, the City of Tombs is a garden one thousand paces square in which dwells Ar-Razzaq, who provides food for all who ask. [*Children of Dune*]

Clairby (15,202–15,245)—Reverend Mother Superior Darwi Odrade's favorite driver, little, vinegary, fast, safe, pinched-faced Clairby drove Odrade, Reverend Mother Tamalane, Bene Gesserit acolyte Aloana Streggi, and several dozen others to the Chapterhouse Desert Watch Center in 15,244. He was mortally wounded in an ornithopter crash in 15,245, and the Bene Gesserit reluctantly transformed him into a cyborg to save his life. Later that year he piloted the small smuggler craft that transported Odrade, Tamalane, Reverend Mother Dortujla, and Bene Gesserit acolyte

Suipol to their meeting with the Honored Matres on Junction. Because shere will not protect a cyborg from a T-probe, Clairby committed suicide in destroying the ship rather than submit to an Honored Matre inspection and risk revealing the location of Chapterhouse. [*Chapterhouse: Dune*]

Coan-Teen—In Fremen mythology, the Coan-Teen is the female death-spirit who walks without feet. In 10,216 the citizens of Arrakeen referred to Regent Alia Atreides as the Coan-Teen. [*Children of Dune*]

Coanua Sietch—Chani brought Lady Jessica a gift of cloth from Coanua Sietch in 10,193, when she flew north to Cave of Birds to revive Paul Atreides after he had transmuted the Water of Life. [*Dune*]

"Collected Legends of Arrakis"—"Collected Legends of Arrakis" is one of the many volumes authored by Princess Irulan. [*Dune*]

"Collected Sayings of Muad'Dib"—"Collected Sayings of Muad'Dib" is one of the many volumes authored by Princess Irulan. [*Dune*]

Colonel—Colonel was a Sardaukar rank between Burseg and Bashar. [*Children of Dune*]

The Commentaries—*The Commentaries* was a volume authored by Stilgar. [*Children of Dune*]

Commission of Ecumenical Translators (C. E. T.)—The Commission of Ecumenical Translators (C. E. T.),

which convened on Earth following the Butlerian Jihad, produced the Orange Catholic Bible and its Commentaries. [*Dune*]

cone of silence—The cone of silence is a distorter field that dampens any vibration, including the human voice, by cancelling it with a counter-vibration 180 degrees out of phase. [*Dune*]

"Conversations with Muad'Dib"—"Conversations with Muad'Dib" is one of the many volumes authored by Princess Irulan. [*Dune*]

Convocation—A Convocation is an extremely rare meeting of all the Bene Gesserit called by the Bene Gesserit Reverend Mother Superior. Convocations occurred when Emperor Leto II seized power in 10,218, when he died in 13,726, and immediately prior to the Bene Gesserit attack on the Honored Matre headquarters on Junction in 15,245. [*Chapterhouse: Dune*]

coriolis storm—A coriolis storm was a major sandstorm on Arraiks; its winds could attain speeds of up to 700 kilometers per hour. [*Dune*]

Corrin, Battle of—Fought in space near Sigma Draconis in 88 B.G., the Battle of Corrin settled the ascendancy to the Imperial throne of the ruling House from Salusa Secundus. Imperial House Corrino took its name from this battle. [*Dune, Chapterhouse: Dune*]

Corrino, House—House Corrino

had been the Imperial House for 81 generations prior to the defeat of Emperor Shaddam IV at the hands of Paul Muad'Dib in 10,193. [*Children of Dune*]

Coss (10,148–10,192)—Coss was one of twenty-six spice miners whom Duke Leto Atreides rescued from a sandworm that consumed their sandcrawler in 10,191. [*Dune*]

Cottages at Cordeville—Sheeana stole Vincent Van Gogh's *Cottages at Cordeville* from Reverend Mother Superior Murbella's quarters at Central on Chapterhouse and took it with her when she escaped from the known universe in the Chapterhouse no-ship with Duncan Idaho ghola number 4, Scytale, Rebecca, the Rabbi, Bene Gesserit Proctor Garimi, a sandworm, and some Futars in 15,245. [*Chapterhouse: Dune*]

"Count Fenring: A Profile"—"Count Fenring: A Profile" is one of the many volumes authored by Princess Irulan. [*Dune*]

crawler—*See* **sandcrawler**. [*Dune*]

crusher—A crusher is an assemblage of many interlocked military space vessels designed to fall on an enemy position and crush it. [*Dune*]

crypt—The crypt was the section of Emperor Leto II's fortress Citadel in the Sareer in which Leto II entombed his deceased Duncan Idaho gholas and the deceased offspring of his breeding program. Ghanima Atreides'

corpse, Harq al-Ada's corpse, and Paul Muad'Dib's water are also there. Leto II often interviewed his Idaho gholas and the offspring of his breeding program, such as Moneo, in the crypt. [*God Emperor of Dune*]

crysknife—A twenty-centemeter-long, double-edged, milk-white blade ground from the tooth of a dead sandworm, the crysknife was the sacred knife of the Fremen on Arrakis. A crysknife could be either "fixed" or "unfixed." A "fixed" crysknife could be stored, but an "unfixed" crysknife would disintegrate if not kept in the proximity of a human body's electrical field. The Shadout Mapes gave an "unfixed" crysknife to Lady Jessica in 10,191, at which time no crysknife had ever successfully been taken off of Arrakis. Any person who had seen a crysknife could not leave Arrakis without the consent of the Fremen. [*Dune*]

Cult of Alia—In the 138th century Duncan Idaho ghola number 3 discovered a Cult of Alia—a group that worshipped Paul Muad'Dib's long-deceased sister—on Giedi Prime. [*God Emperor of Dune*]

Cutteray—A cutteray is a short-range lasgun used as a cutting tool. [*Dune*]

Czigo (10,158–10,191)—Czigo was a Harkonnen trooper who, with Kinet, conveyed the captive Lady Jessica and Paul Atreides to the desert, where they were to be killed, after the fall of

Arrakeen in 10,191. Czigo there loosened Jessica's gag, allowing her to use the Voice, and she then manipulated him into killing Kinet. Paul then killed Czigo with a well-placed thrust of his right foot. [*Dune*]

Dalak (10,171–10,210)—A relative of Count Hasimir Fenring's, Dalak was Princess Wensicia's husband and Prince Farad'n's father. [*Children of Dune*]

Dalamak (9th and 10th centuries B.G.)—Dalamak was Emperor of the known universe on two separate occasions in the eighth and ninth centuries before the Battle of Corrin. [*Dune Messiah*]

Dama, Great Honored Matre—*See* **Great Honored Matre Dama**.

Dan—Dan was a region of the Imperium containing several planets whose inhabitants had agitated for another Jihad against the machines in the 138th century. [*God Emperor of Dune*]

Dan—By the 153rd century Caladan had come to be known as Dan. See **Caladan**. [*Heretics of Dune*]

"Dance Diversion"—A frantic, apparently unrhythmic dance that was related to the Fremen way of sandwalking and that often ended in bloodshed and the death of the dancers, the "Dance Diversion" was the remnant of Siaynoq in the 153rd century. The Bene Gesserit believed that the "Dance Diversion" and other

Rakian dances were a kind of language. [*Heretics of Dune*]

Dance of Propitiation—In the 153rd century the Dance of Propitiation was an almost rhythmless dance, related to the Fremen way of sandwalking, that beseeched Shai-Hulud to forgive his people. The Bene Gesserit believed that the Dance of Propitiation and other Fremen dances were a kind of language. [*Heretics of Dune*]

Danian Marinete—Deep blue Danian Marinete, a very fine brandy from Dan, was Bene Gesserit Supreme Bashar Miles Teg's favorite alcoholic beverage. [*Heretics of Dune, Chapterhouse: Dune*]

Daniel (14,890–15,285)—Marty's partner, Daniel was the grandfatherly Face Dancer in antique farmer's clothing, tending his garden in the Scattering, whom Duncan Idaho ghola number 4 saw in his Mentat visions of "the net" in 15,244 and 15,245. He may have been a leader of the evolved Face Dancers who drove the Honored Matres from the Scattering back into the known universe of the Old Empire in the 153rd century. [*Chapterhouse: Dune*]

Dar-es-Balat—The earliest known no-chamber in the universe, Dar-es-Balat was the site on Rakis (Arrakis) where Hadi Benotto's research team discovered Emperor Leto II's original journals, inscribed by an Ixian dictatel on ridulian crystal paper, in the 143rd century. There was a museum at Dar-es-Balat in the 153rd century. [*God Emperor of Dune, Heretics of Dune*]

Delnay, Professor (15,151–15,463)— In 15,232 Professor Delnay, a winter farmer on Gammu and a professor of martial arts and the history of martial arts, took Bene Gesserit Supreme Bashar Miles Teg to a bar in Ysai where Teg recruited many soldiers who had served under him at Renditai. [*Heretics of Dune*]

Delta Pavonis—Delta Pavonis is the star about which Caladan orbits as well as the planet, in another star system, about which the moon Harmonthep once orbited. [*Dune*]

Desert Botanical Testing Stations— The Desert Botanical Testing Stations were ancient advanced Imperial bases on Arrakis in which supplies and material were stored. Dr. Liet Kynes took Paul Atreides and Lady Jessica to a Desert Botanical Testing Station in which Duncan Idaho was killed during their escape into the desert after the fall of Arrakeen in 10,191. [*Dune*]

Desert Demon—The Desert Demon was Leto Atreides II, his strength and speed amplified by the skin of sand trout that had merged with his body, who in 10,217 and 10,218, before returning to Arrakeen, destroyed the qanats of many new djedidas, making them uninhabitable. [*Children of Dune*]

Desert Watch Center—The Desert Watch Center was a temporary installation on Chapterhouse, established in 15,244, from which Sheeana kept a lookout for any sandworms that might appear in Chapterhouse's expanding equatorial desert. Bene Gesserit Senior Acolyte Assistant Walli assumed command of the Desert Watch Center in 15,245. [*Chapterhouse: Dune*]

Desert of Zan—The desert of Zan was the legendary location of the first trial of the Zensunni Wanderers, the ancestors of the Fremen. [*Children of Dune*]

Desian Gesture—A shortening of the term "Atreidesian Gesture," a Desian Gesture is a dramatic act that one has chosen even though choosing it dictates one's future course of action. [*Chapterhouse: Dune*]

The Desposyni—Arrakis' Oral History termed the caliphate of Emperor Paul Muad'Dib's heirs *The Desposyni*. [*God Emperor of Dune*]

De Vries, Piter (10,145–10,191)—A hawk-featured, sadistic, effeminate, tenor-voiced mentat assassin in the service of Baron Vladimir Harkonnen, Piter de Vries had Fremen-like blue-within-blue eyes as a result of excessive spice consumption. He had devised the plan to destroy House Atreides and end Duke Leto's line by luring the Atreides to Arrakis on Emperor Shaddam IV's orders. He murdered Dr. Wellington Yueh on the Baron's orders, after Yueh had betrayed the Atreides, but was then inadvertently killed by Duke Leto when Leto unsuccessfully attempted to use the poison gas hidden in a false tooth to assassinate the Baron. [*Dune*]

dew collectors—Also known as dew precipitators, dew collectors are four-centimeter-long, chromoplastic, egg-shaped devices that are transparent in darkness but turn white in light. They were used to line small pits in which the Fremen planted vegetation in the desert. They reflect light during the day but cool at night, when the dew that waters their plant forms on them. [*Dune*]

Dhuri (10,167–10,207)—One of Otheym's wives and Lichna's mother, Dhuri was present when Emperor Paul Muad'Dib visited Otheym in the suburbs of Arrakeen in 10,207. [*Dune Messiah*]

Dhyana—Dhyana was the spice-induced internal reality grasped by Leto Atreides II as he escaped from Jacurutu into the Tanzerouft in 10,216. [*Children of Dune*]

dictatel—A dictatel is an Ixian machine that transcribes thought into print. [*God Emperor of Dune*]

"Dictionary of Muad'Dib"—"Dictionary of Muad'Dib" is one of the many volumes authored by Princess Irulan. [*Dune*]

"The Disputation of Armistead and Leandgrah"—"The Disputation of Armistead and Leandgrah" was a play popular in Arrakeen in 10,216. [*Children of Dune*]

distrans—A distrans is a device that produces a temporary neural imprint on the nervous system of a bat or bird. The animal's cry then contains a message that can be separated from the cry itself by another distrans. The distrans was used by the Fremen to transmit messages across the desert. By 10,205 both Emperor Paul Muad'Dib and the Bene Gesserit/Tleilaxu/Guild conspiracy against him were employing human beings to carry distrans messages. [*Dune, Dune Messiah*]

Dit, Dat, and Dot—Dit, Dat, and Dot were puppets from the planet's Winter Show that Bene Gesserit Supreme Bashar Miles Teg remembered from his childhood on Lernaeus. [*Heretics of Dune*]

djedida—A djedida was a type of new town on Arrakis founded after Muad'Dib's Jihad, in the early 103rd century. Djedidas were built above ground level, not in caves, and were designed to take advantage of the increased moisture in the previously more-arid Arrakeen desert. [*Children of Dune*]

Djedida (10,174–10,207)—Secretary to Korba, Djedida was a Fremen Naib who was identified by Bijaz in 10,207 as being one of the Fremen traitors conspiring against Emperor Paul Muad'Dib. [*Dune Messiah*]

dolban screens—An Ixian device popular in the 153rd century with artists and antique dealers, dolban screens are flat black slats ten molecules wide rotating in a transparent liquid medium that admits the full spectrum of a predetermined level of light without diminishing the view. [*Heretics of Dune*]

Domel—The lowest ranking caste among the Tleilaxu Masters, Domel were conditioned to bow to the white khilat, the robe of honor worn by the Tleilaxu Mahai, the Master of Masters. [*Heretics of Dune*]

Dortujla, Reverend Mother (14,892–15,245)—An aging Reverend Mother from the Bene Gesserit punishment planet Buzzell who had been banished for having succumbed to a love affair, Dortujla collected old coins as a hobby, had had dealings with soostone smugglers on Buzzell, and possessed a small no-ship. She brought Reverend Mother Superior Darwi Odrade the message in 15,244 that Futars from the Scattering wanted to join the Bene Gesserit in their fight against the Honored Matres, and she agreed to let Odrade use her as bait on Buzzell to entice the Honored Matres into meeting to negotiate a Bene Gesserit surrender at Junction. In 15,245 she returned to Chapterhouse—ill from experiments the Honored Matres had conducted on her—with the message that the Honored Matres had agreed to attend such a meeting. All three of the Bene Gesserit Reverend Mothers who had accompanied Dortujla to Junction had been killed by the Honored Matres and eaten by Futars, and Dortujla had received all of their other memories prior to their deaths. Odrade subsequently appointed Dortujla to be a special advisor to her Council and then had Dortujla share her other memories with Reverend Mother Bellonda in preparation for having Dortujla accompany Reverend Mother Tamalane and herself to the parlay with the Honored Matres on Junction. Dortujla accompanied Odrade, Tamalane, and Bene Gesserit acolyte Suipol to Junction and was killed there by the Honored Matres during the Miles Teg clone's successful attack on the planet. [*Chapterhouse: Dune*]

Drisq (10,160–10,205)—Drisq was smuggler Staban Tuek's quartermaster in 10,191. He was instructed by Tuek to extend every courtesy to the 74 men still under Gurney Hallek's command after the fall of Arrakeen. [*Dune*]

Drumind (15,037–15,223)—A historian-locutor among the Rakian priests who had been dismissed as evil by Sheeana the day after she had been adopted by the Rakian priesthood, Drumind admonished the other Rakian priests to study Sheeana and was shortly thereafter taken to the desert to be killed by a sandworm on Rakian High Priest Hedley Tuek's orders. [*Heretics of Dune*]

drum sand—On Arrakis, drum sand is a condition of sand compaction that produces a distinct drumming sound when the area affected is struck or stepped on. [*Dune*]

Duana (15,181–15,487)—Duana was Reverend Mother Superior Darwi

Odrade's cook at Chapterhouse Central. [*Chapterhouse: Dune*]

Dune—Dune was the popular name for the desert planet Arrakis. *See* **Arrakis.**

The Dunebuk of Irulan—*The Dunebuk of Irulan* is one of the many volumes authored by Princess Irulan. [*Dune Messiah*]

Dune Tarot—The Dune Tarot was a fortune-telling method employing cards that greatly muddied the currents of time for such prescients as Emperor Paul Muad'Dib, his sister Alia, and the Guild Steersmen. [*Dune Messiah*]

Dur—Homeworld to Honored Matre Field Marshal Jafa Muzzafar, Dur is a jungle planet in the Scattering. [*Heretics of Dune*]

Dur—Dur and Guldur were the names by which Emperor Leto II was known in the Scattering. [*Chapterhouse: Dune*]

dust chasms—Also known as tidal dust basins, dust chasms were any deep depression in the desert of Arrakis that had filled with dust. Indistinguishable from the surrounding area, dust chasms constituted a deadly trap in the desert because any anlmal or human attempting to walk on one would sink and smother. [*Dune*]

D-wolves—Man-high at the shoulders but susceptible to poison, the keen-eyed D-wolves were monstrous pack animals that guarded Emperor Leto II's Citadel fortress in the Sareer in the 138th century. In 13,726 D-wolves in the Forbidden Forest killed the ten companions who had helped Siona Ibn Faud al-Seyefa Atreides steal The Stolen Journals from Leto II's Citadel. [*God Emperor of Dune*]

Earth—Earth was the site of the Commission of Ecumenical Translators (C. E. T.) convention that produced the Orange Catholic Bible and its Commentaries in the aftermath of the Butlerian Jihad. [*Dune*]

Ecaz—The fourth planet orbiting Alpha Centauri B, Ecaz is the native planet of several exotic plants: sapho, the juice of which is used by Mentats to enhance their thinking processes; fogwood, a favorite plant of sculptors because its wood can be shaped solely by human thought; the hufuf vine, from which krimskell fiber is woven; and elacca wood, from which both semuta and the elacca drug is derived. Verite is also a narcotic derived from a plant native to Ecaz. Ecaz eventually became a Bene Gesserit planet and was captured by the Honored Matres in the 153rd century. [*Dune, Chapterhouse: Dune*]

Edric (10,127–10,207)—A Guild Steersman of limited intellect, Edric was a participant in the 10,205–07 conspiracy against Emperor Paul Muad'Dib that also included Reverend Mother Gaius Helen Mohiam, Scytale, and Princess Irulan. An elongated, vaguely humanoid figure with tiny rodent eyes, monstrous finned feet, and fanned, membranous hands who occupied a transparent tank filled with mélange gas, Edric's role in the conspiracy was, as a Guild Steersman with prescience, to shield the conspiracy from Paul's prescience. He became Guild Steersman-Ambassador to Paul's Imperial Court in 10,207 and on that occasion gave the ghola Hayt to Paul as a gift. Later that year he accompanied Chani—with Paul, Bijaz, Hayt, Alia, Mohiam, Scytale disguised as Lichna, Stilgar, Harah, and Irulan—when she returned to the desert, to Sietch Tabr, to give birth. After Chani's death in childbirth, Edric was executed by Stilgar on Alia's orders. [*Dune Messiah*]

Edric (14,992–15,270)—Edric was a Guild Navigator who attempted to aid the Bene Gesserit in 15,243. [*Chapterhouse: Dune*]

Eknekosk, Reverend Mother (13,677–13,746)—Bene Gesserit Reverend Mother Eknekosk was an author of the Welbeck Abridgement, a 13,726 report to the Bene Gesserit. [*God Emperor of Dune*]

elacca drug—Native to Ecaz and commonly used to prepare slave gladiators for the arena, the elacca drug is a narcotic that removes most of the user's will to live. Produced by burning blood-grained elacca wood, it turns the user's skin orange. [*Dune*]

Eldio—Eldio was a Chapterhouse community near the shrinking equatorial sea at which Reverend Mother

Superior Darwi Odrade, Reverend Mother Tamalane, Bene Gesserit acolyte Aloana Streggi, and their entourage spent the night en route from Central to the Desert Watch Center in 15,244. [*Chapterhouse: Dune*]

El Kuds—El Kuds was the holy place on Arrakis, a promontory above Harg Pass, where Duke Leto Atreides' skull was enshrined. [*Dune Messiah*]

Elpa (10,183–10,207)—Blinded in 10,207 by the stone burner that also blinded Emperor Paul Muad'Dib, Elpa was a citizen of Arrakeen who swore than he would commit suicide rather than take Tleilaxu eyes. [*Dune Messiah*]

Elpek, Senior Dame (15,167–15,245)—Senior Dame Elpek was an ancient, powerful Honored Matre who accepted Murbella as an Honored Matre after the battle for Junction and took her to see Great Honored Matre Longo. Elpek assassinated Reverend Mother Superior Odrade as Murbella was murdering Longo, and she was soon thereafter killed by Murbella. [*Chapterhouse: Dune*]

Elrood IX, Emperor (10,079–10,156)—Emperor Shaddam IV's father and the emperor who preceded him, Elrood IX is reputed to have been poisoned by Count Hasimir Fenring. [*Dune*]

el-sayal—The rain of sand that brings the morning, el-sayal was a fall of dust that had been carried to an altitude of about 2,000 meters by a coriolis storm on Arrakis. It frequently brought moisture to ground levels. [*Dune*]

Enemy of Many Faces—Foes of the Honored Matres who drove them from the Scattering back into the known universe of the Old Empire in the 153rd century, the Enemy of Many Faces were the evolved descendants of Face Dancers who had gone out into the Scattering in the 138th century. [*Chapterhouse: Dune*]

Enfeil—Enfeil was the planet on which Farok had led Muad'Dib's Jihad to victory and on which he had first seen a sea. [*Dune Messiah*]

entio—An entio was a tribal leader during the great Zensunni wandering, prior to the arrival of the Fremen on Arrakis. [*Heretics of Dune*]

Epsilon Alangue—Epsilon Alangue is the star about which Poritrin orbits. [*Dune*]

Eridani A—Eridani A is the star about which Richese orbits. [*Dune*]

Extremis Progressiva—Extremis Progressiva is the Bene Gesserit process of mutually sharing all of the other memories of all the Reverend Mothers present when their lives are all in imminent danger. [*Chapterhouse: Dune*]

Face Dancers—Submissive to the Tleilaxu Masters and possessing no sense of self, Face Dancers are Tleilaxu who have the chameleon-like ability to alter their appearance across a wide range of body types and facial features as well as to assume the psyches of the individuals they mimic. When not mimicking another, face dancers are small, chinless, round-faced, pug-nosed males with tiny mouths, black-button eyes, and short-cropped white hair. Although they cannot breed, face dancers are Jadacha hermaphrodites, able to assume the guise of either sex at will. From the 103rd century through to 13,726, Face Dancers impersonated Paul Atreides in the staged drama on Tlielax that awakened the original Duncan Idaho persona of Emperor Leto II's Duncan Idaho gholas. In 13,726 numerous Face Dancers infiltrated the Ixian Embassy on Arrakis, and fifty Face Dancers disguised as Dundan Idaho attempted unsuccessfully to assassinate Leto II as he travelled on the Royal Road to the festival city of Onn. In retribution, and because they also appeared to have posed a threat to his fiancé Hwi Noree, Leto II subsequently had his Fish Speakers slay all the Face Dancers in Onn. The 200 Face Dancers remaining on Arrakis then performed at Leto II's and Hwi Noree's bethrothal ceremony. By the 153rd century, "new" Face Dancers had developed the ability to absorb memories by touching their victims and could transmit those memories to another Face Dancer. By that time the new Face Dancers had infiltrated the highest councils of Ix and the Fish Speakers and had even infiltrated the ranks of the Honored Matres.

However, even the new Face Dancers could be detected by the Bene Gesserit through the unique smell of their pheromones. By the 153rd century Face Dancers had evolved into the dominant force in the Scattering and had driven the Honored Matres back into the known universe of the Old Empire. [*Dune Messiah, God Emperor of Dune, Heretics of Dune, Chapterhouse: Dune*]

The fai—The fai was the water tribute, the principle form of taxation on Arrakis in the 102rd century. [*Dune*]

Fali (15,183–15,516)—Tall, hollow-cheeked, sharp-chinned, thin-mouthed Fali was in the early 153rd century the Orchard Mistress in Pondrille, a Bene Gesserit postulant center near the Desert Watch Center on Chapterhouse. [*Chapterhouse: Dune*]

False Sietch—A kilometer-wide, free-form building of irregular domes on the outskirts of Onn, False Sietch was the first abode and subsequently the school of the Museum Fremen. During the festival of 13,726, Emperor Leto II met the Bene Geserrit delegation in False Sietch. [*God Emperor of Dune*]

Famine Times—The Famine Times, which coincided with the Scattering, was the period of great deprivation in the Old (Atreides) Empire that followed the death of Emperor Leto II in 13,726. [*Heretics of Dune*]

Farad'n, Prince (10,199–10,308)—Emperor Shaddam IV's grandson and the son of Princess Wensicia and Dalak, the unusually intelligent Prince Farad'n was only mildly attracted to the possibility of sitting on the Imperial throne because he had so many other interests, principally history and archaeology. In 10,216 he described one of his dreams to The Preacher, who had been transported from Arrakis to Salusa Secundus on Wensicia's orders by Tyekanik, ostensibly to interpret Farad'n's dreams, but in reality to interest Farad'n in the religion of Muad'Dib so that Farad'n might thereby ingratiate himself to the Fremen. However, The Preacher refused to reveal his interpretation of Farad'n's dream on the grounds that his interpretation would only be misinterpreted. Farad'n was subsequently convinced that the Corrino spy in Regent Alia Atreides' court, Alia's lover Ziarenko Javid, was a double agent. Angered by his mother's plot to assassinate Leto Atreides II and Ghanima, he agrees to banish Wensicia in return for Jessica's offer to teach him the Bene Gesserit way. He also refused Alia's offer to marry him, due to his realization that she would ultimately destroy him, but he accepted an offer to be bethrothal to Ghanima. He grew more sinewy and slender during the months in which he was instructed in the Bene Gesseriut way by Jessica, who had been transported from Arralis to Salusa Secundus by Hayt, and the end result of this tutelage was his transformation from a Corrino into a Bene Gesserit. In

10,218 he travelled with Jessica to Arrakis to be bethrothed to Ghanima. After witnessing Alia's suicide he was appointed Royal Scribe by Emperor Leto II and was renamed Harq al-Ada. He was subsequently Ghanima's lover and consort, and the father of her children, although Ghanima formally married her brother Leto II. *See* **Harq al-Ada**. [*Children of Dune*]

Farok (10,169–10,207)—Farok was a member of Stilgar's band of forty Fremen who found Paul Atreides and Lady Jessica at Tuono Basin after the fall of Arrakeen in 10,191. In 10,207, after having served as a Bashar of the Ninth Legion of Muad'Dib's Jihad, he met Scytale in a suburb of Arrakeen to further the conspiracy against Muad'Dib because he longed for the old days and the old Fremen ways that Muad'Dib had changed. He had joined the Jihad only for the opportunity it afforded to enable him to view a sea, something he could not imagine. He finally saw a sea on Enfeil, and this cured him of any desire to participate further in the Jihad. He was killed in his own home by Scytale's poisoned needle after turning Otheym's daughter Lichna over to Scytale. [*Dune, Dune Messiah*]

Farok's Son (10,185–10,207)—Farok's son, who had been blinded on Naraj by a stone burner during Muad'Dib's Jihad, subsequently lived with his father in a suburb of Arrakeen. In 10,207 he was the human distrans who communicated information about the Fremen conspiracy against Muad'Dib on Arrakis to Scytale while playing the baliset in his father's house. It was he who had addicted Otheym's daughter Lichna to semuta, vainly hoping thus to win a Fremen woman despite his blindness. [*Dune Messiah*]

Faroula (10,153–10,187)—A noted Fremen herbalist, Faroula was Chani's mother, Stilgar's sister, Liet-Kynes' wife, and Emperor Leto II's maternal grandmother. [*God Emperor of Dune*]

Farrukh (10,161–10,201)—Farrukh was a member of Stilgar's band of forty Fremen who found Paul Atreides and Lady Jessica at Tuono Basin after the fall of Arrakeen in 10,191. He, with Larus, was charged with hiding the band's tracks as it proceeded to Sietch Tabr. [*Dune*]

Fash (10,177–10,217)—Fash was a dissident Fremen Naib who fled Arrakis with a stolen worm in 10,207. [*Dune Messiah*]

faufreluches—Faufreluches was the rigid system of class stratification imposed by the Empire in the 102nd century. [*Dune*]

fedaykin—The fedaykin were Paul Muad'Dib's Fremen death commandos. Chatt the Leaper was their captain in 10,193. [*Dune*]

Fenring, Count Hasimir (10,118–10,225)—A dapper and ugly little man, the small, weak-looking, weasel-faced, gray-eyed Count Hasimir Fenring was in his time one of the deadliest fighters in the Empire and was the childhood companion and only real friend to Emperor Shaddam IV. He was reputedly responsible for the chaumurky that killed Emperor Elrood IX in 10,156. As Shaddam IV's Imperial agent on Arrakis during the Harkonnen regime, Count Fenring and his wife, Lady Margot Fenring, had inhabited the palace in Arrakeen prior to the Atreides' 10,191 relocation to Arrakis. Afterwards he was appointed Siridar-Absentia of Caladan. Through dispensing bribes and gifts, he allayed the Landsraad's suspicions about the Emperor's complicity in the Harkonnen's 10,191 victory on Arrakis. He and Lady Fenring, who publicly communicated with one another in a secret humming code, observed Feyd-Rautha Rabban Harkonnen's 100th gladiatorial combat in the arena in Giedi Prime's capital, Harko, later in 10,191. In 10,193 he accompanied Shaddam IV to Arrakis, but he refused to obey the Emperor's order to engage Paul in a duel following the Emperor's defeat at Arrakeen. As Count Fenring was a genetic eunuch and an almost Kwisatz Haderach, Paul's prescience could not perceive him. He joined Shaddam IV in retirement on Salusa Secundus. [*Dune*]

Fenring, Lady Margot (10,151–10,245)—Gray-green-eyed, golden-haired, and willowy, Lady Margot Fenring was a Bene Gesserit and the wife of Count Hassimir Fenring. In 10,191 she left fellow-Bene-Gesserit Lady Jessica a coded message in Arrakeen's ducal palace informing her that the Harkonnens had set a death trap for her son, Paul, and that one of the Atreides retainers was a traitor. She and Count Fenring, who publicly communicated with one another in a secret humming code, observed Feyd-Rautha Rabban Harkonnen's 100th gladiatorial combat in the arena in Giedi Prime's capital, Harko, in 10,191. During that visit to Giedi Prime she seduced and was impregnated by Feyd-Rautha on orders from the Bene Gesserit, who were desperate to preserve Feyd-Rautha's genes. She gave birth to Feyd-Rautha's daughter in 10,192. [*Dune, Children of Dune*]

Feyd-Rautha Rabban Harkonnen (10,175–10,193)—Dark-haired, impatient, immoral, and brave, Feyd-Rautha Rabban Harkonnen was the son of Abulurd Harkonnen Rabban, the younger brother of Count Glossu "Beast" Rabban, and the nephew of Baron Vladimir Harkonnen. He took the name Harkonnen when he joined the Baron's household. During his 100th gladiatorial combat in the arena in Giedi Prime's capital, Harko, in 10,191, on the occasion of his 16th birthday, he was lauded as a hero by the crowd for having defeated an undrugged Atreides soldier-gladiator. However, that the gladiator was not drugged was part of a plot Feyd-Rautha had concocted with Thufir Hawat to make himself appear to be more heroic and intimidating. Feyd-

Rautha attempted unsuccessfully to assassinate Baron Harkonnen by hiding a poisoned needle in a slave boy's thigh in 10,193. As punishment, he was ordered by the Baron to murder his lovers, all of the women in the Harko palace's pleasure wing. Later in 10,193 he accompanied the Baron and Emperor Shaddam IV to Arrakis, where he fought a duel with Paul Muad'Dib and was killed by a crysknife thrust to the brain. [*Dune*]

Fintil, Reverend Mother (15,181–15,427—Fintil had been Reverend Mother Dortujla's trusted acolyte prior to undergoing the Spice Agony to become a Reverend Mother herself in 15,244. [*Chapterhouse: Dune*]

fiqh—Meaning "religious law" or "knowledge" in Chakobsa, fiqh was one of the half-legendary origins of the faith of the Zensunni Wanderers. [*Dune*]

First Moon—The major satellite of Arrakis and the first of its two moons to rise in the night sky, First Moon is notable for the fist pattern on its surface. [*Dune*]

Firus (14,956–15,297)—A native of Lernaeus, Firus was Bene Gesserit Supreme Bashar Miles Teg's son-in-law and Dimela Teg's husband. [*Heretics of Dune*]

Fish Speakers—Fanaticaly devoted to Emperor Leto II, Fish Speakers were Leto II's heavily-muscled, all-female military establishment. They served as Leto II's Imperial Guard on Arrakis as well as in off-planet garrisons. In the 138th century the Fish Speaker School was located in the festival city of Onn, and Fish Speakers were—with the Duncan Idaho gholas, who served as Leto II's Imperial Guard Captains—the only citizens permitted to participate in Siaynoq, the Feast of Leto. In the Famine Times that followed the death of Emperor Leto II in 13,726, the Fish Speakers found and subsequently squandered a vast mélange hoard Leto II had hidden at Seitch Tabr. By the 153rd century the Fish Speakers had become a military force allied with IX and had inherited the core of the old Atreides Empire, but they were led by Tleilaxu Face Dancers disguised as Fish Speakers and were still a less powerful force in the universe than the Bene Gesserit, the Spacing Guild, the Bene Tleilax, or Ix. By the 153rd century the democracy practiced by Fish Speakers who had gone out into the Scattering had devolved into the Honored Matre's autocracy. [*God Emperor of Dune, Heretics of Dune, Chapterhouse: Dune*]

fogwood—Highly prized by sculptors, fogwood is a plant native to Ecaz that can be shaped solely by human thought. [*Dune*]

Fondak—Fondak was a desert Sietch that by 10,216 had been completely taken over by smugglers and had become taboo to the Fremen. It was the secret location of Jacurutu, the legendary sietch of the water stealers. *See* **Jacurutu**. [*Children of Dune*]

Forbidden Forest—Guarded by D-wolves, the Forbidden Forest was in the 138th century a region of Arrakis bordering the last desert of the Sareer, which contained Emperor Leto II's Citadel fortress. [*God Emperor of Dune*]

Foum al-Hout—Foum al-Hout is Arrakis' southern pole star. [*Children of Dune*]

Fourteen Sages—The Fourteen Sages were the fourteen members of the Commission of Ecumenical Translators (C. E. T.) who never recanted the teachings of the Orange Catholic Bible. [*Dune*]

Fremen—The tough, renegade natives of Arrakis who lived in the desert—not in the grabens, sinks, and pans—the Fremen were the descendants of the Zensunni Wanderers. Imbued with a deep hatred of the Harkonnens throughout much of the 102nd century, when they numbered some 20 million, they had the ability to control Arrakis' sandworms and used them for transportation in Arrakis' deep desert. Their eyes were totally blue due to the saturation of their blood with the spice, mélange, and their blood also exhibited the property of ultra-fast coagulation. The Fremen culture was trained to military order as an adaptation to their harsh life in the desert. Their dream was slowly, over a period of centuries, to transform Arrakis into a water-planet. They allied with Paul Atreides and Lady Jessica in 10,191 and were instrumental in the defeat of the Harkonnens in 10,193. [*Dune*]

fremkit—A desert survival kit manufactured by the Fremen, a fremkit contains a stillsuit, a stilltent, a para-compass, thumpers, maker hooks, the Kitab Al-Ibar, a literjohn of water, binoculars, and a knife. A fremkit was hidden by Dr. Wellington Yueh in the ornithopter that transported Paul Atreides and Lady Jessica into the desert of Arrakis when they were captured during the fall of Arrakeen in 10,191 [*Dune*]

Futars—By the 153rd century the Tleilaxu of the Scattering had interbred human beings and large cats to produce Futars, which were used to hunt Honored Matres. Great Honored Matre Dama kept a caged Futar that had been captured on Gammu in her quarters on Junction. In 15,244 a group of Futars who had returned to the Old Empire offered through Reverend Mother Dortujla to ally themselves with the Bene Gesserit against the Honored Matres. Some captive Futars were in the hold of the Chapterhouse no-ship when Duncan Idaho ghola number 4 launched it into the unknown space beyond the known universe of the Old Empire in 15,245. [*Heretics of Dune, Chapterhouse: Dune*]

Galach—Galach, a hybrid Inglo-Slavic tongue, is the official language of the Imperium. [*Dune*]

"Galacian Girls"—"Galacian Girls"

is a bawdy song popular in the 102nd century. [*Dune*]

Gamma Waiping—Gamma Waiping is the star about which Salusa Secundus orbits. [*Dune*]

Gammu—Gurney Hallek changed the name of Giedi Prime to Gammu in the 103rd century. The planet was recolonized and rebuilt by the people of Dan (Caladan) after the Famine Times and the Scattering of the 138th century, when the Harkonnens had abandoned it. By the 153rd century Gammu had become a Bene Gesserit banking center, and the citizens of Gammu by that time possessed a strong Harkonnen and Atreides geneology and had developed especially seductive eyes due to Bene Gesserit backbreeding. Gammu was captured by the Honored Matres in the early 153rd century. *See also* **Giedi Prime**. [*Heretics of Dune, Chapterhouse: Dune*]

Gammu Keep—Forty-five kilometers long, 30 kilometers wide, 950 stories high, and composed entirely of plasteel and armor-plaz, the Gammu Keep is the center of Gammu's capital city, Barony (later, Ysai). From the time of the Old Empire through to the 153rd century, the Gammu Keep had been surrounded by a forest reserve in which the Harkonnens had once hunted human game and grown pilingtam, a valuable wood. [*Heretics of Dune*]

Gamont—The third planet orbiting the star Niushe, Gamont was noted in the 102nd century for its hedonistic culture and exotic sexual practices. It had become a Bene Gesserit planet by the 153rd century, when it was captured by the Honored Matres. [*Dune, Chapterhouse: Dune*]

Gansireed—Gansireed was a planet in the Imperium in the 103rd century. [*Children of Dune*]

Gara Rulen—After merging with the sand trout in 10,217, Leto Atreides II destroyed the qanats at Gara Rulen, Windsak, Old Gap, and Harg to set back the ecological transformation of Arrakis. [*Children of Dune*]

Gare Ruden—In 10,218 Leto Atreides II introduced Gurney Hallek to The Preacher and revealed himself to be the Desert Demon in one of the small rebel sietches in Gare Ruden. [*Children of Dune*]

Garimi (15,115–15,464)—Garimi was a Bene Gesserit Chief Assignment Proctor who spoke at the 15,245 Bene Gesserit Convocation on Chapterhouse. Later that year she escaped from the known universe of the Old Empire in the Chapterhouse no-ship with Duncan Idaho ghola number 4, Scytale, Sheeana, Rebecca, the Rabbi, a sandworm, and some Futars. [*Chapterhouse: Dune*]

Garun of Tuono (13,672–13,744)—Garun was the old-looking, brown-eyed Museum Fremen who greeted Siona Ibn Faud al-Seyefa Atreides, Nayla, and Duncan Idaho ghola number 3 when they entered Tuono Village, the prospective site of Leto II's marriage to Hwi Noree, in 13,726. Although he was not at all like one, Garun wanted desperately to be like a genuine 102nd-century Fremen. [*God Emperor of Dune*]

Geasa, Reverend Mother Luran (15,101–15,427)—A failed Bene Gesserit Reverend Mother, Luran Geasa was Duncan Idaho ghola number 4's chief teacher on Gammu when he was eight years old. She was replaced by Reverend Mother Tamalane in 15,221. [*Heretics of Dune*]

Geoff (10,156–10,181)—Father of Kaleff, Harah's older son, Geoff was Harah's first husband and was slain by Jamis. [*Dune*]

Ghafla—Ghafla is a Bene Gesserit term for possession, a condition that exists when one of the pre-born is overcome by the persona of one of his or her malignant ancestors. [*Children of Dune*]

ghanima—A ghanima is something acquired in battle—or by having slain the previous owner in single combat—and kept as a memento; more generally, it is something that is no longer used for its original purpose. [*Dune, Dune Messiah*]

Ghanima Atreides (10,207–10,317)—Leto Atreides II's twin and the daughter of Emperor Paul Muad'Dib and Chani, red-haired Ghanima was born in Sietch Tabr in 10,207 with full awareness, with all the prescient powers of her father, and with the mem-ories of all of her female ancestors. She participated in the Royal Council while still a child. Although it would allow them to forsee the future, she and Leto II avoided the overdose of melange that would bring on the spice trance because it would also lead to Abomination, to being possessed by one of the ancestors whose persona resided in her consciousness. Instead, she would sometimes assume her mother Chani's persona while Leto II assumed their father Paul's persona to access his memories of his prescient visions. Afterwards, it took a tremendous effort of will for the parent to relinquish her body back to the child. Shortly after arriving on Arrakis in 10,216, Jessica interviewed Ghanima at Sietch Tabr to determine if either Leto II or Ghanima had succumbed to Abomination, as Regent Alia Atreides had. That same year Ghanima was persuaded by Leto II to allow him to pursue the Golden Path forseen but not taken by Paul. Ghanima then snuck out of Sietch Tabr with Leto II, to escape being placed in Alia's custody, and—although wounded in their attack—escaped death in the desert at the paws of the Laza tigers that Princess Wensicia had had sent from Salusa Secundus to Arrakis to assassinate her and Leto II. After Leto II killed one Laza tiger with his poisoned crysknife, she killed the remaining Laza tiger with her poisoned crysknife. She then hypnotized herself into believing that Leto II had been slain by the Laza tigers as Leto II left her to seek Jacurutu. Upon returning to Sietch Tabr alone, Ghanima at first resisted Alia's plan to have her bethrothed to Prince Farad'n, whom Ghanima blamed for the supposed death of Leto II, and swore to kill Farad'n on their wedding night were she to marry him. However, in Arrakeen Alia gave Ghanima permission to slay Farad'n if she accepted the betrothal, and Ghanima accepted under that condition. She was then sent back to Sietch Tabr at the insistence of rebellious Fremen who were negotiating with Alia. She subsequently accompanied Stilgar, Irulan, and Harah into the desert, to join the Fremen rebels, when Stilgar fled Sietch Tabr after slaying Hayt in 10,217. In 10,218 Ghanima was abducted by kidnappers and, with Stilgar and Irulan, returned to Arrakeen. There, reunited with Leto II, she and Leto II confronted Alia as Leto II spoke the trigger phrase, "Secher Nbiw," that released her from the self-imposed hypnotic suggestion that had compelled her to believe that he was dead. After witnessing Alia's suicide, she was wed in a platonic union to her brother, Leto II, but took Farad'n as her future lover and as the future father of her children. [*Dune Messiah, Children of Dune*]

ghola—A product of the Tleilaxu, a ghola is a clone of a deceased individual grown in an axlotl tank from cell scrapings taken from the cadaver. A ghola has no memory of its former life, nor has it the persona of the being it had been, and it was widely believed until 10,207 that a ghola could not be restored to its original self. However, in 10,207 the Tleilaxu succeeded in restoring the memories and persona of his former self, Duncan Idaho, to the ghola Hayt. [*Dune Messiah*]

Ghufran—Ghufran is the cleansing ritual a Tleilaxu must perform, to beg pardon for having had contact with the sins of aliens, once he has returned to Tleilax after having been offworld among the powindah. [*Heretics of Dune*]

Giedi Prime—Orbiting Ophiuchi B (36), a yellow-green star, Giedi Prime was in the 102nd century the homeworld of House Harkonnen. Its day is 31.27 standard hours long, and its year is 949.65 standard days long. Its capital city in the 102nd century was Barony (later, Ysai). In the 103rd century the planet was renamed Gammu by Gurney Hallek. *See also* **Gammu**. [*Dune, Heretics of Dune*]

Ginaz, House of—One-time allies of Duke Leto Atreides, the House of Ginaz was defeated by Grumman, ruled by house Moritani, in the War of Assassins. [*Dune*]

glowglobes—Glowglobes are suspensor-buoyed illuminating devices that are self-powered by organic batteries. [*Dune*]

God's Way—God's Way was an avenue in Keen (Arrakeen) in the 153rd century that had been Emperor Leto II's route into the festival city of Onn in the 138th century. [*Heretics of Dune*]

Golden Path—The Golden Path was Paul Atreides' final prescient vision of how the future could best be negotiated—a path that Paul could not bring himself to take but that he left for his son Leto Atreides II to pursue. The Golden Path mandated that Leto II physically merge with Arralkis' sand trout to lose his humanity and become a new, hybrid creature with near-invulnerability, super-human speed, and super-human strength who would rule humanity as a tyrannical living god for up to 4,000 years and during that time impose such severe repression that humanity would erupt into a new excess of freedom on his death. Leto II foresaw that humanity would have become extinct by some hideous process before the 138th century had he not accepted the Golden Path, his metamorphosis, and become humanity's God Emperor. [*Children of Dune, God Emperor of Dune*]

gom jabbar—The gom jabbar is a poisoned needle tipped with metacyanide that is used by the Bene Gesserit to test for human awareness. Reverend Mother Gaius Hellen Mohiam tested Paul Atreides with a gom jabbar on Caladan in 10,191, and Lady Alia Atreides assassinated Baron Vladimir Harkonnen with a gom jabbar in 10,193 during the battle of Arrakeen. [*Dune*]

Goygoa—Known as Shuloch in the 103rd century, Goygoa was a village built of black stones to which Fish Speaker Inmeir flew Siona Ibn Faud al-Seyefa Atreides and Duncan Idaho Ghola number 3 in 13,726. One of Emperor Leto II's 103rd-century brides came from Shuloch/Goygoa, and Duncan Idaho ghola number 2's children—two sons and a daughter—lived in Goygoa in 13,726. *See* **Shuloch**. [*God Emperor of Dune*]

graben—Created when movement in the underlying crustal layers caused the ground to sink, a graben was a long, habitable geological ditch on Arrakis. [*Dune*]

The Great Belief—The Great Belief, which maintains that Emperor Leto II was God's prophet, is the core religious doctrine of the Bene Tleilax. [*Heretics of Dune*]

Great Convention—The Great Convention was the universal truce within the Empire, enforced until the late 102nd century, that was made possible by the balance of power maintained by the Imperial House, the Landsraad, and the Spacing Guild. Its primary proscription prohibits the use of atomic weapons against human populations. [*Dune*]

Great Honored Matre Dama (15,166–15,245)—Also know as the High One by the Honored Matres and called "Spider Queen" by Bene Gesserit Reverend Mother Superior Darwi Odrade, small, ancient, scrawny, plain, oval-faced, weak-chinned, brown-eyed Great Honored Matre Dama interviewed Rebecca and Reverend Mother Lucilla on Junction in 15,243 to get information about the Bene Gesserit. She killed Lucilla in a rage while interviewing her again on Junction in 15,244. Dama was poisoned in her private workroom on Junction in 15,245 by Honored Matre Longo—who assumed the title of Great Honored Matre on Dama's demise—while parlaying with Bene Gesserit Reverend Mother Superior Darwi Odrade, who observed the assassination. [*Chapterhouse: Dune*]

Great Messenger—The Great Messenger is an Islamiyat term for Emperor Leto II, whom the Bene Tleilax believed was God's prophet. [*Chapterhouse: Dune*]

Great Sharing—The Great Sharing was the public veneration of Emperor Leto II that occurred once every ten years in the festival city of Onn. [*God Emperor of Dune*]

Great Spice Hoard—Ledgend maintained that a mountain-sized hoard of mélange, the Great Spice Hoard, was hidden underground on a planet distant from Arrakis in the years before the first Empire and the Spacing Guild. This legend also maintained that Paul Muad'Dib still lived beside the hoard and was kept alive by it. [*God Emperor of Dune*]

Great Square of Keen—In the 153rd century the Great Square of Keen was a huge public marketplace in Keen (formerly Arrakeen) that was one kilometer wide and four kilometers long. [*Heretics of Dune*]

growler—A growler was a type of sandworm that frequently dug in its foreplates while driving itself forward with its tail. This caused part of its body to rise clear of the sand in a moving hump while also producing rumbling sounds. [*Children of Dune*]

Grumman—The second planet orbiting the star Niushe, Grumman was ruled by House Moritani and is remembered primarily for the feud between House Moritani and House Ginaz. [*Dune*]

Guild, the Spacing—After the Bene Gesserit school, the Spacing Guild was the second mental-physical training school established following the Butlerian Jihad. The Imperial calendar begins in the year in which the Spacing Guild established its monopoly on space travel and transport. With the Emperor and the Landsraad, it was one leg of the political tripod that maintained the Great Convention in the 102nd century. Dependent on mélange, which enable their navigators to foresee the future and thus to travel between star systems safely, the Spacing Guild throughout the late the 102nd century collected a huge spice bribe from the Fremen to keep Arrakis free of surveillance satellites. At the conclusion of the Fremen insurrection of 10,193, the Guild allowed thousands of ships, crammed with the soldiers of every Great House, to orbit Arrakis, but the ships were withdrawn when Paul Muad'Dib threatened to destroy all spice on Arrakis with the Water of Death if the Guild did not capitulate. In the 138th century the Guild and the Bene Gesserit conspired with Ix to create a machine that would replace Guild Navigators, but it is likely that the scientists of Ix were only conning the Guild and the Bene Gesserit by having them support research on a machine that could not yet be developed. However, by the 153rd century Ixian navigation devices had broken the Guild monopoly on space travel, and the Tleilaxu had become the Guild's only secure source of mélange. [*Dune, God Emperor of Dune, Heretics of Dune*]

Guild Key—The Guild Key was the cypher the Spacing Guild used to translate both The Stolen Journals, in 13,726, and, 1000 years later, the ridulian-crystal-paper maunscripts inscribed by Emperor Leto II and found in an ancient Ixian no-globe at Dar-es-Balat on Rakis (formerly Arrakis). [*God Emperor of Dune*]

Guldur—In the 153rd century a sect on Gammu still worshipped Emperor Leto II under the name Guldur, a name by which Leto II was also known in the Scattering. [*Heretics of Dune, Chapterhouse: Dune*]

Habbanya Erg—Habbanya Erg is the extensive dune area on Arrakis where Paul Atreides first mounted and rode a sandworm without assistance in 10,193. [*Dune*]

Habbanya Ridge—Habbanya Ridge is the area in Arrakis' northern hemisphere where Paul Atreides re-encountered Gurney Hallek among a band of smugglers in 10,193. [*Dune*]

hadhdhab—The hadhdhab was a Fremen's sense of the immense omnipresence of the desert. [*Children of Dune*]

Hagal—The second planet in the Theta Shaowei system, Hagal is known as the "Jewel Planet" even though it was mined out during the reign of Emperor Shaddam I. Emperor Shaddam IV's throne was carved from a single piece of Hagal quartz. [*Dune*]

hajra—In the Fremen language, a "hajra" is a journey or quest. [*Dune*]

Haker (15,055–15,245)—Dark, muscular, heavy-browed Haker was the Miles Teg clone's personal aide during the Bene Gesserit's 15,245 attack on the Honored Matre position on Junction. After the battle he was given custody of Great Honored Matre Longo and other captured Honored Matres, but he was then killed by the Honored Matre's secret weapon. [*Chapterhouse: Dune*]

Hakka, Honored Matre (15,175–15,253)—Hakka, who had an injured right foot, was the Honored Matre under whom Murbella had studied while on Gammu. [*Chapterhouse: Dune*]

Hall of Mirrors—The Hall of Mirrors is a term that refers to the Mentat's confrontation with his or her own ego-core. It is difficult for the Mentat to escape from the endless fascination evoked by this confrontation. [*Chapterhouse: Dune*]

Hallek, Gurney (10,147–10,234)—The baliset-playing Atreides' troubadour-warrior, Gurney Hallek was a rolling, ugly lump of a man with wispy blond hair and a beet-colored ink-vine scar on his chin who was renowned for his ability to produce a biblical quotation to match almost any occasion. Duke Leto Atreides had previously saved Hallek from the Harkonnen slave pits, where Hallek had acquired his ink-vine scar at the hands of Glossu "Beast" Rabban. The only one of Leto's lieutenants to escape the 10,191 fall of Arrakeen, Hallek remained on Arrakis to avenge himself against Rabban and joined a smuggler band led by Staban Tuek. He was reunited with Paul Atreides at Habbanya Ridge in 10,193 while investigating a false spice blow with Tuek's band of smugglers. Still believing that Lady Jessica had been the Atreides traitor, Hallek tried to slay her when Paul subsequently reunited them in Cave of Birds, but Paul intervened and revealed to Hallek that Dr. Wellington Yueh had been the traitor. During the 10,193 battle to retake Arrakeen, Hallek detonated the Atreides' family atomics to shatter the Shield Wall and allow a coriolis storm to strike the basin in which Arrakeen was located. After Paul seized the Imperial throne, he made Hallek an earl and appointed him Governor of Caladan. After having lived for twenty-three years on Caladan, Hallek returned to Arrakis with Jessica in 10,216. Jessica then ordered him to use his connections among the smugglers to seek legendary Jacurutu because it had been a feature of Leto Atreides II's prescient dreams. Later, also on Jessica's orders, he captured Leto II in the desert—after Leto II's escape from Sietch Tabr and the Laza tigers—and took him to Jacurutu to be quizzed and tested by Namri, the inquisitor chosen by Hallek. Still obeying Jessica's orders, Hallek repeatedly injected Leto II with spice essence to force him to experience prescient visions and to confront the ancestors residing in his consciousness. But on learning that Namri was really Regent Alia Atreides' ally intent on murdering him, Hallek killed Namri in self defense in Jacurutu. He subsequently fled to Staban Tuek's sietch—a smugglers' hideaway on the inner lip of False Wall—by mounting and riding a sandworm. In 10,218 Leto II introduced him to The Preacher, whom he realized was Paul, in one of the small rebel sietches in Gare Ruden. Leto II in the guise of the Desert Demon then brought Hallek, with The Preacher, to Shuloch. After Leto II became Emperor, Hallek returned to Sietch Tabr with Stilgar as Leto II's advisor to Stilgar's council. Later in the 103rd century Hallek changed the name of Giedi Prime to Gammu. [*Dune, Children of Dune, Heretics of Dune*]

handlers —Handlers were humans from the Scattering, probably Face Dancers, who managed Futars. Futars will attack an Honored Matre only on orders from a handler. [*Chapterhouse: Dune*]

Harah (10,163–10,228)—Olive-skinned, dark-haired, sharp-featured Harah was a citizen of Stilgar's Sietch Tabr. Widow to both Geoff and Jamis, and the mother of Kaleff and Orlop, Harah was accepted by Paul Atreides as his servant after Paul had slain Jamis in Cave of Ridges in 10,191. She subsequently became the infant Lady Alia Atreides' nurse, guardian, and companion and took on the task of explaining Alia's strangeness to the other Fremen of Sietch Tabr, where she eventually became one of Stilgar's wives. In 10,207 she accompanied Chani—with Paul, Stilgar, Bijaz, Hayt, Alia, Edric, Reverend Mother Gaius Helen Mohiam, Scytale disguised as Lichna, and Irulan—when she returned to the desert, to Sietch Tabr, to give birth to the twins Leto and Ghanima. When Stilgar slew Hayt in Sietch Tabr in 10,217, she accompanied him, Ghanima, and Irulan into the desert to hide among the Fremen rebels. [*Dune, Dune Messiah, Children of Dune*]

haram—In the 153rd century "haram" was a Fremen gutter term for that which was most evil. [*Heretics of Dune*]

Harg—After merging with the sand trout in 10,217, Leto Atreides II de-stroyed the qanats at Harg, Gara Rulen, Windsack, and Old Gap to set back the ecological transformation of Arrakis. [*Children of Dune*]

Harg Pass—Harg Pass was the site of the shrine on Arrakis housing Duke Leto Atreides' skull. [*Dune*]

harj—In the Fremen language, a "harj" is a desert journey or migration. [*Dune*]

Harko—Harko was the Harkonnen capital city on Giedi Prime in the 102nd century, the time of Muad'Dib. [*Dune*]

Harkonnen, Baron Vladimir (10,110–10,193)—Basso-voiced, addicted to food and to perverse sex with boys, and so grossly fat that he required portable suspensors attached to his body to support his weight, Baron Vladimir Harkonnen engaged in 10,191 in a conspiracy with Emperor Shaddam IV to destroy House Atreides by luring the Atreides from their secure base on Caladan to Arrakis, the former Harkonnen fief, where the Atreides would be more vulnerable. However, the Baron's overarching goal was eventually to betray the Emperor and to place a Harkonnen on the Imperial throne. With the assistance of the Emperor's Sardaukar and an Atreides traitor, Dr. Wellington Yueh, the Baron defeated the Atreides on Arrakis; but Paul Atreides and Lady Jessica escaped Harkonnen captivity and fled into the desert. The Baron narrowly evaded death while interrogating a captive Duke Leto Atreides when the helpless Leto attempted to assassinate him with poison gas hidden in a false tooth. After Leto's death the Baron appointed Count Glossu "Beast" Rabban to govern Arrakis. However, the Baron went to Arrakis himself in 10,193, with the Emperor and his Sardaukar, to attempt to quell a Fremen insurrection led by Paul. He was killed by a captive Lady Alia Atreides' gom jabbar during the Fremen attach on Arrakeen. However, in 10,216 the persona of the deceased Baron Harokonnen that existed within Alia's consciousness struck a bargain with her: The Baron's persona would protect her from the multitude of other ancestral personae also inhabiting her consciousness if she would allow it contact with her senses while she was intimate with her lovers. The Baron's persona then advised her to take Ziarenko Javid as her lover and to kill him in her bed if he ever revealed that he had betrayed her. The Baron's persona came by degrees to possess Alia and worked through her to wreak its revenge on the Atreides by attempting, through the planet's ecological transformation, to destroy all the sandworms on Arrakis. Its influence over Alia ended with Alia's suicide in 10,218. [*Dune, Children of Dune*]

Harkonnen, Bashar Abulurd (138–78 B.G.)—A direct-line ancestor of Baron Vladimir Harkonnen, Bashar Abulurd Harkonnen was banished for cowardice after the Butlerian Jihad's Battle of Corrin. [*Dune*]

Harkonnen no-globe—Constructed on Gammu by the Harkonnens at great expense in the 138th century and some 200 meters in diameter, the Harkonnen no-globe was discovered by Patrin, in the 150th century, when he was a teenager. The skeletons of the 21 artisans who had built the no-globe were preserved in transparent plaz along one of the no-globe's walls, and the no-globe also contained automata that existed in violation of the Butleriuan Jihad's proscription against thinking machines. In 15,232 Bene Gesserit Supreme Bashar Miles Teg, Reverend Mother Lucilla, and Duncan Idaho ghola number 4 escaped from the Bene Gesserit Keep on Gammu to the Harkonnen no-globe, where they hid for more than three months. During this time Teg restored the ghola's Duncan Idaho persona by subjecting the ghola to intense physical and emotional pain. [*Heretics of Dune*]

Harkonnens—Sworn enemies of the Atreides, the Harkonnens—who were descendants of the Greeks, the Pathans, and the Mamelukes—ruled Arrakis under a CHOAM company contract from 10,111 to 10,191. They had previously become a wealthy Great House through adroit manipulation of the whale fur trade. Their homeworld was Giedi Prime. [*Dune*]

Harmonthep—No longer in existence, Harmonthep was a moon of

Delta Pavonis and the sixth stop in the Zensunni Wanderers' (the Fremnen) migration. [*Dune*]

Harq al-Ada—Harq al-Ada, which means "Breaking of the Habit" in the Fremen tongue, was the new name bestowed on Prince Farad'n by Emperor Leto II ofter Leto II appointed Farad'n to be his Royal Scribe in 10,218. Harq al-Ada was the author of *The Butlerian Jihad, The Holy Metamorphosis, Leto Atreides II, The Mahdinate, An Analysis, The Prescient Vision, Riddles of Arrakis,* and *The Story of Liet Kynes. See* **Farad'n, Prince.** [*Children of Dune*]

Harum (prehistoric)—A despot and the ancient founder of an Earthly dynasty that lasted 4,000 years, Harum was Leto Atreides II's ultimate ancestor, the oldest ancestor whose persona existed in his consciousness, and the ancestor who finally possessed him. [*Children of Dune*]

harvesters—Also known as "crawlers," harvesters were huge machines—often 40 by 120 meters—used to mine mélange on the surface of Arrakis. They consisted of a long, bug-like body moving on independent sets of wide tracks. [*Dune*]

Hawat, Thufir (10,097–10,193)—Grizzled, weather-leathered, brown-eyed Thufir Hawat was Duke Leto Atreides' Mentat Master of Assassins. He had served three generations of Atreides dukes by the time the Atreides had relocated to Arrakis in 10,191,

by which time his lips and teeth were cranberry-colored from imbibing sapho juice. In 10,191 he ordered Duncan Idaho to keep the Lady Jessica—whom he believed might be a traitor—under constant surveillance. After the fall of Arrakeen Hawat joined forces with the Fremen but was captured by Sardaukar troops wearing Harkonnen uniforms, some 200 kilometers southeast of Arrakeen, and was delivered to Baron Vladimir Harkonnen, who had a residual poison administered to Hawat but also gave orders that the antidote should be administered to him regularly. Motivated by a desire to wreak vengeance on Emperor Shaddam IV and on Lady Jessica, whom he still believed to be a traitor, Hawat then became Baron Harkonnen's Mentat, replacing the deceased Piter de Vries. In 10,193 he informed Baron Harkonnen of Feyd-Rautha Rabban Harkonnen's plot to assassinate him by placing a poisoned needle in a slave boy's thigh. Later that year he accompanied Baron Harkonnen to Arrakis and, after refusing to obey the Emperor's order to kill Paul Atreides with a hidden poisoned needle, died in Paul's arms of the residual poison that had been administered to him in 10,191. [*Dune*]

Hawt—Lady Alia Atreides was known as Hawt, The Fish Monster, on the out-worlds conquered by Muad'Dib's Jihad. [*Dune Messiah*]

Hayt (10,192–10,217)—A Tleilaxu ghola grown from the cells of the deceased Duncan Idaho, Hayt was the first Duncan Idaho ghola and was given to Emperor Paul Muad'Dib as a gift from the Guild by Edric when Edric became Steersman-Ambassador to Paul's Imperial Court in 10,207. As a ghola, Hayt had no memory of his former life as Idaho but retained Idaho's skills as a swordsman; his central compulsion as Hayt was to learn who he had been as Idaho. Hayt had metal Tleilaxu eyes that were intended to remind Paul of Hayt's Tleilaxu origins, and he had also been trained by the Tleilaxu to be a Mentat and a Zensunni philosopher, which made him doubly truthful. In his first interview with Paul he readily admitted that he had been given to Paul in order to destroy him, as a weapon to be used against him. But, unbeknownst to him initially, the Tleilaxu had fashioned him to be a weapon against Alia as well. After Paul was blinded by a stone burner, Hayt was charged with questioning Bijaz in order to learn what the Tleilaxu had wanted Bijaz to do on Arrakis. Bijaz revealed that he had been created to awaken the Dundan Idaho persona in Hayt. He then activated Hayt's Tleilaxu-born compulsion to attempt to assassinate Paul when Paul said the words "She is gone" and conveyed to Hayt, as a hypnotic suggestion, a message to be delivered to Paul at that moment—that the Tleilaxu would create a precise duplicate of Chani, with Chani's persona, in return for Paul's empire and his renunciation of the Religion of Muad'Dib and its

Qizarate. Soon thereafter Hayt saved Alia from having taken a massive overdose of spice by having her stomach pumped, and he subsequently admitted to her that he loved her. He then accompanied Chani—with Paul, Alia, Bijaz, Edric, Reverend Mother Gaius Helen Mohiam, Scytale disguised as Lichna, Stilgar, Harah, and Princess Irulan—when she returned to the desert, to Sietch Tabr, to give birth to the twins Leto II and Ghanima. When Paul subsequently learned that Chani had died in childbirth and uttered the words "She is gone," Hayt's compulsion to kill Paul was triggered; but this created such a conflict with Hayt's submerged, loyal Idaho persona that the Idaho persona emerged—and Hayt stayed his hand from striking Paul and knew himself to be Idaho, was restored to his original self. When Bijaz then reiterated the dead Scytale's offer to create a similarly-restored Chani in return for Paul's empire, Hayt killed Bijaz on Paul's orders. Now possessing Idaho's persona, Hayt married Alia within a month of Paul's disappearance into the desert in 10,207. In 10,216 Hayt was summoned by The Preacher via a secret signal known only to Paul. Also in that year, shortly after Jessica's arrival on Arrakis, Alia ordered Hayt to abduct Jessica in such a way as to make it look like an act of House Corrino's. Hayt's Mentat computations deduced from her behavior that Alia had become possessed by one of her ancestors, was an Abomination, and that Alia wanted Jessica abducted because Jessica had observed the same thing. This realization broke Hayt's heart. He also realized that Alia really wanted Jessica dead and sent a warning to Jessica. Operating as a Mentat, Hayt realized as well that the garments sent to Arrakis from Salusa Secundus as a gift posed a mortal danger to Leto Atreides II and Ghanima. Acting on Alia's orders that he abduct her, Hayt met Jessica at Red Chasm Sietch and then took her to Prince Farad'n on Salusa Secundus. Bound with shigawire during his and Jessica's first interview with Farad'n, Hayt unsuccessfully attempted suicide (by severing an artery with his shigawire bonds) when Farad'n acknowledged that Alia had offered to be his bride. He later declared to Jessica on Salusa Secundus that he had formally removed himself from enemy territory and had abandoned House Atreides to serve Farad'n at the behest of The Preacher. He then returned to Arrakis to report to Alia that Jessica was training Farad'n in the Bene Gesserit way, and he was subsequently sent by Alia to Sietch Tabr to spy on Ghanima and Irulan. Alia had planned to have her chief amazon Ziarenka Valefor fly Hayt to Sietch Tabr and for Hayt to have a fatal "accident" en route. Suspecting this, however, Hayt did not wait for Valefor but flew himself to Sietch Tabr, where in 10,207 he killed Ziarenko Javid, the Master of Appointments with whom Alia had cuckolded him, and in doing so defiled the neutrality of Stilgar's sietch. Suicidal, he then grossly insulted Stilgar, who killed him in a murderous rage. *See* **Idaho, Duncan**. [*Dune Messiah, Children of Dune*]

heighliner—A heighliner is an enormous Guild transport used in interstellar travel. [*Dune*]

Hesterion, Sister (15,125–15,464)—Bene Gesserit Sister Hesterion from Archives, a Mentat, was the advisor to Reverend Mother Superior Alva Mavis Taraza who had suggested that it was a Tleilaxu ambition to produce Face Dancers who were complete prana-bindu mimics. With Taraza and Reverend Mother Bellonda, Hesterion was the only Bene Gesserit to possess all the memories of the unbroken line of Bene Gesserit Mother Superiors. [*Heretics of Dune*]

hiereg—A hiereg was a temporary desert camp set up by Fremen. [*Heretics of Dune*]

hiereg hangings—Delicate tapestries depicting figures from Fremen mythology, hiereg hangings adorned Emperor Paul Muad'Dib's immense keep in Arrakeen. [*Dune Messiah*]

Hobars (10,162–10,207)—Hobars was a dissident Fremen Naib who attended the trial of Korba, presided over by Alia, in 10,207. [*Dune Messiah*]

Holtzman generator—A Holtzman generator produces either a shield's protective field or a suspensor field, depending on the energy phase employed. It also enables Guild ships to fold space and thus to travel faster than the speed of light. [*Dune, Chapterhouse: Dune*]

The Holy Metamorphoisis—*The Holy Metamorphosis* was a volume authored by Harq al-Ada. [*Children of Dune*]

Honored Matres—Descendants of a Fremen Bene Gesserit Reverend Mother and Fish Speakers who had gone out into the Scattering of the 138th century, and subsequently bureaucrats in the Scattering who had rebelled successfully against their masters, in the 153rd century the Honored Matres—who by then outnumbered the Bene Gesserit 10,000 to 1—returned to the Old Empire to infiltrate and conquer it. They fled a biological weapon from the Scattering that made vegetables of them, and they wanted to acquire from the Bene Gesserit their immunity from disease. By that time the Fish Speaker democracy that had gone out into the Scattering had devolved into Honored Matre autocracy. Honored Matres have an uncannily high reaction speed, which develops in them in puberty. While they can employ Voice themselves, Honored Matres are trained to kill by reflex anyone who attempts to use Voice on them. They customarily kill with their feet. Instead of mélange, Honored Matres used an inferior, tart-smelling stimulant that flects the whites of their eyes orange; when an Honored Matre succumbs to murderous rage, the whites of her eyes turn completely orange. Honored Matres enslave men by eliciting the total sensual involvement of the male in magnified sensations of the orgasmic platform that transmit multiple orgasmic waves throughout the male body. They can also make themselves poisonous to Futars, human-cat hybrids that have been bred in the Scattering to hunt Honored Matres. By the 153rd century the Honored Matres had evolved beyond depravity to the point where they would sacrifice anything to satisfy their own desires and ambitions, but, like addicts, they could not be satisfied and constantly required more and more of whatever it was that simulated pleasure. They were also adrenaline addicts who revelled in and prefered chaos. In 15,219 two Honored Matres were killed in known space by Tleilaxu Master of Masters Tylwyth Waff and replaced by Face Dancers. In 15,232 the Honored Matres destroyed Arrakis in an unsuccessful attempt to kill Duncan Idaho ghola number 4. They subsequently destroyed all of the Bene Tleilax planets, nearly exterminating the Tleilaxu, and then destroyed or captured all but a handful of the Bene Gesserit planets. The Honored Matres were successfully co-opted by the Bene Gesserit in 15,245 when Bene Gesserit Reverend Mother Superior Murbella, an Honored Matred who had become a Bene Gesserit, killed Great Honored Matre Longo and became the Great Honored Matre as well as the Bene Gesserit Reverend Mother Superior. [*Heretics of Dune, Chapterhouse: Dune*]

Huanui-naa—Huanui-naa was the Fremen term for the greatest sandstorms on Arrakis, which were also known as the Earth's Deathstill. [*Children of Dune*]

hufuf vine—Native to Ecaz, the hufuf vine is the plant from which krimskell fiber is woven. [*Dune*]

"The Humanity of Muad'Dib"— "The Humanity of Muad'Dib" is one of the many volumes authored by Princess Irulan. [*Dune*]

hunter-seeker—A common assassination device, a hunter-seeker is a suspensor-buoyed metal sliver controlled by a near-by operator. Paul Atreides was threatened by a hunter-seeker hidden in his bedroom shortly after his arrival on Arrakis in 10,191. [*Dune*]

Hutye (13,702–13,726)—One of Siona's ten companions in the theft in 13,726 of The Stolen Journals from Emperor Leto II's Citadel fortress in the Sareer, Hutye was killed by a pack of D-wolves in Arrakis' Forbidden Forest following the raid on the Citadel. [*God Emperor of Dune*]

hypnobong—The hypnobong was a mesmerizing device composed of whirling lights that was outlawed on all of the more-civilized worlds of the 153rd century, but not on Gammu. [*Heretics of Dune*]

ichwan—On Arrakis, an "ichwan" was a band of brothers—as opposed to a "taif," a company of men held together by mutual self-interest. [*Children of Dune*]

ichwan bedwine—The ichwan bedwine was the brotherhood of all Fremen on Arrakis. [*Dune*]

Idaho, Duncan (10,136–10,191)—Born and raised on Giedi Prime and tortured by the Harkonnens in its capital city, Barony, Duncan Idaho was rescued from Harkonnen bondage by the Atreides. Loyal, proud, truthful, ruthless, and moral, flat-faced, curly-haired Idaho was a Swordmaster of Ginaz, an Atreides retainer, and Paul Atreides instructor in weaponry on Caladan. His extraordinarily quick reflexes made him the greatest swordsman of his age. In 10,191 he was named the Atreides ambassador to the Fremen and also ordered by Thufir Hawat to keep the Lady Jessica under constant surveillance as a suspected traitor. That same year he killed the pilot and escaped the fall of Arrakeen in a Harkonnen ornithopter, and he subsequently rescued Paul and Lady Jessica from the desert and conveyed them to an underground Imperial Ecological Testing Station, where he killed nineteen Sardaukar before he was slain defending Paul from Sardaukar pursuers in Harkonnen uniforms. After his death Idaho's cadaver was preserved by a Sardaukar commander and shipped to the Tleilaxu, who created a Mentat ghola from

Idaho's dead cells. Renamed Hayt, the ghola was sold to the Spacing Guild as a gift to be given to Emperor Paul Muad'Dib that was intended to poison his psyche and also to seduce his sister, Alia. *See also* **Hayt**, **Idaho Ghola number 2**, **Idaho Ghola number 3**, and **Idaho Ghola number 4**. [*Dune, Dune Messiah, Children of Dune, God Emperor of Dune, Heretics of Dune*]

Idaho ghola number 2 (13,644–13,726)—Irti's husband, Idaho Ghola number 2 had served Emperor Leto II as Commander of his Royal Guard for sixty years when, in 13,726, he tried to assassinate Leto II with a lasgun and was killed by Leto II's thrashing pre-worm body. Hundreds of Idaho gholas were created by the Tleilaxu for Leto II between the creation of Hayt (the first Idaho ghola) in the 103rd century and the creation of Idaho ghola number 2 in the 137th century. [*God Emperor of Dune*]

Idaho ghola number 3 (13,701–13,788)—More reckless than any of the hundreds of previous Idaho gholas created from the original, deceased Dundan Idaho's cells by the Tleilaxu for Emperor Leto II, Idaho ghola number 3 joined Leto II's court as the Commander of his Imperial Guard and as leader of the Fish Speakers in 13,726. Later that year he helped thwart a Tleilaxu assassination attempt against Leto II along the Royal Road to Onn by stripping naked to distinguish himself from the fifty clothed Face Dancer

mimics who had impersonated him during the attack. He was subsequently, with Siona, flown by a squad of Fish Speakers to Goygoa and was returned the next day to Onn to participate in Leto II's Feast of Siaynoq. Later, although Leto II had forbidden it, Idaho ghola number 3 met, fell in love with, and had sexual relations with Hwi Noree, Leto II's fiancé. Moneo subsequently informed Idaho ghola number 3 and Hwi Noree that Leto II had decreed that they were never to see one another again. In an attempt to save the ghola's life, Moneo then sent Idaho ghola number 3, Siona, and Nayla to Tuono Village so that they would be absent during Hwi Noree's and Leto II's wedding ceremony, which was to have occurred in Tabur Village, but Leto II then relocated the nuptials to Tuono Village. On the morning of Leto II's wedding day, Idaho ghola number 3 scaled the sheer cliff wall separating Tuono Village from the Royal Road and lowered a rope that allowed Siona, Nayla, some other Fish Speakers, and some Museum Fremen to scale the cliff wall also. At the summit, acting on Siona's orders, Nayla severed the supports to the bridge over the Idaho River with a lasgun and tumbled Leto II, Hwi Noree, and Moneo to their deaths. Idaho ghola number 3 then killed Nayla with her own lasgun because her actions had murdered Hwi Noree. Like all of the Idaho gholas, Idaho ghola number 3 was fascinated by the idea of all the Idaho gholas who had preceded him. [*God Emperor of Dune*]

Idaho ghola number 4 (15,213–15,578)—The twelfth Duncan Idaho ghola to be provided to the Bene Gesserit in the 152nd and 153rd centuries by the Tleilaxu, who had themselves killed the previous eleven Idaho gholas in the series, Duncan Idaho ghola number 4 was created with an advanced nerve-muscle system that was superior to that of a normal 153rd-century human being. An especially thoughtful iteration of Duncan Idaho, this ghola was raised and educated on Gammu by Bene Gesserit Reverend Mothers Geasea and Tamalane and, afterwards, by retired Bene Gesserit Supreme Bashar Miles Teg. By the age of nine he had come to hate Bene Gesserit Reverend Mother Schwangyu, who then commanded the Gammu Keep, for having punished guards he had considered his friends. By the age of fifteen he had fallen in love with Reverend Mother Lucilla, who was under Bene Gesserit orders to seduce him, but he successfully resisted her advances because he did not want to become a stud for the Bene Gesserit. Later that year Teg saved him and Lucilla from an attack by a Face Dancer disguised as Teg whom Schwangyu's minions had allowed into the Keep. Teg then led the ghola and Lucilla into the forest northeast of the Keep, to evade Schwangyu's treachery, and to an ancient Harkonnen no-globe that Teg's aide Patrin had discovered when a teenager and had kept secret for well over two hundred years. While they hid for three months inside the no-globe, Teg restored the ghola's original Duncan Idaho persona by subjecting the ghola to intense physical and emotional pain. With the assistance of Bene Gesserit BasharAlef Burzmali, the ghola, Teg, and Lucilla escaped from the no-globe and the ghola was disguised as a Tleilaxu Master named Wose. He was then taken by Tormsa—a Gammu native disguised as a Face Dancer who was also known as Ambitorm—to an abandoned factory on the outskirts of Ysai, where Tormsa was killed and the ghola was taken prisoner by Honored Matre Murbella. Murbella subsequently attempted to enslave the ghola by using Honored Matre sexual amplification techniques on him, but this only resulted in his recovering the memories of all of his hundreds of past ghola iterations and simultaneously triggered the special ability the Tleilaxu had implanted in him: the ability to enslave any woman by subjecting her to similar sexual amplification techniques. The ghola and Murbella then enslaved one another in an amplified mutual orgasm during which the ghola impregnated Murbella. The ghola, Murbella, Burzmali, and Lucilla were then transported to Rakis in a no-ship from the Scattering that had been captured by Teg. In 15,232, on Teg's orders, the ghola, Sheeana

Brugh, Murbella, Reverend Mother Superior Darwi Odrade, and a sandworm from Rakis were transported in the no-ship from Rakis to Chapterhouse, where the ghola—with Murbella and Scytale—was kept confined in the no-ship until 15,245. During his thirteen years in the no-ship Idaho ghola number 4 trained the Miles Teg clone in weapons mastery, fathered four children with Murbella, and trained in the techniques of sexual amplification men who were then sent out to plague the Honored Matres. In 15,244 he convinced Reverend Mother Bellonda, who had long wanted him killed, that he was of greater value to the Bene Gesserit than he was a danger to them. In that year, using an ancient Atreides hand code, he secretly discussed with Sheeana the possibility of having her attempt to sexually imprint the Teg clone as a more-humane way of activating his original persona and memories than the painful process usually employed to activate a ghola's or clone's original persona and memories. Idaho ghola number 4 subsequently won Odrade over to this plan, and Sheeana used this method to restore the eleven-year-old clone's persona and memories in 15,245. Idaho ghola number 4 later helped Murbella to survive the Spice Agony in the Chapterhouse no-ship. In a Mentat dream he visualized a way to miniaturize Holtzmann Generators and also deduced Odrade's plot to defeat the Honored Matres, and in his Mentat vision of "the net" he perceived the Face Dancers in the Scattering who had driven the Honored Matres back into the Old Empire of the known universe. In 15,245 he launched the Chapterhouse no-ship into the unknown space beyond the Old Empire, taking with him as passengers and cargo Sheeana, Scytale, Rebecca, the Rabbi, Bene Gesserit Proctor Garimi, some Futars, and a sandworm. [*Heretics of Dune*, *Chapterhouse: Dune*]

Idaho River—Dug by Ixian machines in the 108th century, the Idaho River was a river on Arrakis that in the 138th century bordered the Forbidden Forest. Emperor Leto II was killed by immersion in the Idaho River in 13,726. [*God Emperor of Dune*]

Iduali—The Iduali were ancient Fremen tribes who made it a practice to steal water from other Fremen. They had inhabited Jacurutu but had been wiped out there by other Freman tribes who had banded together to destroy them. The word "iduali" means "water insects" in the Fremen tongue. [*Children of Dune*]

Ignat—Ignat was a month in the old Fremen calendar. Sheeana Brugh was born in Ignat. [*Heretics of Dune*]

ijaz—In the Fremen tongue, an" ijaz" is an undeniable, immutable prophecy. [*Dune*]

Ikonicre (12,174–12,414)—Ikonicre was Emperor Leto II's majordomo in 12,334. [*God Emperor of Dune*]

ilm—In Chakobsa, "ilm" means "theology." [*Dune*]

Imperial Conditioning—Developed by the Suk Medical Schools, Imperial Conditioning at its highest level supposedly made it impossible for the person conditioned to take a human life. Those with Imperial Conditioning wear a diamond tattoo on their foreheads and bind their long hair with a silver Suk ring. Dr. Wellington Yueh's Imperial Conditioning was broken by Baron Vladimir Harkonnen, even though it is widely believed that Imperial Conditioning cannot be broken without killing the individual conditioned. [*Dune*]

Imperial Council—In 10,207 the Imperial Council consisted of Emperor Paul Muad'Dib, his wife Irulan, his sister Alia, his lover Chani, his Quizara and panegyrist Korba, and his Minister of State Stilgar. In 10,216 numerous Fremen signed a petition demanding that Jessica be placed on the Imperial Council. [*Dune Messiah, Children of Dune*]

Imperial House—In the 102nd century, the time of Muad'Dib, the Imperial House was House Corrino and was one leg, with the Landsraad and the Spacing Guild, of the political tripod that maintained the Great Convention. House Corrino was supplanted by House Atreides in 10,193. [*Dune*]

"In My Father's House"—"In My Father's House" is one of the many volumes authored by Princess Irulan. [*Dune*]

Inineg (13,704–13,726)—One of Siona's ten companions in the theft in 13,726 of The Stolen Journals from Emperor Leto II's Citadel fortress in the Sareer, Inineg was killed by a pack of D-wolves in Arrakis' Forbidden Forest following the raid on the Citadel. [*God Emperor of Dune*]

inkvine—A creeping plant native to Giedi Prime, the inkvine was often used as a whip in the Harkonnen slave cribs. The scar it leaves causes residual pain for many years. Gurney Hallek had an inkvine scar on his jaw. [*Dune*]

Inmeir (13,700–13,746)—Brawny Inmeir was the Fish Speaker ornithopter pilot who in 13,726 flew Idaho ghola number 3 and Siona from Onn to Goygoa and, the next day, flew Idaho ghola number 3 back to Onn and Siona to Leto II's Citadel fortress. [*God Emperor of Dune*]

Irti (13,675–13,749)—A resident of Goygoa and a Fish Speaker, Irti was the wife of Idaho ghola number 2. Oval-faced, dark-eyed, and full-mouthed, she strongly resembled Lady Jessica. [*God Emperor of Dune*]

Irulan, Princess (10,176–10,268)—Eldest daughter of Emperor Shadam IV and Anirul, and sister to Chalice, Wensicia, Josifa, and Rugi, the tall, blonde, green-eyed, beautiful Princess Irulan in 10,193 accompanied Shadam to Arrakis, where she was betrothed to Paul Atreides as a condition of Shaddam's surrender. Never Paul's lover, however, she subsequently devoted her life to being Paul's biographer. She was permitted by Paul to take lovers, so long as she was discrete and bore no children. Nonetheless, aiming to become eventually the founding mother of the royal dynasty, she secretly administered a contraceptive to Emperor Paul Muad'Dib's lover Chani, to prevent her from bearing children, from 10,193 to 10,207. She was during this time forced by Paul to serve as his secretary at Imperial Council meetings. She was a participant in a 10,205–07 conspiracy against MuaD'dib, crafted on Wallach IX, that also included Reverend Mother Gaius Helen Mohiam, Scytale, and Edric. Her part in the conspiracy was to continue to spy on Paul and to continue to prevent Chani from having any children. On being instructed by Mohiam in 10,207 to engineer Chani's death, to conclusively prevent her from giving Paul an heir, Irulan realized that the conspiracy against Paul to which she was a party now considered her to be expendable. She subsequently accompanied Chani—with Paul, Hayt, Bijaz, Alia, Edric, Mohiam, Scytale disguised as Lichna, Stilgar, and Harah—when Chani returned to the desert, to Sietch Tabr, to give birth. After a blinded Paul wandered off into the desert following Chani's death in childbirth, Irulan denounced the Bene Gesserit and swore to spend her life educating Paul's

newborn twins, Leto II and Ghanima. She was present when Jessica landed in Arrakeen on returning to Arrakis from Caladan in 10,216. Later that year, at Regent Alia Atreides's urging, she tried to convince Ghanima to accept bethrothal to Prince Farad'n, but she argued heatedly against Ghanima's and Alia's plot to have Ghanima then slay Farad'n at the first opportunity. She accompanied Stilgar, Ghanima, and Harah into the desert, to the Fremen rebels opposing Alia, when Stilgar fled Sietch Tabr after he had slain Hayt in 10,217. In 10,218 she was abducted by kidnappers acting on Alia's orders and, with Ghanima and Stilgar, returned to Arrakeen and imprisoned. She was released when Leto II became Emperor later that year. She is the author of "Analysis: The Arrakeen Crisis," "Arrakis Awakening," "A Child's History of Muad'Dib," "Collected Legends of Arrakis," "Collected Sayings of Muad'Dib," "Conversations with Muad'Dib," "Count Fenring: A Profile," "Dictionary of Muad'Dib," *The Dunebuk of Princess Irulan*, "The Humanity of Muad'Dib," "In My Father's House," "A Manual of Muad'Dib," "Muad'Dib: Conversations," "Muad'Dib, Family Commentaries," "Muad'Dib, the Man," "Muad'Dib: The Ninety-nine Wonders of the Universe," "Muad'Dib: The Religious Issue," "Private Reflections on Muad'Dib," "The Sayings of Muad'Dib," "Songs of Muad'Dib," and "The Wisdom of Muad'Dib." [*Dune, Dune Messiah, Children of Dune*]

Islamiyat—Islamiyat is the ancient, native language of the Tleilaxu; it was the language spoken by the Tleilaxu Masheikh in kehl. [*Heretics of Dune*]

istislah—Among the Fremen, istislah is the law that requires the performance of an act for the welfare of all, usually an act of brutal necessity. [*Dune*]

Ix—Having, with Richese, escaped the more severe effects of the Butlerian Jihad, Ix—the ninth planet from its sun—had developed an advanced machine culture by the 102nd century, the time of Muad'Dib. Although they were forbidden to his subjects, Emperor Leto II traded with Ix for outlawed machines throughout his reign (10,218–13,726). By the 153rd century Ixian navigational devices had broken the Guild monopoly on space travel, but by then the new Theilaxu Face Dances had infiltrated the highest councils of Ix, which had produced no technical innovations in centuries, and its influence was on the decline. *The Last Jihad*, by Sumer and Kautman, examines the forces that had allowed Richese and Ix to evade the Buterlian Jihad's anti-machine proscriptions. [*Dune, Dune Messiah, God Emperor of Dune, Heretics of Dune, Chapterhouse: Dune*]

Ixian Confederacy—The Ixian Confederacy was a union of planets led by IX that submitted to the rule of Muad'Dib in 10,207. However, the Confederacy subsequently agitated for a constitution and complained

about how much they must pay in Imperial taxes. [*Dune Messiah*]

Ixian Core—The Ixian Core was the heartland of the technological federation goverened by Ix. Although it was know to Emperor Leto II, the location of the Ixian Core was a secret. [*God Emperor of Dune*]

Ixian probe—Like a T-probe from the Scattering, an Ixian probe is a machine than can reveal the contents of a mind up until the point when the individual brain cells die, even after death. Shere is a drug that protects one from an Ixian probe, and the Tleilaxu are naturally immune to its effects. [*Heretics of Dune*]

Iylyo, Bashar Nyshae (13,676–13,756)—A descendant of Harq al-Ada who had family on Salusa Secundus, tall, bone-thin, dignified Nyshae Iylyo was the bashar commanding the Fish Speakers who had suppressed the 13,726 Tleilaxu/rebel attack on the Ixian Embassy in Onn. [*God Emperor of Dune*]

Jacaranda—Jacaranda is a veined, deep-brown wood grown on Caladan or Dan. [*Heretics of Dune*]

Jacurutu—Jacurutu, the sietch of the water stealers, was a legendary location on Arrakis that Leto Atreides II had dreamed of in his earliest prescient dreams. Consequently, in 10,216 Jessica ordered Gurney Hallek to use his connections among the smugglers to locate it. It was hidden in the open as Fondak, a sietch completely taken over by smugglers that had become taboo among the Fremen, and that same year Leto II escaped from Sietch Tabr to Jacurutu after faking his own death at the paws of the Laza tigers sent to Arrakis from Salusa Secundus to assassinate him and Ghanima. [*Children of Dune*]

Jadacha hermaphrodites—Tleilaxu Face Dancers are Jadacha hermaphrodites, able to assume the guise of either sex at will. [*Dune Messiah*]

Jalahud-Din—Namri's family marks were carved on the Shield Wall at Jalahud-Din. [*Children of Dune*]

Jalal, Abedi (10,189–10,138)—Abedi Jalal was the nephew of Namri's who had seen Namri's family marks carved on the Shield Wall at Jalahud-Din. [*Children of Dune*]

Jalanto (15,134–15,500)—Jalanto was a Bene Gesserit Suk doctor who in 15,245 entered the Chapterhouse noship to deliver Murbella's fourth child by Duncan Idaho clone number 4 and to spy on Scytale. [*Chapterhouse: Dune*]

Jamis (10,162–10,191)—Harah's second husband, Orlop's father, and Kaleff's step-father, Jamis was a member of Stilgar's Sietch Tabr and one of the forty Fremen led by Stilgar who found Paul Atreides and the Lady Jessice at Tuono Basin, in the desert of Arrakis, after the fall of Arrakeen in 10,191. He demanded there that Paul and Jessica be killed for their water, but he was disarmed and injured by Paul as Paul scrambled for sanctuary among the rocks when Jessica then attacked Stilgar. After invoking the amtal rule, Jamis was killed by Paul in a knife fight in Cave of the Ridges. [*Dune*]

Jandola—Jandola was a Tleilaxu planet destroyed by the Honored Matres shortly after the 15,232 destruction of Rakis. [*Chapterhouse: Dune*]

Javid, Ziarenko (10,190–10,217)—Round-cheeked, shadow-eyed, surley, repellant, and intelligent, Ziarenko Javid was a priest in the religion of Muad'Dib, as well as one of Regent Alia Atreides' Society of the Faithful, who greeted Jessica on her arrival in Arrakeen, after her twenty-three-year absence from Arrakis, in 10,216. He harbored a secret hatred for the Atreides and was, in fact, a spy on Alia in the employ of Princess Wensicia. Nonetheless, that same year he became Alia's Master of Appointments and, at the instigation of the Baron Harkonnen persona that inhabited Alia's consciousness, Alia's lover. He subsequently conspired with Alia to have one of her priests assassinate Jessica during one of Alia's morning audiences, but the assassination attempt failed. Alia's husband Hayt (who then possessed Duncan Idaho's persona) killed him in Sietch Tabr in 10,217. [*Children of Dune*]

Jessica, Lady (10,154–10,256)—Duke Leto Atreides' concubine since 10,175 and the mother of Paul Atreides and

Lady Alia Atreides, tall, slender, regal, bronze-haired, oval-faced, green-eyed Lady Jessica was (according to Bene Gesserit breeding records) the unacknowledged daughter of Baron Vladimir Harkonnen and Tanidia Nerus, a Bene Gesserit, although her parentage was initially unknown to her. After having been Reverend Mother Gaius Helen Mohiam's pupil and serving wench for fourteen years while attending the Bene Gesserit Mother School on Wallach IX, Jessica bore a son to Duke Leto despite her orders from the Bene Gesserit to give birth only to a female child. Trained in business on Wallach IX, she also served as Duke Leto's secretary. In 10,191, after the Atreides relocation to Arrakis, she was given an unfixed crysknife by the Shadout Mapes. Soon thereafter she was drugged by Dr. Wellington Yueh and captured by the Harkonnens during the fall of Arrakeen, but she escaped with Paul into the desert through Dr. Yueh's intervention. Rescued from the desert by Duncan Idaho and Dr. Liet Kynes, she was taken with Paul to an underground Imperial Ecological Testing Station, where Idaho was killed while Kynes directed them to a hidden ornithopter in which she and Paul escaped the Harkonnens again by piloting the craft into a coriolis storm in which the Harkonnens believed they had perished. She and Paul were then found by Stilgar's band of forty Fremen and taken to Cave of the Ridges and then to Seitch Tabr, where she successfully transmuted the Water of Life to become a Bene Gesscrit Reverend Mother even though she was pregnant. After transmuting the Water of Life she received all of dying Fremen Reverend Mother Romallo's life's memories. She later gave birth to Alia, who had also, pre-natally, become a Bene Geserrit Reverend Mother when Jessica had transmuted the Water of Life. In 10,193 Jessica was threatened in Seitch Tabr by Gurney Hallek, who believed that she had been the Atreides traitor, but she was saved when Paul intervened. After Paul became Emperor in 10,193 she retired with Hallek to Caladan. Jessica returned to Arrakis twenty-three years later, in 10,216, to visit her grandchildren Leto Atreides II and Ghanima. On her arrival she perceived that Alia had succumbed to Abomination (had become possessed by the persona of one of her ancestors), a condition that made Alia and Jessica mortal enemies. Jessica then ordered Hallek to use his connections among the smugglers to find the legendary Jacurutu because it had been a feature of Leto II's prescient dreams. She subsequently interviewed Ghanima in Sietch Tabr in an attempt to determine if Ghanima and Leto II, as well as Alia, had succumbed to Abomination. Deciding that they had probably not succumbed, she interviewed Leto II the following day and was told that Alia planned to abduct her and to place the blame on Princess Wensicia and House Corrino, but that she should allow herself to be abducted. While urged to denounce The Preacher by Ziarenko Javid, who was acting on Alia's behalf, Jessica refused to renounce him even though he railed against House Atreides. Subsequently, during one of Alia's morning audiences, one of Alia's priests tried to assassinate Jessica with a maula pistol, but Jessica dodged the maula pellet and, concluding that the assassination attempt had been the result of a conspiracy involving Alia and Javid, she publically accused Alia of having tried to kill her. She then recognized that Alia had been possessed by the Baron Harkonnen's persona and that the Baron was working through Alia to destroy all the sandworms on Arrakis, through the planet's ecological transformation, as a way of wreaking his vengeance on the Atreides. With the help of Fremen Naib Ghadhean al-Fali she then escaped to al-Fali's Red Chasm Sietch, where she met Hayt (now possessing Duncan Idaho's persona), who took her to Salusa Secundus, where she agreed to teach Prince Farad'n the Bene Gesserit Way. While on Salusa Secundus she also accepted Hayt's declaration that he had withdrawn from serving the Atreides. In 10,218 she returned with Farad'n to Arrakis and there witnessed Alia's suicide. She spent her last years on Caladan, as a teacher of Bene Gesserit acolytes. [*Dune, Children of Dune, Chapterhouse: Dune*]

Jews—Despite the widespread belief that the Jews had died out shortly after the Second Interspace Migrations, a secret society of insular, unassimilated Jews existed on Gammu and elsewhere in the 153rd century. The Jews had served the Bene Gesserit as a secret society, in times of need, since the Battle of Corrin, and by the 153rd century they had interbred with Siona Ibn Faud al-Seyefa Atreides' descendants and were thus invisible to prescient awareness. [*Chapterhouse: Dune*]

Jihad—*See* **Butlerian Jihad** and **Muad'Dib's Jihad**.

Joshua (15,221–15,556)—Young, short, slender, triangle-faced, dark-haired, brown-eyed Joshua was a Jew who had built the small, barrel-shaped nochamber in which he, the Rabbi, and Rebecca had hidden on Gammu in 15,244–45. [*Chapterhouse: Dune*]

Josifa, Princess (10,182–10,256)—One of Emperor Shaddam IV's five daughters by Anirul, Josifa accompanied Shaddam IV into retirement on Salusa Secundus in 10,193. [*Dune*]

J-rays—A form of radiation emitted by a stone burner, J-rays cause blindness in anyone in close proximity to the detonation. [*Dune Messiah*]

jubba cloak—The jubba cloak is the all-purpose garment commonly worn over a stillsuit on Arrakis. It can be converted to hammock or shelter, and it can be set either to reflect or to admit radiant heat. [*Dune*]

Judge of the Change—In the 102nd century the Judge of the Change was the official charged by the Emperor and the Landsraad High Council with the task of monitoring a kanly negotiation, a formal battle in a War of Assassins, or a change of fief. Dr. Liet Kynes was the Judge of the Change charged with overseeing the change of fief on Arrakis in 10,191. [*Dune*]

Junction—Junction was a Guild planet that was conquered by the Honored Matres in the early 153rd century. The Honored Matres then set up their Old Empire headquarters in Junction's Citadel. The planet was successfully attacked and occupied by Bene Gesserit forces led by the Miles Teg clone in 15,245. [*Chapterhouse: Dune*]

Kadesh—Kadesh is a planet of the Imperium on which it was the custom in the early 103rd century for men to wear shoulder-length hair. [*Children of Dune*]

Kadrish—Kadrish was one of the many planets in the Imperium where it was fashionable in the early 103rd century to wear imitation stillsuits. [*Children of Dune*]

Kagga Basin—Kagga Basin was an area of Arrakis near Arrakeen whose qanats were destroyed in 10,216 by Fremen raiders from the Broken Lands. [*Children of Dune*]

Kaitain—The seat of Empire and home to the Royal Court in the 102nd century, the time of Muad'Dib, Kai-

tanin became the homeworld of House Corrino after House Corrino evacuated Salusa Secundus. [*Dune*]

Kaleff (10,181–10,203)—Kaleff was Harah's older son, fathered by Geoff, and Orlop's half-brother. [*Dune*]

kanawa—"Kanawa" is the Fremen word for intense jealousy. [*God Emperor of Dune*]

kanly—Kanly is a formal feud or vendetta carried out under the rules of the Great Convention, which were originally designed to protect innocent bystanders. In the 102nd century a state of kanly existed between the Atreides and the Harkonnens. [*Dune*]

karama—In the Fremen tongue, "karama" is a miracle or action initiated by the spirit world. [*Dune*]

Kautman (10,058–10,137)—Kautman was, with Sumer, the author of *The Last Jihad*, a study that examines the forces that allowed Richese and Ix to evade the anti-machine proscriptions of the Butlerian Jihad. [*Dune*]

Kayamakam—A Kayamakam was a planetary governor under Alia Atreides' Regency, in the early 103rd century. [*Children of Dune*]

Kaza—A Kaza was a leader of Alia Atreides' priestly guards. [*Children of Dune*]

Kedem—Kadem was the Fremen word for Arrakis' inner desert. [*Dune Messiah, Children of Dune*]

Keen—By the 153rd century Arrakeen had come to be known as Keen. [*Heretics of Dune*]

Keeper of Jessica's Light—The Keeper of Jessica's Light was the chief priestess of the Cult of Alia, which flourished on Giedi Prime in the 138th century. [*God Emperor of Dune*]

keffiya—A keffiya was the knotted headdress worn by a Fremen Naib. [*Children of Dune*]

Keke (10,162–10,217)—Keke was a dissident Fremen Naib who fled Arrakis with a stolen worm in 10,207. [*Dune Messiah*]

ketman—Also known as *taquiyya* among the ancient Fremen, *ketman* is the practice of concealing one's identity when revealing it might be harmful. [*God Emperor of Dune*]

khasadar—The khasadar were the Tleilaxu soldiers who policed the Tleilaxu frontier. [*Heretics of Dune*]

Khel—Khel is the Tleilaxu ritual that reaffirms Bodal, the ultimate revenge sought by the Tleilaxu. [*Heretics of Dune*]

khilat—The white kihlat is the Tleilaxu robe of honor, worn by the Mahai, to which all Domel were conditioned to bow. [*Heretics of Dune*]

Kievemo (13,701–13,743)—Kievemo was a heavy-set Fish Speaker Guard Captain who was promoted by Emperor Leto II to the rank of sub-bashar for informing him in 13,726 that Hwi

Noree had survived the Tleilaxu/rebel attack on the Ixian Embassy in Onn. [*God Emperor of Dune*]

Kinet (10,153–10,191)—Kinet was a deaf, scar-faced Harkonnen trooper who, with Czigo, conveyed Paul Atreides and the Lady Jessica to the desert to die after the two were captured by the Harkonnens during the 10,191 fall of Arrakeen. Czigo stabbed Kinet to death in their ornithopter at Jessica's instigation. [*Dune*]

Kipuna (15,187–15,232)—Fuzzy-haired, round-featured Kipuna was a Rakian native of the priestly caste and a Bene Gesserit acolyte who spied on the Rakian priests. She had taken over much of Sheeana Brugh's physical training by the time Sheeana was 14. She was to have conveyed to the Bene Gesserit Keep in Keen Sheeana's command that the Rakian priests bring her Senior Security Mother Darwi Odrade; however, she was decapitated before she could execute this order—while protecting Sheeana from a hunter-seeker trailing a length of shigawire that had been deployed by the Tleilaxu and the Ixians. [*Heretics of Dune*]

Kitab Al-Ibar—The Kitab Al-Ibar was a combination Fremen religious manual and desert survival handbook. There was a Kitab Al-Ibar in the fremkit that Dr. Wellington Yueh hid in the ornithopter in which he hoped that Paul Atreides and the Lady Jessica would be transported to the desert after the fall of Arrakeen in 10,191. [*Dune*]

Kobat, Iyo (13,671–13,746)—Tall, thin, brown-eyed, bushy-browed, narrow-mouthed Iyo Kobat was the Ixian Ambassador to Arrakis who was dismissed in disgrace by Emperor Leto II for having supplied the lasgun with which Duncan Idaho ghola number 2 had attempted to assassinate Leto II in 13,726. Kobat subsequently met with Siona, Topri, Nayla, and other members of Siona's rebellion against Leto II in order to receive copies of the journals Siona had stolen from Leto II's Citadel to take back with him to Ix to have translated. [*God Emperor of Dune*]

kontar—A unit of measure, one kontar was 2/3rd's the amount of spice that a camel could carry. That is, 1.5 kontars equalled one camel-load of spice. [*Dune Messiah*]

Korba (10,169–10,207)—Korba was one of Paul Muad'Dib's Fedaykin. He was present when Paul was reunited with Gurney Hallek at Habbanya Ridge in 10,193 and when Paul and his Fremen subsequently captured three Sardaukar disguised as smugglers in Cave of Birds. (It was Korba who had failed to detect the Sardaukar's weapons while initially inspecting Hallek's smuggler companions.) Korba then joined Paul, Stilgar, Chatt the Leaper, and Otheym in making battle plans against the Harkonnens. By 10,207 Korba was bald, dark-featured, a Quizara (a priest in the Qizarate), a member of the Imperial Council, and Emperor Paul Muad'Dib's panegyrist. He was arrested following the detonation of the stone burner that blinded Paul, as it was Korba who had ordered that the stone burner be transported from Tarahell to Arrakis. Following his trial for conspiring against Paul, presided over by Alia Atreides, he was executed on Alia's orders. [*Dune, Dune Messiah*]

Kralizek—Kralizek was, in Fremen legend, the Typhoon Struggle, the battle at the end of the universe. [*Children of Dune*]

krimskell fiber—Also known as krimskell rope, krimskell fibre is woven from strands of the hufuf vine native to Ecaz. Krimskell fiber tightens when pulled; thus, anyone bound with krimskell rope only tightens the rope in struggling to break free. [*Dune*]

Kronin—Kronin was a planet on which Bene Gesserit Bashar Supreme Miles Teg had once broken the anti–Sisterhood forces. Subsequently a Bene Gesserit planet, it was captured by the Honored Matres in the early 153rd century. [*Heretics of Dune, Chapterhouse: Dune*]

Krustansik (15,148–15,232)—Stiros' nephew, Krustansik was a wise Rakian priest who in 15,232 headed a faction of priests who wanted to replace Rakian High Priest Hedley Tuek. He successfully conspired with Senior Security Mother Darwi Odrade and Tleilaxu Master of Masters Tylwyth Waff to have a Tleilaxu Face Dancer replace Tuek after Tuek had been murdered by Waff. He was killed in the destruction of Rakis. [*Heretics of Dune*]

Kudu, Umman (10,146–10,191)—Boot-toe-chinned Umman Kudu was the Captain of Baron Vladimir Harkonnen's personal guard in 10,191. He was inadvertently killed when a captive Duke Leto Atreides attempted to use the poison gas hidden in a false tooth to assassinate the Baron. [*Dune*]

Kuentsing—Kuentsing is the star about which Bela Tegeuse orbits. [*Dune*]

kulon—a domesticated desert ass employed by some smugglers on Arrakis, the kulon is descended from the wild ass of Earth's Asiatic steppes. [*Dune*]

Kwisatz Hadderach—"Kwisatz Hadderach" means "the shortening of the way" in Chokabsa. The goal of the Bene Gesserit breeding program was the Kwisatz Hadderach, a male Bene Gesserit whose organic mental powers would transcend space and time. Lady Jessica felt that her son Paul Atreides might be the Kwisatz Hadderach. [*Dune*]

Kwuteg (13,699–13,726)—One of Siona Ibn Faud al-Seyefa Atreides' ten companions in the theft in 13,726 of The Stolen Journals from Emperor Leto II's Citadel fortress in the Sareer, Kwuteg was killed by a pack of D-wolves in Arrakis' Forbidden Forest following the raid on the Citadel. He

delayed the pack of D-wolves sufficiently to allow Siona to escape to the safety of the Idaho River. [*God Emperor of Dune*]

Kynes, Dr. Liet (10,146–10,191)—Proud, regal, strong, tall, thin, sandy-haired, sparsely-bearded, mustachioed, thick-browed Dr. Liet Kynes was the son of Pardot Kynes, the father of Chani, the grandfather of Leto II and Ghanima, and Emperor Shaddam IV's planetary ecologist or planetologist on Arrakis. He had gone native and adopted the ways and attitudes of the Fremen while still a child. Charged with monitoring the change of fief on Arrakis from the Harkonnens to the Atreides in 10,191, as Judge of the Change he was expected by the Emperor to favor the Harkonnens and to betray the Atreides. Shortly after their arrival on Arrakis, Kynes provided Duke Leto Atreides and Paul Atreides with stillsuits and jubba cloaks prior to taking them to the desert to observe spice mining operations. He began to like Duke Leto when he saw on that excursion that Leto prioritizes the lives of the men in a sandcrawler over the value of the spice lost when the crawler was consumed by a sandworm. He was subsequently won over to the Atreides cause when he heard Lady Jessica state at an Arrakeen banquet that she intended to hold the plants in the Ducal Palace's wet-world conservatory in trust until the time comes when such plants could be grown in the open on Arrakis. At that banquet Kynes indicated his sympathy with the Atreides by challenging a terrified Guild banker to a duel. After the fall of Arrakeen Kynes, with Duncan Idaho, rescued Paul and Jessica from the desert and took them to an underground Imperial Ecological Testing Station, from which he directed their escape in a hidden Fremen ornithopter while the station was under attack by Sardaukar in Harkonnen uniforms. To punish him for having aided the Atreides, the Harkennens abandoned Kynes in the desert without a stillsuit. Although he was then killed by the desert when a spice blow erupted beneath him, Kynes had already sent a message to the Fremen instructing them to find and save Paul. Dr. Liet Kynes was the author of *The Arrakis Workbook*. [*Dune, Children of Dune*]

Kynes, Pardot (10,110–10,165)—The father of Dr. Liet Kynes who was killed in a cave-in at Plaster Basin when his son was nineteen, the intensely single-minded Pardot Kynes was the first Imperial Ecologist or Planetologist on Arrakis. He had originated the 500-year plan, subsequently embraced by the Fremen, to hoard water on Arrakis until enough had been conserved to change the planet's ecology. [*Dune*]

Kynes Sea—Lying beyond the last desert of the Sareer, the Kynes Sea was a large body of water on Arrakis in the 138th century. [*God Emperor of Dune*]

Laab—Laab was one of the spring-time months on Arrakis. [*Children of Dune*]

Lake Azrak—Lake Azrak was a gypsum plane, west of Jacurutu, where there had once been open water on Arrakis—in the time before the sandworms. [*Children of Dune*]

Lame (10,165–10,209)—Lame was a dissident Fremen Naib who fled Arrakis with a stolen worm in 10,207. [*Dune Messiah*]

Lampadas—A Bene Gesserit school planet and stronghold, Lampadas was the planet to which Miles Teg was sent to be educated at the age of twelve, in 14,935. It was destroyed by the Honored Matres in 15,243. Bene Gesserit Supreme Bashar Alef Burzmali and four million Bene Gesserit soldiers died on Lampadas; the sole survivor of the attack was Reverend Mother Lucilla, who fled to Gammu in a no-ship. [*Heretics of Dune, Chapterhouse: Dune*]

Laoujin—Laoujin is the star about which Wallach IX orbits. [*Dune*]

Landsraad—The Landsraad is the union of Great Houses that is one leg—with the Imperial Household and the Spacing Guild—of the political tripod maintaining the Great Convention in the 102nd century. [*Dune*]

Larus (10,169–10,198)—Larus was one of the band of forty Fremen, led by Stilgar, who found Paul Atreides and the Lady Jessica in the desert after the Fall of Arrakeen in 10,191. He, with Farrukh, was charged with hiding the band's tracks. [*Dune*]

lasgun—Expensive and difficult to maintain, a lasgun is a continuous-wave laser weapon. The lasgun beam produces explosive subatomic fusion when it intersects an active shield; thus, lasguns are of limited use in a culture that employs shields. [*Dune*]

Lashkar—A Lashkar is a Tleilaxu war party seeking Bodal, the Tleilaxu's ultimate revenge. By extension, it is also any adventure that takes a Tleilaxu Master among the Powindah. [*Heretics of Dune*]

Last Desert of the Sareer—In the 138th century the sole remaining desert on Arrakis was the Last Desert of the Sareer. It is here that Emperor Leto II had built his Citadel fortress. [*God Emperor of Dune*]

The Last Jihad—A study conducted by Sumer and Kautman, *The Last Jihad* examines the forces that allowed Richese and Ix to evade the anti-machine proscriptions of the Butlerian Jihad. [*Dune*]

Laza tigers—Laza tigers were a special breed of tigers brought to Salusa Secundus in the 3rd millennium after the Butlerian Jihad. They often had servo-stimulators implanted in their brains while cubs that made them the pawns of whoever possessed the transmitter. In 10,216, on orders from Princess Wensicia, two Laza tigers were trained by Sardaukar on Salusa Secundus to attack Leto Atreides II and Ghanima. The tigers did attack Leto II and Ghanima on Arrakis later that year, but the two survived the attack. [*Children of Dune*]

Legg (10,058–10,207)—Legg was a dissident Fremen Naib who attended the trial of Korba, presided over by Alia, in 10,207. [*Dune Messiah*]

Lemil (10,167–10,201)—Lemil was one of the band of forty Fremen, led by Stilgar, who found Paul Atreides and the Lady Jessica in the desert after the Fall of Arrakeen in 10,191. He was sent by Stilgar to find glowglobes once the band had reached Cave of the Ridges. [*Dune*]

Lernaeus—The planet, orbiting a yellow star, on which Bene Gesserit Supreme Bashar Miles Teg had been born and raised and on which the Teg family had lived for three generations, Lernaeus was the planet on which Teg was living in retirement when Reverend Mother Superior Alma Mavis Taraza charged him with the task of guarding Duncan Idaho ghola number 4 and the Bene Gesserit Keep on Gammu. [*Heretics of Dune*]

Leto (10,192–10,193)—The natural son of Paul Atreides and Chani, Leto was killed in infancy in a Sardaukar raid on a relocated Sietch Tabr that occurred immediately prior to the 10,193 Fremen assault on Arrakeen. [*Dune*]

Leto Atreides II (10,207–13,726)—The natural son of Paul Atreides and

Chani, twin brother to Ghanima, and the grandson of Duke Leto Atreides, Lady Jessica, Dr. Liet Kynes, and Faroula, rusty-haired Leto Atreides II was born in Sietch Tabr in 10,207 with full awareness, with all the prescient powers of his father, and with the memories of all his ancestors. Shortly after his birth he allowed the blind Paul to see through his eyes, enabling Paul to kill Scytale with a thrown crysknife as Scytale threatened the lives of Leto II and his newborn sister. While still a child he participated in the Royal Council, and he had begun to have prescient dreams by the age of nine. Although it would allow them to forsee the future, he and Ghanima avoided the overdose of melange that would bring on the spice trance because it would also lead to Abomination, to being possessed by the persona of one of the ancestors who resided in their consciousnesses. Instead, to avoid Abomination, Leto II would sometimes assume his father Paul's persona, to access Paul's memories of his prescient visions, while Ghanima assumed their mother Chani's persona. Afterward, it took a supreme effort of will for the parent to relinquish his body back to the child. However, this parent game persuaded Leto II that he must pursue the Golden Path that Paul had forseen but had not taken. On being interviewed by his grandmother Jessica in 10,216, Leto II informed Jessica that Regent Alia Atreides planned to have her abducted and

to place the blame on Princess Wensicia and House Corrino. Subsequently, he took Stilgar into the desert, near the Attendant, and ordered him to flee from Sietch Tabr with Ghanima should Leto II be slain on that spot. He subsequently snuck out of Sietch Tabr with Ghanima, to escape being placed in Alia's custody, and then evaded death in the desert at the paws of the Laza tigers that Wensicia had had transported from Salusa Secundus to Arrakis to assassinate him and Ghanima. Leto II, hidden in a shallow cave, killed one Laza tiger with the blade of a poisoned crysknife while Ghanima killed the remaining Laza tiger with her poisoned crysknife. Leto II then set out for Jacurutu on a sandworm while Ghanima hypnotized herself into believing that Leto II had been slain by the Laza tigers before she returned to Sietch Tabr. However, Leto II was captured while approaching Jacurutu by Gurney Hallek, who took him as a prisoner to Jacurutu, where he was questioned by Namri and made to understand that Namri would kill him if his answers were unsatisfactory. On Jessica's orders he was subsequently injected with spice essence by Hallek, to force him to have prescient visions and to confront the ancestors who resided in his consciousness, but the persona of Paul residing in his consciousness vowed to protect him from being possessed. In Jacurutu Leto II had prescient visions of wearing a skin that was not his own and of an Arrakis that was without sandworms and without spice. He also encountered Harum, his ultimate ancestor and the persona inhabiting his consciousness, who finally did possess him. Eventually he escaped Jacurutu—by hypnotizing his guard, Sabiha, into falling asleep—and headed south, through a great sandstorm, into the Tanzerouft wasteland and towards Shuloch (the secret desert sietch of the Cast Out) and The Preacher. Leto II survived the sandstorm by burying himself in a stilltent in the sand and putting himself into a dormancy trance that slowed his metabolic functions. The next day he encountered Muriz, who took him to Shuloch, where he again met Sabiha. He subsequently merged himself with the sand trout of Shuloch, which covered his entire body except his face with a thin, incredibly tough membrane, forming a living stillsuit. This sand-trout skin amplified his movements and gave him super-speed, super-strength, and command of the sandworms, but it also made him a hybrid being who was no longer human. The following day he smashed the qanats of Gara Rulen, Windsack, Old Gap, and Harg to set back Alia's ecological transformation of Arrakis; these attacks were attributed to the Desert Demon. He subsequently encountered The Preacher and his young guide, Assan Tariq, in the Tanzerouft and had a battle of prescient visions with The Preacher from which Leto II's vision of the

future emerged victorious. When Assan, in the midst of this contest, tried to murder both The Preacher and Leto II by activating a pseudo-shield in the desert to attract a maddened sandworm, Leto II killed him, threw the pseudo-shield a great distance, and declared that he was The Preacher's new guide. For the next year, in the guise of the Desert Demon, Leto II repeatedly destroyed the qanats of numerous djedida—new Fremen towns—to continue to halt Arrakis' ecological transformation. In 10,218 Leto II introduced The Preacher to Hallek in one of the small rebel sietches in Gare Ruden, where he also revealed to Hallek that he was the Desert Demon. He subsequently brought The Preacher and Hallek back to Shuloch, where he was worshipped as a god, and then returned to Arrakeen as The Preacher's guide. In Arrakeen he was reunited with Ghanima and together, after Leto II had slain her guards, they confronted Alia. Leto II offered Alia the choice of a Trial of Possession or suicide, and Alia chose suicide and threw herself from a window of her temple. Leto II subsequently assumed the mantle of Emperor and wed his sister, Ghanima, but appointed Prince Farad'n to be Ghanima's consort and his Royal Scribe. In 12,334, in the 2116th year of his reign, Leto II executed nine historians in his Citadel for their pretentious lies. By the 138th century Leto II's metamorphosis into a sandworm had reached the pre-worm stage. His body, which weighed five tons, was seven meters long and more than two meters in diameter; it had a human face, humanoid arms and hands, and flippers instead of legs and feet. His skull had dissolved and his brain had grown without limits in ganglia along his spinal column. He had extremely acute sight and hearing but little sense of touch. By this time Leto II no longer comnsumed any mélange, as his pre-worm body manufactured all the spice his addiction required. To distract and amuse himself he would often go on extended "safaris" among the memories of his ancestors and, due to his prescience and longevity, his greatest wish and keenest delight was to be surprised. In 13,726 he survived a Tleilaxu attempt to assassinate him that employed fifty Face Dancers disguised as Museum Fremen and then as Duncan Idaho. This attempt occurred near the Idaho River as Leto II traversed the Royal Road from his Citadel fortress in the Sareer to the festival city of Onn. During the 13,726 festival in Onn Leto II had the Tleilaxu Ambassador to Arrakis, Duro Nunepi, publically flogged as punishment for the Tleilaxu attempt on his life. Later that year Leto II fell in love with and proposed marriage to Hwi Noree, the newly appointed Ambassador from Ix. He also that year personally participated in suppressing the Tleilaxu/rebel attack on the Ixian Embassy in Onn. Through an interview with her in his Citadel

Leto II subsequently determined that Siona Ibn Faud al-Seyefa Atreides was ready to be tested, and he took her into the Sareer to test her. On their fifth day in the Sareer, when she was dying of thirst, Leto II permitted Siona to nurse water mixed with spice essence from the curled flaps of the cowl that protected his face, and this imparted to her a vision of the Golden Path. After learning that Idaho ghola number 3 had had sexual relations with Hwi Noree, Leto II decreed that they must never see one another again. And on then learning that Moneo had sent Siona, Nayla, and Idaho ghola number 3 to Tuono Village so that they would miss his and Hwi Noree's nuptials, which were to have occurred in Tabur Village, Leto II changed the location of his wedding ceremony to Tuono Village. He was then killed when Nayla, acting on Siona's orders, severed the supports to the bridge over the Idaho River as he, in his Royal Cart with Hwi Noree, crossed over the river on his peregrination to Tuono Village. When Leto II's body contacted the Idaho River it disintegrated into sand trout that eventually grew into mature sandworms that each contained a pearl of Leto II's consciousness. During Leto II's reign the number of wars in the known universe dropped to 2% of what it had been previously. The Tleilaxu of the 153rd century saw Leto II as being God's prophet whose true message only they have heard. Leto II was the author of The Stolen Journals and of the histories ascribed to, as well as the biography of, Noah Arkwright. [*Dune Messiah, Children of Dune, God Emperor of Dune, Heretics of Dune*]

Leto Atreides II—*Leto Atreides II* was a volume authored by Harq al-Ada. [*Children of Dune*]

Leto's Peace—Leto's Peace was the 3,508 years of repressive tranquility imposed on the human universe by Emperor Leto II during his reign, 10,218–13,726. [*God Emperor of Dune*]

Levenbrech—Levenbrech was a Sardaukar rank, beneath the rank of Bator, often assumed by an aide to a Bashar. [*Children of Dune*]

Licallo (prehistoric)—Licallo was a composer whom Emperor Leto II believed was as gifted as J. S. Bach. [*God Emperor of Dune*]

Lichna (10,186–10,207)—Otheym's daughter by his wife Dhuri, Lichna was addicted to semuta by Farok's son. She was in 10,207 led from Farok's house by Scytale disguised as Farok, whom Scytale had killed with a poisoned needle. Her remains, which were later found in the desert, indicated that she had been killed by a poison of Tleilaxu origin called "the throat of hell"; however, no Fremen woman had been reported missing because after her death Lichna was impersonated by Scytale. [*Dune Messiah*]

Lidiche—Prior to the 153rd century, the Jews of Secret Israel had endured

a pogrom on the planet Lidiche. [*Chapterhouse: Dune*]

Linchine (15,165–15,243)—Linchine was an inept Bene Gesserit acolyte with whom Darwi Odrade had been paired in learning to fly an ornithopter on Lanpadas, a Bene Gesserit school planet. While she was neither intelligent nor emotionally balanced, Linchine carried genes valuable to the Bene Gesserit. [*Chapterhouse: Dune*]

Lisan Al-Gaib—In Fremen legend the Lisan Al-Gaib is a messianic prophet from another planet, the "Voice from the Outer World." The Fremen and the other natives of Arrakis hoped that Paul Atreides would prove to be the Lisan Al-Gaib shortly after his 10,191 arrival on their planet. *See* **Mahdi**. [*Dune*]

litany against fear—The litany against fear is a Bene Gesserit mantra designed to mitigate anxiety. [*Dune*]

Little Citadel—150 meters in diameter and 3,000 meters high, the Little Citadel was a vantage tower Leto II had had built in the central Sareer. It was connected to his Citadel fortress by a secret tunnel, and it took Leto II less than an hour to travel by Royal Cart from his Citadel fortress to the Little Citadel. In 13,726 Leto II interviewed Siona Ibn Faud al-Seyefa Atreides in the Little Citadel and determined that she was ready to be tested. [*God Emperor of Dune*]

little maker—A stage in the sandworm lifecycle, the little maker or sand trout was a hand-sized, half-plant-half-animal deep-sand vector that joined together with others of its kind to encapsulate water beneath the desert and turn it into a pre-spice mass with their excretions. By encapsulating water and converting it into mélange, the little makers created the arid planetary conditions on Arrakis necessary for the survival of the adult sandworm, to which water is fatal. [*Dune*]

London—London is a village on the planet Gansireed. [*Children of Dune*]

Longo, Honored Matre Grand Dame/Great Honored Matre (15,196–15,245)—Golden-haired, thin-lipped, rheumy-eyed, viscious Longo was an Honored Matre Grand Dame and a senior aide to Great Honored Matre Dama when, in 15,245, she eschewed the Honored-Matre tradition of killing with the feet and poisoned Dama to become the Great Honored Matre while Longo was parlaying with Bene Gesserit Reverend Mother Superior Odrade on Junction. After the Miles Teg clone's victory at Junction, Longo surrendered to Odrade but quickly took command of the situation again when the Honored Matre's secret weapon killed nearly all of the Bene Gesserit attackers except for Odrade and the Teg clone. Soon thereafter Senior Dame Elpek took Reverend Mother Superior Murbella to Longo, who was goaded into attacking Murbella and perished in the attempt. [*Chapterhouse: Dune*]

The Lost Ones—The Lost Ones were the megatrillions who had left the known universe during the Scattering, which began in the 138th century. [*Heretics of Dune*]

Lucilla, Reverend Mother (15,192–15,244)—Solid, ample-breasted, brown-haired, cautious Reverend Mother Lucilla was a Bene Gesserit Imprinter with seductive eyes who greatly resembled Senior Security Mother Darwi Odrade in everything except body type and age. A direct descendant of Lady Jessica and the Atreides line, with strong backbreeding from Siona Ibn Faud al-Seyefa Atreides' descendants, she had borne three children for the Bene Gesserit on Gammu by the time she was assigned to seduce and imprint Duncan Idaho ghola number 4. While she succeeded in making the Idaho ghola fall in love with her, the ghola successfully resisted her sexual advances because he did not want to be a stud for the Bene Gesserit. Lucilla was sexually attracted to the much older Bene Gesserit Supreme Bashar Miles Teg, but he succeeded in resisting her sexual overtures as well. In 15,232 Teg saved the ghola and Lucilla from an attack by Face Dancers disguised as Teg whom Reverend Mother Schwangyu's minions had allowed into the Gammu Keep. He then led the ghola and Lucilla into the forest northeast of the Keep, to evade Schwangyu's treachery, and to an ancient Harkonnen no-globe that Teg's aide Patrin had discovered as a teenager and kept a secret for well over two hundred years. While the three hid in the no-globe for three months, Lucilla attempted unsuccessfully to carry out her orders to make the ghola irrestible to most women, through sexual imprinting, in order to facilitate the Bene Gesserit plan to have the ghola seduce Sheeana Brugh on Rakis. With the assistance of Bene Gesserit Bashar Alef Burzmali, Lucilla and the ghola escaped the no-globe and Lucilla was disguised by Gammu native Sirafa as a postulant of the Honored Matres named Pira who was working on Gammu as a playfem. She and Burzmali, disguised as her client, Skar, traversed Ysai and encountered Honored Matre Murbella, who had already captured the ghola, in an abandoned factory on Ysai's outskirts. Lucilla, Burzmali, the ghola, and Murbella were then taken to Rakis in a no-ship from the Scattering that had been captured by Teg. Lucilla, the ghola, and Murbella, with Sheeana Brugh and a captive sandworm, were transported in the same no-ship to Chapterhouse just before Rakis was destroyed by the Honored Matres. Lucilla was Vice Chancellor on Lampadas, a Bene Gesserit school planet, when it fell to the Honored Matres in 15,243. The only survivor, she was afterwards interrogated for several weeks on Junction by Great Honored Matre Dama, who finally killed her in a murderous rage by kicking her in the temple. [*Heretics of Dune, Chapterhouse: Dune*]

Luli (13,699–13,770)—Graceful, slender, almond-eyed, high-cheekboned Luli was a member of Emperor Leto II's Imperial Guard who welcomed Duncan Idaho ghola number 3 as her commander in Onn in 13,726. [*God Emperor of Dune*]

Luyseyal, Reverend Mother Marcus Claire (13,691–13,808)—Red-haired, sensous, oval-featured, headstrong Reverend Mother Marcus Claire Luyseyal was a Bene Gesserit Truthsayer who attended the 13,726 festival in Onn with Reverend Mother Tertius Eileen Anteac. The two were informed by Othwi Yake that Tleilaxu Face Dancers had infiltrated Arrakis' Ixian Embassy and intended to assassinate Emperor Leto II during his peregrination to the festival city of Onn, and they conveyed this intelligence to Leto II via his Fish Speakers. Luyseyal and Anteac then conversed with Leto II when he subsequently met the Bene Gesserit delegation to Arrakis in False Sietch. Luyseyeal brought with her to this interview a vial of spice essence that she thought incorrectly might harm Leto II, but Leto II detected and confiscated it. [*God Emperor of Dune*]

Madinat assalam—Madinat assalam was, in the Fremen tongue, the Abode of Peace that comes with death. [*Children of Dune*]

magchutes—Magchutes were magnetic transport bases that had carried goods or raw materials to factories on Gammu in the 138th century. [*Heretics of Dune*]

The Mahai—The Mahai is the Tleilaxu Master of Masters. Tlywyth Waff had been the Mahai for centuries prior to his death in 15,232. [*Heretics of Dune*]

Mahdi—Mahdi is the Fremen term for their anticipated messiah, the one who will lead them to paradise. *See* **Lisan Al-Gaib**. [*Dune*]

Mahdinate—Alia Atreides' rule over Arrakis and the Empire as Regent, from 10,207 to 10,218, was known as the Mahdinate. [*Children of Dune*]

The Mahdinate, An Analysis—*The Mahdinate, An Analysis* was a volume authored by Harq al-Ada. [*Children of Dune*]

Mahdi Spirit Club—The Mahdi Spirit Club composed the Tabla Memorium, which was the source material for the Muad'Dib Concordance. [*Dune Messiah*]

maker hooks—Maker hooks are telescoping, barbed, whip-like shafts with plasteel hooks at one end that were used by Fremen to capture, mount, and steer a sandworm. They are about 1.5 meters long and are roughened at the end opposite the hook to provide a firm grip. Maker hooks are among the artifacts in the fremkit that Dr. Wellington Yueh hid in the ornithopter in which Kinet and Czigo transported Paul Atreides and Lady Jessica to the desert after the 10,191 fall of Arrakeen. [*Dune*]

Malky (13,655–13,726)—Gray-haired, oval-faced, brown-eyed, heavy-browed, cruel, industrious, hedonistic Malky was Hwi Noree's uncle and an Ixian Ambassador to Arrakis. Emperor Leto II was Malky's favorite companion because Malky judged him to be ultimately civilized. The Bene Gesserit believed that both Malky and his niece Hwi Noree had been genetically bred to serve as Ixian Ambassadors to Leto II's court, and Leto II believed that Malky might also have been Hwi Noree's father. When Malky returned to Ix in 13,726 he was hidden from Leto II's prescience by the Ixian no-globe. He was subsequently captured on Ix by Fish Speakers and returned to Arrakis, somewhat injured, where he met Moneo and Leto II at the Little Citadel and was executed by Moneo on Leto II's orders. [*God Emperor of Dune*]

Mamulut, Reverend Mother (13,680–13,802)—Bene Gesserit Reverend Mother Mamulut was an author of the Welbeck Abridgement, a 13,726 report to the Bene Gesserit. [*God Emperor of Dune*]

Manri (10,190–10,248)—Manri was a citizen of Jacurutu whom Muriz suspected may have told Leto Atreides II about Shuloch. [*Children of Dune*]

"A Manual of Muad'Dib"—"A Manual of Muad'Dib" is one of the many volumes authored by Princess Irulan. [*Dune*]

Maometh (907–945)—Maometh was the so-called third Muhammed, whose teachings were denounced by Ali Ben Ohashi, leader of the original Zen-sunni, in about 1,381. [*Dune*]

Mapes, the Shadout (10,128–10,191)— Knobby, gray-haired, stringy-voiced, wrinkled, and desiccated, the Shadout Mapes was the head housekeeper of the ducal palace in Arrakeen when the Atreides arrived on Arrakis in 10,191. (The title "shadout" means "well-dipper" in the Fremen tongue.) She soon thereafter gave an unfixed crysknife to Lady Jessica, whom she believed to be the mother of the Fremen Mahdi or Lisan Al-Gaib. She was then almost killed by a hunter seeker that threatened Paul Atreides, but Paul saved her life, and in return she warned him that the Atreides had a traitor in their midst. Less than a month later she was stabbed to death by the traitor, Dr. Wellington Yueh, in the Arrakeen palace. [*Dune*]

Marcus, Wanna (10,092–10,186?)— Wife to Dr. Wellington Yueh, Wanna Marcus was a Bene Gesserit truthsayer who was captured, tortured, and executed by the Harkonnens. [*Dune*]

Markow, Battle of—The battle of Markow was won entirely by Bene Gesserit Supreme Bashar Miles Teg's reputation, which compelled the enemy to surrender. [*Heretics of Dune*]

Marquis of the Inner Desert—The Marquis of the Inner Desert were Fremen rebels against Alia Atreides'

Regency who cursed House Atreides and Muad'Dib. [*Children of Dune*]

Martin (14,926–15,238)—Martin was an old soldier and one of Bene Gesserit Supreme Bashar Miles Teg's house guards on Lernaeus. [*Heretics of Dune*]

Marty (14,901–15,305)—Daniel's partner, Marty was the grandmotherly Face Dancer tending her garden in the Scattering that Duncan Idaho ghola number 4 saw in his 15,244 and 15,245 Mentat visions of "the net." She may have been a leader of the evolved Face Dancers who drove the Honored Matres from the Scattering back into the known universe of the Old Empire in the 153rd century. [*Chapterhouse: Dune*]

The Masheikh—The Masheikh are the highest rank caste of the Tleilaxu Masters and the caste that is master of the genetic code. [*Heretics of Dune*]

mashhad—To the Fremen of Arrakis, a "mashhad" was a spiritual test. [*Children of Dune*]

The Masters—Among the Tleilaxu, the Masters are the ruling subgroup who command the subservient Face Dancers, the other sub-group. [*Heretics of Dune*]

matar—On Arrakis, matar was a rain of sand dropped from high altitudes by a dying sandstorm. [*Children of Dune*]

Mater Felicissima—Mater Felicissima was an ancient term for a Bene Gesserit Council member. [*Chapterhouse: Dune*]

Materly (15,191–15,232)—Sincere, green-eyed, square-jawed Materly was a female minion of the Honored Matres who played the role of the friendly, compassionate interrogator when Bene Gesserit Supreme Bashar Miles Teg was subjected to a T-probe after having been captured by the Honored Matres during Reverend Mother Lucilla's and Duncan Idaho ghola number 4's escape from the Harkonnen no-globe on Gammu. Teg killed Materly in escaping from the T-probe's influence after the agony it had caused him had lifted him to a new level of ability. [*Heretics of Dune*]

Mattai (10,164–10,191)—One of Gurney Hallek's Atreides troopers, Mattai died at Staban Tuek's smuggler base soon after the 10,191 fall of Arrakeen to the Harkonnens. [*Dune*]

maula pistol—A projectile weapon used by the Fremen in the desert, where it is unwise to employ shields, a maula pistol is spring-loaded, fires poisoned darts, and has a range of forty meters. [*Dune*]

mélange—Popularly known as "spice," mélange is a blue, highly alkaline by-product of the sandworm lifecycle that until the 16th millennium occurred naturally only on Arrakis and could not be synthesized. At one time extremely expensive—as much as 620,000 solaris per decagram when Arrakeen mélange was most readily available, during the 102nd century, and a handful of spice would buy a home on Tupile—it extends life but is mildly addictive when consumed in small quantities and highly addictive when consumed in large quantities (two grams daily per seventy kilos of body weight). Prodigious consumption of mélange can extend an individual's life to as many as 400 years. (The geriatric properties of mélange were first noted by Yanshuph Ashkoto, royal chemist during the reign of Shakkad the Wise.) When consumed in large quantities mélange also turns the whites of the eyes blue due to mélange saturation of the blood. It smells like cinnamon, never tastes the same way twice, makes food taste better, and imparts a natural immunity to most poisons in the average person. Mélange also enables Guild Navigators to pilot faster-than-light space vessels by giving them a limited power to foresee the future, and exposure to mélange unlocked Paul Atreides' more-extensive prophetic abilities in 10,191. More than 10 billion solaris in mélange was mined by the Harkonnens on Arrakis each year during much of the 102nd century. Due to the ecological transformation of Arrakis that began after Muad'Dib's Jihad, by 10,218 melange production on Arrakis had fallen to 10% of what it had been at its peak under the Harkonnens. By the 138th century the only mélange in the universe was contained in the Spacing Guild and the Bene Gesserit storehouses, in the holdings of a few remaining Great Houses, and in Emperor Leto II's gigantic hoard hidden in his Citadel fortress on Arrakis. By the 153rd century the vast bulk of the mélange in the known universe was produced in huge quantities in Tleilaxu axlotl tanks, and the Bene Tleilax hoped to monopllize mélange production through a never-materialized alliance with the priests of Rakis. Due to the ready availability of mélange produced in the Tleilaxu axlotl tanks, the human lifespan had lengthened to 300–400 years by the 153rd century. Melange is interchangeable with the adrenaline-based substitute used by the Honored Matres. [*Dune, Children of Dune, God Emperor of Dune, Heretics of Dune, Chapterhouse: Dune*]

Melides (10,170–10,233)—A short man with a gourd-like body and ugly, spindly legs, Melides was in 10,217 a citizen of Tuek's smugglers' sietch on the inner lip of False Wall. [*Children of Dune*]

Memar (13,705–13,726)—One of Siona Ibn Faud al-Seyefa Atreides' ten companions in the theft in 13,726 of The Stolen Journals from Emperor Leto II's Citadel fortress in the Sareer, Memar was killed by a pack of D-wolves in Arrakis' Forbidden Forest following the raid on the Citadel. [*God Emperor of Dune*]

"**Memory Poem**"—"Memory Poem" is a verse by Emperor Leto II that he had had inscribed on the wall at Dar-es-Balat. [*Chapterhouse: Dune*]

Mentat—A Mentat is a human trained to possess computer-like logic and computational ability. A Mentat's abilities are heightened through the use of sapho juice. The Order of Mentats was founded by Gilbertus Albans. Many Mentats were trained on Tleilax, but no Mentats were trained during the reign of Emperor Leto II, from 10,218 to 13,726, because Mentat schools formed a nucleus of independent opposition to his rule. Notable Mentats in history include Paul Atreides, Thufir Hawat, Piter DeVries, several Duncan Idaho gholas, and Bene Gesserit Supreme Bashar Miles Teg. [*Dune, God Emperor of Dune, Chapterhouse: Dune*]

Merkur (10,166–10,209)—Merkur was a dissident Fremen Naib who fled Arrakis with a stolen worm in 10,207. [*Dune Messiah*]

Metulli Family—In 10,218 the Metulli Family sold half of the planet Novebruns for 321 liters of mélange. [*Children of Dune*]

Million Planets—The Million Planets was a term used by the Honored Matres to refer to the Old Empire, the known universe ruled by Emperor Leto II during his 3,508-year reign (10,218–13,726). [*Chapterhouse: Dune*]

minah—In the Fremen tongue, minah is the time of year for testing the young to determine if they are ready for adulthood. [*Dune*]

minimic film—Minimic film is a one-micron in diameter length of shigawire often used to transmit espionage and counterespionage data. [*Dune*]

Mirlat (13,629–18,747)—Mirlat was a Tleilaxu Masheikh of the innermost Kehl and one of Master of Masters Tylwyth Waff's nine councilors. His persona had been alive during the time of Emperor Leto II, he had aspired to become The Mahai in the 138th century, and his current body was centuries old in the 153rd century. [*Heretics of Dune*]

Mirzabah—In Fremen mythology Mirzabah is the Iron Hammer with which the dead are beaten who cannot answer correctly the questions they must answer to gain entry into paradise. [*Children of Dune*]

misr—Meaning "the people" in the Fremen tongue, "misr" is the word that the Zensunni (the Fremen ancestors) used to refer to themselves. [*Dune*]

Missionaria Protectiva—A propaganda arm of the Bene Gesserit, the Missionaria Protectiva was a cadre of missionary-like sisters of the order who seeded the known universe with prophecy patterns for the protection of other Bene Gesserit personnel who might venture to backwater worlds. Such prophecy patters were sown on Arrakis and were capitalized on by Lady Jessica and her son Paul Atreides. [*Dune*]

Mitha (7,802–7,864)—Mitha was a Zensunni Wanderer during the time when the Fremen inhabited Bela Tegeuse. [*Dune*]

Modibo (10,157–10,225)—Modibo, the bent one, was in 10,217 Stilgar's messenger in Sietch Tabr. At Stilgar's behest he sent for Buer Agarves so that Agarves could witness the dead bodies of Hayt and Ziarenko Javid. [*Children of Dune*]

Mohalata—Mohalata is the partnership one of the pre-born can have with benign ancestors to protect him or her from malignant ancestors. [*Children of Dune*]

Mohandis, Tagir (10,191–10,283)—Tall, bold, intelligent, virile, golden-haired Tagir Mohandis was a baliset player and a Kadeshian troubadour on Hajj on Arrakis in 10,216 who approached Regent Alia Atreides during her morning audience to complain that he had been drugged and robbed by Arrakeen mercenaries and to ask for money with which to travel to Salusa Secundus to join Prince Farad'n's court. Having been given the authority to do so by Alia, Jessica granted his request. [*Children of Dune*]

Mohiam, Reverend Mother Gaius Helen (10,114–10,207)—Reverend Mother Gaius Helen Mohiam, who had silver metal teeth and bird-bright eyes, was Jessica's teacher and the Proctor Superior at the Bene Gesserit school on Wallach IX and, later, Emperor Shaddam IV's truthsayer. She tested Paul with the gom jabbar on Caladan in 10,191 and predicted the demise of Duke Leto to Paul and Jessica prior to the Atreides relocation from Caladan to Arrakis. She accompanied Shaddam IV to Arrakis in 10,193. She was a principal party to the 10,205–07 conspiracy against Paul Muad'Dib hatched on Wallach IX that also involved Scytale, Edric, and Princess Irulan. In 10,207 she arrived in Arrakeen space on the Guild heighliner that brought Edric to Arrakis as the Guild's Steersman-Ambassador to Paul's Imperial Court. She was removed from the heighliner as a prisoner at Paul's command. On Arrakis, having concluded that Paul would never impregnate Irulan, she subsequently told Irulan that the possibility of mating Paul with Alia must be explored, as a way to preserve the Atreides genes for the Bene Gesserit breeding program, and that Chani must be killed to prevent her from giving Paul an heir. She later accompanied Chani—with Paul, Bijaz, Hayt, Alia, Edric, Scytale disguised as Lichna, Stilgar, Harah, and Irulan—when Chani returned to the desert, to Sietch Tabr, to give birth. After Chani's death in childbirth, Stilgar executed Mohiam on Alia's orders. [*Dune, Dune Messiah*]

Moneo (13,608–13,726)—A product of Emperor Leto II's breeding program, sandy-haired, gray-eyed, flat-featured, hawk-nosed, loyal Moneo was a direct descendant of Ghanima Atreides and Harq-al-Ada who also had one of Leto II's Duncan Idaho gholas in his ancestry. He was Siona Ibn Faud al-Seyefa Atreides' father and, during the late 137th and early 138th centuries, was the major-domo and chief aide to Leto II. In 13,726 Leto II put Moneo in charge of planning his wedding to Hwi Noree; and Moneo informed Hwi Noree and Duncan Idaho ghola number 3, after they had had sexual relations, that it was Leto II's decree that they must never see one another again. In an attempt to save Idaho ghola number 3's life, Moneo sent the ghola, Siona, and Nayla to Tuono Village so that they would not be able to attend Leto II's wedding ceremony, which was to have occurred in Tabur Village, but which Leto II then relocated to Tuono Village. Moneo executed Malky at the Little Citadel on Leto II's orders. He was killed in falling from the bridge above the Idaho River, near Tuono Village, when Nayla severed the bridge supports with a lasgun and assassinated Leto II and Hwi Noree. Moneo and Siona are the two participants in the brief dialogue contained in the "Welbeck Fragment." [*God Emperor of Dune*]

Mother of Moisture—"Mother of Moisture" was a Fremen title bestowed on Jessica when she returned to Arrakis in 10,216. [*Children of Dune*]

Mount Idaho—Mount Idaho was a mountain to the north of Arrakeen that was visible from the Attendant, a rock outcropping near Sietch Tabr. [*Children of Dune*]

Mount Syubi—Mount Syubi is a mountain that is visible from Castle Caladan. [*Dune*] m'smow—In the Fremen tongue, "m'smow" was the foul odor on a summer night that was the harbinger of death at the hands of demons. [*Children of Dune*]

Muad'Dib—The Fremen name for the adapted kangaroo mouse of Arrakis admired by the Fremen for its ability to survive in the open desert, Muad'Dib is also the word Paul Atreides took as a part of his public Fremen name, Paul Muad'Dib, at Cave of Birds after killing Jamis in a knife fight in 10,191. See **Atreides, Paul**. [*Dune, Dune Messiah*]

Muad'Dib Concordance—Copied from the Table Memorium of the Mahdi Spirit Cult, the Muad'Dib Concordance attempted to dispel myth and to humanize Paul Muad'Dib and his sister Alia. [*Dune Messiah*]

"Muad'Dib: Conversations"— "Muad'Dib: Conversations" is one of the many volumes authored by Princess Irulan. [*Dune*]

"Muad'Dib, Family Commentaries"—"Muad'Dib, Family Commentaries" is one of the many volumes authored by Princess Irulan. [*Dune*]

"Muad'Dib, the Man"—"Muad'Dib, the Man" is one of the many volumes authored by Princess Irulan. [*Dune*]

"Muad'Dib: The Ninety-nine Wonders of the Universe"—"Muad'Dib: The Ninety-nine Wonders of the Universe" is one of the many volumes authored by Princess Irulan. [*Dune*]

"Muad'Dib: The Religious Issue"— "Muad'Dib: The Religious Issue" is one of the many volumes authored by Princess Irulan. [*Dune*]

Muad'Dib's Jihad—Muad'Dib's Jihad was the period of violent consolidation of Emperor Paul Muad'Dib's rule, from 10,193 to 10,207, that saw the subjugation of 10,000 worlds and the deaths of 61 billion people. [*Dune Messiah*]

Muadh Quran—The Muadh Quaran of Caladan, with its pure Ilm and Fiqh, is one of the Ancient Teachings that shaped the religious beliefs of the Imperium of the 102nd century, the time of Muad'Dib. [*Dune*]

Mudir Nahya—Roughly translated as "Demon Ruler," Mudir Nahya was the Fremen name for Count Glossu "Beast" Rabban. [*Dune*]

Murbella, Honored Matre/Reverend Mother/Reverend Mother Superior/ Great Honored Matre (15,212– 15,597)—A native of the Scattering planet Roc who spoke nine languages, oval-faced, willowy, green-eyed, full-lipped Murbella was recruited by the Honored Matres when she was four years old. As a newly-robed Honored Matre, in 15,232 she encountered Reverend Mother Lucilla and Bashar Alef Burzmali in an abandoned Gammu factory on the outskirts of Ysai after she had captured Duncan Idaho ghola number 4 and killed his Gammu guide, Tormsa (also known as Ambitorm). She then inadvertently induced the ghola, who already possessed the original Duncan Idaho's memories, to recover the memories of his hundreds of previous ghola iterations in attempting to enslave him by using Honored Matre sexual amplification techniques. This exposure to Honored Matre sexual amplification techniques also triggered the secret ability the Tleilaxu had built into the ghola, the ability to enslave women by using similar sexual amplification techniques, and Murbella and the ghola thus enslaved one another in an amplified mutual orgasm during which Murbella was impregnated. Murbella, the ghola, Lucilla, and Burzmali were then taken to Rakis in a no-ship from the Scattering that had been captured by Bene Gesserit Supreme Bashar Miles Teg; and Murbella, Lucilla, and the ghola, with Sheeana Brugh and a captive sandworm, were transported in the same no-ship to Chapterhouse just before Rakis was destroyed by the Honored Matres in 15,232. Murbella was kept captive in the no-ship by the Bene Gesserit—with the Idaho ghola, Scytale, and the Miles Teg clone—from 15,232 to 15,245, during which time she gave birth to four children fathered by the ghola. During her captivity in the no-ship Murbella fell in love with the ghola and also began to use mélange instead of the Honored Matres' orange, adrenaline-based substitute. In 15,245, due to the fact that the clone was only eleven years old, she opposed the Bene Gesserit plan to restore the Miles Teg clone's original memories by having him have intercourse with Sheeana. Shortly after the birth of her fourth child she underwent the Spice Agony, which nearly killed her, and became a Bene Gesserit Reverend Mother. Soon thereafter, she shared other memories with Reverend Mother Superior Darwi Odrade prior to Odrade's trip to parlay with the Honored Matres on Junction. In a separate ship she travelled to Gammu with the Teg clone and there ordered the clone to rescue the Rabbi and Rebecca. She was also present, in a separate ship, during the Teg clone's successful attack on Junction. After the Honored Matres' secret weapon killed the attack force and Bene Gesserit acolyte Streggi on Junction, Murbella descended alone to the planet's surface in a one-man lighter, identified herself as an Honored Matre who had learned all of the Bene Gesserit's secrets, and was taken to Great Honored Matre Longo, whom she goaded into attacking her and easily killed, thus becoming the Great Honored Matre herself. She then absorbed Odrade's most recent memories, as Odrade had been killed by Honored Matre Senior Dame Elpek as Murbella was dispatching Longo, and returned to Chapterhouse with an Honored Matre entourage to claim the title of Bene Gesserit Reverend Mother Superior, thus unifying the Bene Gesserit and the Honored Matres. She subsequently ordered the surviving Bene Gesserits, whom the Honored Matres greatly outnumbered, to teach the Honored Matres how to be Bene Gesserit, thus co-opting them while ostensibly preparing them to return to the Scattering to defeat their enemies. [*Heretics of Dune, Chapterhouse: Dune*]

Muriz (10,181–10,241)—Assan Tariq's father and a citizen of Shuloch, the secret desert sietch of the Cast Out, Muriz was a leathery Fremen smuggler who encountered Leto Atreides II in the desert after Leto II had escaped from Jacurutu and who, with Behaleth, flew him to Shuloch. [*Children of Dune*]

Muriz (10,195–10,216)—A citizen of Sietch Tabr, weak-willed Muriz was Palimbasha's lover and a traitor to the Atreides who was working for House Corrino. [*Children of Dune*]

Museum Fremen—The last remnants of 102nd-century Fremen culture in the 138th century, Museum Fremen imitated and performed flawlessly the lifestyle and rituals of 102nd-century Fremen for tourists on Arrakis but had none of the 102nd-century Fremen qualities or perspectives. [*God Emperor of Dune*]

mushtamal—A mushtamal was a small garden annex to a Fremen dje-dida—a new town established in the desert of Arrakis in the early 103rd century. [*Children of Dune*]

musky—Also known as "murky" or "chalmurky," "musky" is poison administered in one's drink. [*Dune*]

Muzzafar, Field Marshal Jafa (15,181–15,232)—Tall, ruddy, big-nosed, gray-green-eyed Field Marshal Jafa Muzzafar was the regional commander of the forces of Dur, his homeworld in the Scattering, who met Bene Gesserit Supreme Bashar Miles Teg in Ysai and took him to an abandoned bank to meet an ancient, wrinkled Honored Matre. Muzzafar was killed with the building's other fifty occupants when Teg then used his newly-acquired super-speed to slaughter everyone in the building and escape. [*Heretics of Dune*]

"My Woman"—A traditional Caladanian song, "My Woman" was sung by Gurney Hallek to Mattai, a dying Atreides soldier, in 10,191. [*Dune*]

naib—A naib is a Fremen leader of a sietch who has sworn an oath never to be taken alive by an enemy. In the Fremen tongue, "naib" means "servant of the sietch." [*Dune, Childern of Dune*]

Namri (10,169–10,217)—Ziarenko Javid's father, Ziamad's nephew, Abedi Jalal's uncle, Sabiha's uncle, and a citizen of Jacurutu, dark-skinned, sharp-featured Namri was the human gom jabbar who had the authority to kill Leto Atreides II in Jacurutu should he prove to be an Abomination. Namri saw himself vis-à-vis Leto II as being Mirzabah, the Iron Hammer with which the dead are beaten who cannot answer correctly the questions they must answer to gain entry into paradise. He had been chosen to serve as Leto II's inquisitor by Gurney Hallek, but he finally revealed himself to be an ally of Regent Alia Atreides and was slain in Jacurutu by Hallek. [*Children of Dune*]

Naraj Worlds—The Naraj Worlds were planets conquers by Muad'Dib's Jihad sometime between 10,193 and 10,205. Farok's son lost his eyes to a stone burner in the conquest of Naraj. [*Dune Messiah*]

Narcal—Narcal was a planet on which Duke Leto had lost a tooth in battle. Dr. Wellington Yueh subsequently replaced the lost tooth with a false one. [*Dune*]

Navachristianity of Chusuk—The Navachristianity of Chusuk is one of the Ancient Teachings that shaped the dominant religious beliefs of the Imperium in the 102nd century, the time of Muad'Dib. [*Dune*]

Nayla (13,697–13,726)—Square-faced, ivory-haired, green-eyed, thin-lipped, wide-mouthed, square-jawed, thick-fingered, muscular, honest, and patient, Nayla was Emperor Leto II's devoted servant and his spy on Siona, to whom Leto II had had Nayla swear a vow of obedience. A Fish Speaker, she had served in a garrison on Serprek before joining Leto II's Imperial Guard. Leto II had then had a transmitter through which he could communicate with her implanted in her head and had given her a genuine crysknife that had once belonged to one of Stilgar's wives. Wearing a cibus hood and known to him only as "Friend," Nayla, with Luli, greeted Duncan Idaho ghola number 3 when he arrived in Onn, on Arrakis, in 13,726, and tentatively determined that the ghola had probably not been tampered with by the Tleilaxu. Following the Tleilaxu attempt to assassinate Leto II, Nayla gave Tleilaxu Ambassador to Arrakis Duro Nunep twenty lashes in Onn's public plaza. Later, Nayla informed Moneo that his daughter Siona had survived the test to the death to which Leto II had subjected her in the Sareer. Placed under Siona's Command, Nayla was then ordered by Leto II to attend his wedding to Hwi Noree as the only Fish Speaker present who would be permitted to carry a lasgun. Contrarily, she was also ordered to accompany Idaho ghola number 3 and Siona to Tuono Village during the nuptuals, which were to have occurred in Tabur Village until Leto II changed their location to Tuono Village. With Idaho ghola number 3, Siona, some other Fish Speakers, and some Museum Fremen, Nayla climbed from Tuono Villaga to the Royal Road above it where, acting on Siona's orders, which she believed to be a test of her loyalty to Leto II, she severed the Royal Road's bridge supports and disabled the suspensors on Leto II's Royal Cart with her lasgun, tumbling

Leto II, Hwii Noree, and Moneo to their deaths in the Idaho River below. She was then killed by Idaho ghola number 3 with her own lasgun because her actions had caused Hwi Noree's death. [*God Emperor of Dune*]

Nebirds—The Nebirds were one of the Imperium's houses minor in the 103rd century. Essas Paymon was widely believed to be working for House Nebirds, but he was actually a CHOAM spy on Arrakis. [*Children of Dune*]

Nefud, Iakin (10,154–10,193)—Flat-faced, green-eyed, yellow-haired, thick-lipped Iakin Nefud was the Harkonnen guard corporal who was promoted to captain of Baron Vladimir Harkonnen's personal guard on the death of the previous captain, Umman Kudu, who was inadvertently killed in 10,191 when a captive Duke Leto Atreides attempted to assassinate the Baron with poison gas hidden inside a false tooth. Nefud was addicted to semuta. [*Dune*]

Nerus, Tanidia (10,124–10,177)—According to Leto Atreides II and the Bene Gesserit breeding records, Tanida Nerus was Lady Jessica's mother. [*Children of Dune*]

net—The net was Duncan Idaho ghola number 4's name for the Mentat vision he had experienced in the Chapterhouse no-ship, in 15,244 and 15,245, of a shimmering, multi-colored net of jeweled ropes through which was visible a benign, older Face Dancer cou-

ple—Daniel and Marty—who seemed to preside in a god-like way over the Scattering. [*Chapterhouse: Dune*]

nezhoni scarf—A nezhoni scarf was the scarf-pad worn on the forehead, beneath a stillsuit, by Fremen women who had given birth to a son and who were married or romantically attached to a Fremen male. [*Dune*]

Nilotic al-Ourouba—Nilotic al-Ourouba was the original planet from which the Fremen's Sunni ancestors had fled. [*Dune*]

Nisai (1,331–1,408)—Nisai was the wife of Ali Ben Ohashi, leader of the Zensunni sect that broke away from the teachings of Maometh in about 1,381. [*Dune*]

Niushe—Niushe was a Bene Gesserit planet captured by the Honored Matres in the 153rd century. [*Chapterhouse: Dune*]

Niushe—Niushe is the star about which the planets Gamont and Grumman orbit. [*Dune*]

no-globe—A no-globe is an Ixian machine invented in the late 137th century that shields itself and its contents from prescient awareness. Hwi Noree was conceived, born, and raised in an Ixian no-globe. [*God Emperor of Dune*]

Noree, Hwi (13,700–13,726)—Dark skinned, brown-eyed, brown-haired, oval-faced Hwi Noree was conceived, born, and raised in an Ixian no-globe to be exceptionally good, sweet, sincere, gentle, patient, truthful, honest, delicate, sensible, grave, and calm—the antithesis of all that is mechanical and non-human—so as to attract the affection of Emperor Leto II. She was educated by the Bene Gesserit but never became one. Cloned from Malky's cells and raised as Malky's niece, she was bred to be his opposite in every way, and the Bene Gesserit believed that she and her uncle had both been genetically engineered to serve as Ixian Ambassadors to Arrakis and that both had been designed to be temptations, although in opposite ways, to Leto II. Hwi Noree replaced Iyo Kobat as Ixian Ambassador to Arrakis in 13,726, and while on Arrakis she agreed to be Leto II's bride despite the fact that she was strongly attracted to Duncan Idaho ghola number 3, with whom she fell in love and had sexual relations shortly after her bethrothal. Subsequently, Moneo informed her and Idaho ghola number 3 that they were never to see one another again. She was killed on her way to her nuptuals in Tuono Village when Nayla, acting on Siona's orders, severed the supports to the bridge over the Idaho River and plunged Hwi Noree, Leto II, and Moneo to their deaths. By the 153rd century the priests of Rakis had come to believe, erroneously, that Hwi Noree had been a secret Bene Gesserit Reverend Mother. [*God Emperor of Dune, Heretics of Dune*]

no-ship—A no-ship is an interstellar vehicle that shields itself and its con-tents from prescient awareness. A moat of no-ships surrounding a planet can also shield the entire planet from prescient awareness. No-ships can be as small as 140 meters in diameter. [*Heretics of Dune, Chapterhouse: Dune*]

Novebruns—In 10,218 half of the planet Novebruns was sold by the Metulli Family for 321 liters of mélange. [*Children of Dune*]

nullentropy bins—No-globes are equipped with nullentropy bins, which store any items within them indefinitely with no deterioration or change of any kind. [*Heretics of Dune*]

Nunepi, Duro (13,678–13,749)—Proud, flinty, gray-eyed Duro Nunepi was the Tleilaxu Ambassador to Arrakis in 13,726. Unwilling to acknowledge that his entourage had been attacked by Tleilaxu Face Dancers on the Royal Road to Onn, Emperor Leto II instead accused the Tleilaxu of spreading lies about his sexual practices, a complete fabrication, and then had Nayla flog Nunepi in Onn's public plaza. [God Emperor of Dune]

Oala (13,706–13,726)—One of Siona Ibn Faud al-Seyefa Atreides' ten companions in the theft in 13,726 of The Stolen Journals from Emperor Leto II's Citadel fortress in the Sareer, Oala was killed by a pack of D-wolves in Arrakis' Forbidden Forest following the raid on the Citadel. [*God Emperor of Dune*]

Obeah Ritual—The Obeah Ritual was one of the Ancient Teachings that shaped the religious beliefs of the Imperium in the 102nd century, the time of Muad'Dib. [*Dune*]

Odrade, Senior Security Mother/ Reverend Mother Superior Darwi (15,162–15,245)—Bene Gesserit Supreme Bashar Miles Teg's daughter, tall, supple, willowy, muscular, fullmouthed Senior Security Mother Darwi Odrade was a workaholic Bene Gesserit with seductive eyes who took great care over details and who greatly resembled Bene Gesserit Imprinter Reverend Mother Lucilla except in body type and age. Her mother had been a Bene Gesserit Sister and a descendant of the Atreides and the Corrinos, and Odrade possessed a prescient instinct for detecting threats to the Bene Gesserit sisterhood and the ability to cut through obfuscating details to the core of a conflict. Raised by foster parents on the Gammu seacoast, she thought of herself approvingly as "Sea Child." She had received her early education on the inhospitable, artificial Bene Gesserit world Al Dhanab, was taught to fly an ornithopter on Lampadas, and had later been Reverend Mother Superior Alma Mavis Taraza's mentee at the Bene Gesserit School on Chapterhouse. She subsequently bore nineteen children (two of whom were executed) for the Bene Gesserit, returned to Al Dhanab to prepare herself for her mission on Rakis shortly after having survived the Spice Agony, and wrote "The Atreides Manefesto" on Taraza's orders. In 15,229 she met Teg on a Guild ship in orbit above Gammu and was taken with Teg and Taraza to the Gammu Keep. That same year she succeeded Reverend Mother Tamalane as the commander of the Bene Gesserit Keep in Keen, on Rakis, and soon thereafter defended Sheeana Brugh from an attack against her and the Rakian priests launched by the Tleilaxu and Ix. Despite Rakian High Priest Hedley Tuek's resistance, Odrade successfully wrested guardianship of Sheeana from the Rakian priests in 15,232. That same year she broke both of Tleilaxu Master of Masters Tylwyth Waff's arms in apprehending him after he had murdered Tuek with a poisoned dart in Keen's temple, and under cover of setting his bones she collected samples of Waff's cells that might be of use to the Bene Gesserit breeding program. Soon thereafter she, Waff, and Sheeana went into the desert near Dar-es-Balat to summon and ride a sandworm, which took them to a ruined wall that had once bordered Emperor Leto II's Sareer and to the site of an ancient, dry, subterrainean Fremen water-storage basin, attached to what once had been Sietch Tabr, where Leto II had hidden a vast hoard of mélange. Investigating the ruin, Odrade discovered 90,000 long tons of mélange and a message for the Bene Gesserit, predicting their eventual demise, that Leto II had inscribed on the walls. After they returned to Keen, Odrade allied the Bene Gesserit with the Bene Tleilax—

and against the Honored Matres of the Scattering—by striking a bargain with Waff that was based on Waff's misapprehension that the Bene Gesserit shared the Tleilaxu's Great Belief and would serve as its missionaries. When Taraza subsequently arrived on Rakis, Odrade realized that she had broken free of her Bene Gesserit conditioning and was functioning, as Taraza wanted her to function, as an independent and rebellious Bene Gesserit. Taraza then offered to give Odrade to the Bene Tleilax as the Atreides she had promised them they could use for breeding purposes. A week later Odrade, Taraza, Waff, Rakian priest Tulushan, and Sheeana returned to the desert near Dar-es-Balat to summon another worm, but they were attacked by Honored Matres in ornithopters, Taraza was mortally wounded, and Odrade absorbed Taraza's other memories before she died to succeed Taraza as Reverend Mother Superior. Odrade then escaped into the desert with Sheeana and they rode a worm to Wind Trap, where they met Teg, Reverend Mother Lucilla, Bene Gesserit Bashar Alef Burzmali, and Duncan Idaho ghola number 4. On Teg's Instructions and just prior to the destruction of Rakis, Odrade took the ghola and a sandworm, with Lucilla, Sheeana, and Honored Matre Murbella, to Chapterhouse on the no-ship from the Scattering that had been captured by Teg. As Reverend Mother Superior, Odrade attempted to think like an Honored Matre in

order to contend with and, finally, to co-opt the Honored Matres. In 15,244 she travelled to Chapterhouse's Desert Watch Center with Bene Gesserit acolyte Streggi, Reverend Mother Tamalane, and an entourage. Later that year she interviewed Sheeana there and invited Sheeana to replace Tamalane on the Bene Gesserit Council, which Sheeana did in 15,245. Odrade subsequently used Reverend Mother Dortujla as bait on Buzzell to entice the Honored Matres into agreeing to a parlay on Junction. In 15,245 Odrade brought Scytale from the Chapterhouse no-ship to Central (where he encountered Sheeana and the first small, one-meter-long, captive sandworm to appear on Chapterhouse), observed Murbella as she underwent the Spice Agony in the Chapterhouse no-ship, and called a very rare Bene Gesserit Convocation on Chapterhouse. Shortly thereafter Odrade made Dortujla a special advisor to her Council and accepted the Miles Teg clone's plan to feint against the Honored Matres at Gammu as a prelude to a full attack on Junction, where Odrade would serve as his spy while parlaying with the Honored Matres. Odrade then shared her other memories with Reverend Mother Bellonda, Tamalane, Murbella, and Sheeana prior to going to Junction with Tamalane, Dortujla, and Bene Gesserit acolyte Suipol. On Junction Odrade was interviewed by Great Honored Matre Dama in Dama's private work room in the Citadel and was given a drink that contained a substance that could nullify shere and thus make Odrade susceptible to a T-probe had she not detected the substance and altered it to make it harmless. She then witnessed Honored Matre Grand Dame Longo poison Dama to become the Great Honored Matre herself, and Longo then took Odrade to a tower from which they observed the Teg clone's successful ground attack on the Citadel. After the Bene Gesserit victory on Junction Longo surrendered to Odrade. The Teg clone then found them both in the Citadel, where Odrade observed the Honored Matre's secret weapon kill Streggi and was then murdered herself by Honored Matre Senior Dame Elpek while Murbella killed Longo. Murbella then absorbed Odrade's most recent memories from her corpse and killed Elpek. Odrade was susceptible to feelings of love, which were anathema to the Bene Gesserit of the 153rd century, and she guarded herself against such feelings. Her favorite dish was oyster stew as prepared by Chef Placido Salat, and she disliked chairdogs. [*Heretics of Dune, Chapterhouse: Dune*]

Ohashi, Ali Ben (1,321–1,384)—Husband to Nisai, Ali Ben Ohashi was the leader of the Zensunni sect that broke away from the teachings of Maometh in about 1,381. [*Dune*]

oil lens—Hufuf oil held in static tension by a force field within a viewing tube, an oil lens is the most accurate mechanism for manipulating visible light because each lens element can be adjusted individually one micron at a time. There were oil-lens binoculars in the fremkit that Dr. Wellington Yueh hid in the ornithopter in which Kinet and Czigo transported a captive Paul Atreides and Lady Jessica to the desert after the 10,191 fall of Arrakeen to the Harkonnens. [*Dune*]

Old Empire—Also known as the Million Planets by the Honored Matres, the known universe ruled by Emperor Leto II during his 3,508-year reign (10,218–13,726) was referred to as the Old Empire by those returning to it from the Scattering in the 153rd century. [*Chapterhouse: Dune*]

Old Father Eternity—Old Father Eternity was one of the names that the Fremen bestowed on the sandworms of Arrakis, Shai-Hulud. [*Children of Dune*]

Old Gap—North of the Tanzerouft, Old Gap was the crevase in the Shield Wall through which the first Fremen had migrated to the desert of Arrakis. After merging with the sand trout in 10,217, Leto Atreides II destroyed the qanats at Old Gap—and at Gara Rulen, Windsack, and Harg—to set back the ecological transformation of Arrakis. [*Children of Dune*]

"The Old Man's Hymn"—"The Old Man's Hymn" is a profoundly beautiful Fremen religious song. [*Dune*]

Old Maria—Old Maria was an ancient dragline harvester from the days of Arrakis' first Imperial ecologist that was still in operation in 10,191, when the Atreides relocated to Arrakis. [*Dune*]

"On Awakening a Ghola's Original Memories"—"On Awakening a Ghola's Original Memories" was a 153rd-century Bene Gesserit manual. [*Chapterhouse: Dune*]

Onemao (13,703–13,726)—One of Siona Ibn Faud al-Seyefa Atreides' ten companions in the theft in 13,726 of The Stolen Journals from Emperor Leto II's Citadel fortress in the Sareer, Onemao was killed by a pack of D-wolves in Arrakis' Forbidden Forest following the raid on the Citadel. [*God Emperor of Dune*]

Onn—Built in the region of Arrakis that had once been the Tanzerouft, around the more-ancient city of Arrakeen and on the spot where Paul Muad'Dib had blown a hole in the Shield Wall with the Atreides family atomics in 10,193, Onn, the festival city, was a major population center on Arrakis in the 138th century. It was designed to facilitate its primary purpose, the public veneration of Emperor Leto II, which occurred once every ten years at the Great Sharing. Arrakis' embassies and the Fish Speaker School were located in Onn. [*God Emperor of Dune*]

Opafire—Opafire is one of the rare opaline jewels of Hagal. [*Dune*]

Ophiuchi B (36)—Ophiuchi B (36) is the star about which Giedi Prime orbits. [*Dune*]

Oral History—The Oral History was the folk history of Arrakis; it was often more accurate than the official histories approved by Emperor Leto II. [*God Emperor of Dune*]

Orange Catholic Bible—The religious text produced by the Commission of Ecumenical Translators (C. E. T.), the Orange Catholic Bible contains elements of most of the ancient religions—including the Maometh Saari, Mahayana Christianity, Zensunni Catholicism, and Buddislamic traditions—and was a source of Muad'Dib's religious commentaries in "The Pillars of the Universe." Dr. Wellington Yueh gave Paul Atreides (Muad'Dib) a miniature, antique Orange Catholic Bible prior to the Atreides relocation from Caladan to Arrakis in 10,191. [*Dune*]

Orlop (10,183–10,203)—Orlop was Harah's younger son, fathered by Jamis, and Kaleff's half-brother. [*Dune*]

ornithopter—Popularly known as a "'thopter," an ornithopter is any flying machine that propels itself with bird-like, beating wings. [*Dune*]

Otheym (10,153–10,207)—One of Muad'Dib's (Paul Atreides') Fedaykin, Otheym joined Paul, Stilgar, Chatt the Leaper, and Korba in making battle plans against the Harkonnens in Cave of Birds in 10,193. He soon thereafter greeted Chani and took her to Lady Jessica after Chani had flown from the south to revive Paul in Cave of Birds after Paul had transmuted the Water of Life. Eavesdropping as

Chani revived Paul from his three-week coma, Otheym informed the Fremen that Paul had successfully transmuted the Water of Life. Having subsequently contracted the splitting disease on Tarahell during Muad'Dib's Jihad, in 10,207 Otheym summoned Paul to his home in the suburbs of Arrakeen to warn Paul of a plot against him being hatched by Fremen. He then gave Paul Bijaz, a dwarf he claimed was a human distrans who had recorded the names of all the Fremen traitors. Almost immediately thereafter, Otheym was killed as his house was consumed by a stone burner. [*Dune, Dune Messiah*]

Our Lady of Dune—Our Lady of Dune was a Fremen term for Jessica in the early 103rd century. [*Children of Dune*]

Palimbasha (10,191–10,216)—A mathematics teacher in Sietch Tabr's schools and the grandson of a Fremen Naib whose sons had fallen in service to the Atreides, red-faced, blotchy-nosed Palimbasha was the Fremen traitor who had controlled the Laza tigers that attacked Leto Atreides II and Ghanima in the desert of Arrakis. He was killed in an entrance to Sietch Tabr by Ghanima's poisoned needle when Ghanima returned, wounded by the tigers, from the desert. [*Children of Dune*]

palm lock—A palm lock is a lock keyed to one individual's hand shape and palm lines. The oval door to the airlock to the wet-planet conservatory

in Arrakeen's Ducal Palace was secured with a palm lock. [*Dune*]

Palma—Home to 1,100 Reverend Mothers, Palma was a Bene Gesserit planet that fell to the Honored Matres without a fight in 15,243. [*Chapterhouse: Dune*]

pan—On Arrakis, a pan was any low-lying region or depression. The presence of a pan indicates that the area in question was once covered by open water. [*Dune*]

Panoplia Propheticus—The panoplia propheticus is the body of infectious superstitions sewn throughout the known universe by the Bene Gesserit's Missionaria Protectiva. [*Dune*]

paracompass—A paracompass is a compass sensitive to local magnetic anomalies that is used on planets whose total magnetic field is unstable or subject to disruption by magnetic storms. A paracompass is one of the items contained in the fremkit Dr. Wellington Yueh hid in the ornithopter in which Kinet and Czigo transported a captive Lady Jessica and Paul Atreides to the desert after the 10,191 fall of Arrakeen to the Harkonnens. [*Dune*]

paradan—A soft mellon from Caladan, paradan was Duncan Idaho's favorite fruit. [*God Emperor of Dune*]

Pardee (10,136–10,191)—Pardee was a key man in the Harkonnen underground in Arrakeen in 10,191. [*Dune*]

Parella—Parella is a planet in the Imperium whose inhabitants had agitated for another Jihad against the machines in the early 138th century. [*God Emperor of Dune*]

patiyeh—A common experience among the Fremen in the open desert, "patiyeh" was a Fremen word for "the thirst at the edge of death." [*God Emperor of Dune*]

Patrin (14,966–15,232)—A native of Gammu, blond, thin, old, wrinkled Patrin was Bene Gesserit Supreme Bashar Miles Teg's most trusted aide and batman. As a teenager he had found in the forest northeast of the Gammu Keep, and then kept secret for over 200 years, an ancient Harkonnen no-globe that was eventually occupied by Teg, Reverend Mother Lucilla, and Duncan Idaho ghola number 4. Patrin assisted Teg in training the ghola on Gammu. Following the 15,232 Tleilaxu attack on the Gammu Keep instigated by Reverend Mother Schwangyu, Patrin created a false trail for Schwangyu's minions to follow and thus allowed Teg, Lucilla, and the ghola to escape the Keep. He subsequently sacrificed himself by committing suicide to avoid being captured. [*Heretics of Dune*]

Paul-Muad'Dib—Paul-Muad'Dib was the public Fremen name bestowed on Paul Atreides after he killed Jamis in Cave of Ridges in 10,191. *See* **Atreides, Paul**. [*Dune*]

Paymon, Essas (10,176–10,216)—Essas Paymon was a dark, little man believed to be employed by the Nebirds, one of Arrakis' houses minor, who traded in holy artifacts and small decorative items. In reality he was a CHOAM spy whose task it was to assess the annual spice crop. He was brought to Regent Alia Atreides for judgement in 10,216, and Alia initially spared his life out of admiration for his audacity, but less than an hour later she condemned him to death when Ziarenko Javid told her that Paymon had spoken out against the Bene Gesserit. Alia's doubt as to whether Paymon were truly guilty, or if Javid had merely lied to her, was the immediate concern that enabled the Baron Harkonnen's persona within Alia's consciousness to strike the bargain with her that ultimately led to her being possessed by the Baron's persona. [*Children of Dune*]

Perinte, Reverend Mother (15,204–15,264)—Reverend Mother Perinte was sent into the Bene Gesserit Sisterhood Scattering in 15,244. [*Chapterhouse: Dune*]

pilingitam—Featuring distinctive lime-green leaves, pilingitam is a highly-valued wood grown in the forest reserve that surrounds the Gammu Keep. It works like a soft wood when newly cut and endures like a hardwood when dried and aged. It is anti-fungal, is not eaten by any known insect, and is fire resistant. The living pilingitam tree grows outward from an enlarged and empty tube at its core. [*Heretics of Dune*]

"The Pillars of the Universe,"—"The Pillars of the Universe" is the book of religious commentaries authored by Muad'Dib (Paul Atreides). Its content is derived from the Commission of Ecumenical Translators' (C. E. T.) Orange Catholic Bible, with its Liturgical Manual and Commentaries, and from the teachings of the Fremen-Zensunni. It was interpreted to the masses by the priests in the religion of Muad'Dib, the Quizara Tafwid. [*Dune*]

Pira (15,194–15,232)—Reverend Mother Lucilla escaped from Gammu disguised as Pira, an Honored Matre playfem and a fifth-stage adept in the Order of Hormu who was killed by Sirafa so that Lucilla could assume her identity. [*Heretics of Dune*]

plasteel—Plasteel is steel that has been stabilized by growing stravidium fibers into its crystal structure. [*Dune*]

poison snooper—A poison snooper is a device used by the nobility throughout the Imperium to detect poison in one's food or drink. [*Dune*]

polastine—Commonly known as "tine," polastine is a cheap, mass-produced, artificial material often used—with polaz and pormabat—in the 153rd century in place of wood. [*Heretics of Dune*]

polaz—Commonly known as "laz," polaz is a cheap, mass-produced, artificial material often used—with polastine and pormabat—in place of wood. [*Heretics of Dune*]

Polyana, Yasnaya (prehistoric)—Yasnaya Polyana was a childhood com-

panion to Count Leo Nikolayevich Tolstoy. [*Chapterhouse: Dune*]

Ponciard, The Battle of—The Battle of Ponciard was an engagement in which Bene Gesserit Supreme Bashar Miles Teg's forces were victorious. [*Heretics of Dune*]

Pondrillle—Pondrille was a postulant center on Chapterhouse located along the way from Central to the Desert Watch Center. [*Chapterhouse: Dune*]

Pook, Ledden (12,417–18,932)—Ledden Pook had been the Tleilaxu envoy to Rakis when Hedley Tuek's father had been Rakian High Priest. [*Heretics of Dune*]

Poritrin—The third planet orbiting Epsilon Alangue, Poritrin is one of the earliest planets occupied by the Zensunni Wanderers (the Fremen). [*Dune*]

pormbat—Commonly known as "bat," pormabat is a cheap, mass-produced, artificial material often used—with polastine and polaz—in place of wood. [*Heretics of Dune*]

powindah—To the Bene Tleilax, all people who are not Tleilaxu are powindah. [*Heretics of Dune*]

Praska (15,166–15,508)—Praska was a Bene Gesserit Proctor at Central, on Chapterhouse, who voted in 15,244 to retain Darwi Odrade as Bene Gesserit Reverend Mother Superior, a vote of confidence that Odrade carried by only one vote. [*Chapterhouse: Dune*]

The Preacher—Old before his time as a consequence of excessive spice consumption, The Preacher appeared in the desert of Arrakis and preached against the religion of Muad'Dib from 10,207 to 10,216. Like Muad'Dib, he was blind, had scarred eye sockets that suggested that he had been blinded by a stone burner, and had an uncannily commanding voice that suggested that he had received Bene-Gesserit Voice training. In 10,216 he was transported from Arrakis to Salusa Secundus by Bashar Tyeranik, on Princess Wensicia's orders, ostensibly to interpret Prince Farad'n's dreams, but in reality to interest Farad'n in the religion of Muad'Dib. While on Salusa Secundus The Preacher wore a supposed Ixian mask that reportedly enabled the blind to see, but it was really just a simple mask and not an Ixian machine. He refused to share his interpretation of Farad'n's dream with Farad'n on the grounds that his interpretation would only be misinterpreted. However, in return for having heard Farad'n's dream, he promised to send Hayt (now with Dunca Idaho's persona) to Salusa Secundus to be Farad'n's and Wensicia's agent. He then returned to Arrakis, where he continued to preach against the religion of Muad'Dib in Arrakeen and revealed himself to be Paul Atreides to his sister Regent Alia Atreides. Months later, in the Tanzerouft, he encountered Leto Atreides II, who had recently followed the Golden Path that Paul had rejected and merged with Arrakis' sand trout to gain near-invurnerability, super-speed, super-strength, and command over Arrakis' sandworms. The Preacher and Leto II then had a battle of prescient visions in the desert, and Leto II's vision was victorius. In 10,218 Leto II introduced The Preacher to Gurney Hallek in one of the small rebel-Fremen sietches in Gare Ruden. Subsequently Leto II brought The Preacher, with Hallek, to Shuloch and then accompanied the Preacher, as his guide, back to Arrakeen, where The Preacher denounced Alia to the crowd gathered outside her temple and was slain with a cryknife by one of Alia's priests. *See* **Atreides, Paul**. [*Children of Dune*]

pre-born—The pre-born are those who attain consciousness before birth, often through the influence of such mélange derivatives as the Water of Life or through a genetic predisposition. The pre-born possess within their consciousnesses the personae of their ancestors and run the risk of being possessed by one of their ancestors and becoming an Abomination. Alia Atreides, Leto Atreides II, and Ghanima were among the pre-born. [*Children of Dune*]

The Prescient Vision—*The Prescient Vision* was a volume authored by Harq al-Ada. [*Children of Dune*]

Prester (15,218–15,546)—Prester was Sheeana Brugh's Bene Gesserit acolyte aide and senior assistant at the Desert Watch Center on Chapterhouse in 15,244. [*Chapterhouse: Dune*]

Priest Guardians—Exceptionally tall priests and priestesses, the Priest Guardians were the police force of the Rakian priesthood. They wore short robes and yellow helmets with high crests. [*Heretics of Dune*]

"Private Reflections on Muad'Dib"—"Private Reflections on Muad'Dib" is one of the many volumes authored by Princess Irulan. [*Dune*]

process verbal—The process verbal was a semi-formal report of a crime against the Empire. [*Dune, Children of Dune*]

Proctor—A Proctor is a Bene Gesserit judge. Proctors can arrive at any decision they desire, regardless of the law. [*Chapterhouse: Dune*]

Proctor Superior—Popularly know as a "Bene Gesserit with the Sight," a Proctor Superior is a Bene Gesserit Reverend Mother who is also regional director of a Bene Gesserit School. Reverend Mother Gaius Helen Mohiam was Proctor Superior to the Bene Gesserit School on Wallach IX in the 102nd century, the time of Muad'Dib. [*Dune*]

protomor—Popular with tourists on Arrakis in the 138th century, protomor was an authentic, old, dried Fremen food that contained a slight quantity of mélange. [*God Emperor of Dune*]

pseudo-shield—A pseudo-shield was a weapon developed on Arrakis that simultaneously summoned and maddened a sandworm. [*Children of Dune*]

pundi rice—A mutated rice grain, high in natural sugar, that is capable of achieving lengths of up to four centemeters, pundi rice is Caladan's chief export. [*Dune*]

pyretic conscience—Popularly known as "the conscience of fire," the pyretic conscience is that inhibitory level of consciousness touched by Imperial conditioning. [*Dune*]

Qadis as-Salaf—The Qadis as-Salaf were the holy fathers of Fremen mythology. [*Children of Dune*]

Qizarate—In reality an organization of spies, the Qizrate was the assembly of priests in the religion of Muad'Dib. [*Dune Messiah*]

quizara—A quizara was a priest in the religion of Muad'Dib. [*Dune Messiah*]

Quizara Tafwid—The Quizara Tafwid was the body of Fremen priests and holy men in the religion of Muad'Dib who interpreted Muad'Dib's "The Pillars of the Universe" to the masses. [*Dune*]

Rabban, Abulurd Harkonnen (10,098–10,179)—Father of Count Glossu "Beast" Rabban and Feyd-Rautha Rabban Harkonnen, and youngest half-brother to Baron Vladimir Harkonnen, Abulurd Harkonnen Rabban renounced the Harkonnen name and all rights to the title of Baron when given the subdistrict governorship of Rabban-Lankiveil. [*Dune*]

Rabban, Count Glossu "Beast"
(10,132–10,193)—The low-built, grossly
fat Count of Rabban-Lankiveil, Glossu
"Beast" Rabban was the eldest nephew
of Baron Vladimir Harkonnnen, the
son of the Baron's half-brother Abulurd Rabban, and the older brother of
Feyd-Rautha Rabban Harkonnen. He
had been regent-siridar on Arrakis
prior to the arrival of the Atreides
in 10,191, and he was appointed by
Baron Harkonnen to govern Arrakis
again after the fall of Arrakeen to the
Harkonnens later that year. He was
killed in the successful 10,193 Fremen
attack on Arrakeen. [*Dune*]

Rabban-Lankiveil—Abulurd Harkonnen Rabban renounced the Harkonnen name and all rights to the title of
Baron when given the subdistrict governorship of Rabban-Lankiveil. He
was succeeded as Count of Rabban-
Lankiveil by his eldest son Glossu
"Beast" Rabban. [*Dune*]

Rabbi (15,041–15,293)—An ancient,
intense, broad-faced, brown-eyed,
bearded Jew who wore old-fashioned
spectacles, the Rabbi was a Suk doctor
who informed the Bene Gesserit via
CHOAM spies in 15,243 that Lampadas, their school planet, had fallen
to the Honored Matres. He subsequently gave sanctuary to Reverend
Mother Lucilla on Gammu and in
15,244–45 hid with Rebecca and
Joshua in a small (12.5 meters long),
barrel-shaped no-chamber on Gammu.
He was rescued during the Miles Teg
clone's successful attack on Gammu

and was aboard the Teg clone's command ship during the subsequent attack on Junction. He was afterwards
confined in the Chapterhouse no-
ship with Rebecca and finally escaped
from the known universe in that no-
ship with Rebecca, Duncan Idaho
ghola number 4, Scytale, Sheeana,
Bene Gesserit Proctor Garimi, some
Futars, and a sandworm. [*Chapterhouse: Dune*]

rachag—Rachag is a stimulant similar
to caffeine that is made from the
yellow berries of the akarso. [*Dune*]

Radi (13,704–13,726)— One of Siona
Ibn Faud al-Seyefa Atreides' ten companions in the theft in 13,726 of The
Stolen Journals from Emperor Leto
II's Citadel fortress in the Sareer, Radi
was killed by a pack of D-wolves in
Arrakis' Forbidden Forest following
the raid on the Citadel. [*God Emperor
of Dune*]

Rajia (10,197–10,262)—Darkly ascetic
Rajia was Harah's niece and one of
Stilgar's lieutenants during Stilgar's
flight from Sietch Tabr in 10,218.
[*Children of Dune*]

Rajifiri (10,161–10,207)—An ally of
Korba's in the Fremen conspiracy
against Muad'Dib, Rajifiri was a dissident Fremen Naib who attended
Korba's trial, presided over by Alia, in
10,207. [*Dune Messiah*]

Rakis—By the 143rd century Arrakis
had come to be known as Rakis. *See*
Arrakis. [*God Emperor of Dune*]

Ramallo, Reverend Mother (10,085–10,191)—The wrinkled, ancient, stick-like Reverend Mother to the Fremnen of Stilgar's Sietch Tabr, Reverend Mother Ramallo shared in her dying moments her life's memories and her other memories with Lady Jessica after Jessica had ingested and transmuted the Water of Life to become a Reverend Mother herself. [*Dune*]

Rasir (10,127–10,209)—A Fremen companion to Paul Muad'Dib (Paul Atreides) from his days in Sietch Tabr, Rasir was an old man in 10,207, when he guided a disguised Paul through the streets of Arrakeen to Otheym's dwelling in Arrakeen's suburbs. [*Dune Messiah*]

razzia—In the Fremen tongue, a razzia is a piratical raid. [*Children of Dune*]

rebec—A rebec is the musical instrument used to produce semuta music. [*Dune Messiah*]

Rebecca (14,934–15,257)—Dark-gray-haired, wrinkled, blue-within-blue-eyed Rebecca was a Jew who had survived the Spice Agony and successfully transmuted the Water of Life to acquire the abilities of a Bene Gesserit Reverend Mother. She had once been married to Sholem, a Truthsayer. She received the other memories of Reverend Mother Lucilla and the 7,622,013 other Reverend Mothers on Lampadas, a Bene Gesserit school planet, prior to that planet falling to the Honored Matres in 15,243. She subsequently received an eye-transplant, so that she could go among the Honored Matres without revealing that she had undergone the Spice Agony, and an organic implant that administered to her measured doses of shere and mélange. In 15,244 she was brought before Great Honored Matre Dama, who wanted to gather intelligence about the Bene Gesserit, and was then returned from Junction to Gammu, where she hid in a small (12.5 meters long), barrel-shaped no-chamber for several months with the Rabbi and Joshua. She was rescued, with the Rabbi, when the Miles Teg clone's forces successfully attacked Gammu in 15,245; she subsequently shared the other memories of the millions from Lampadas with those Bene Gesserit Reverend Mothers aboard a no-ship in space during the Teg clone's attack on Junction; and she was afterwards confined to the Chapterhouse no-ship with the Rabbi. She finally escaped from the known universe in that no-ship with the Rabbi, Duncan Idaho ghola number 4, Scytale, Sheeana, Bene Gesserit Proctor Garimi, some Futars, and a sandworm. [*Chapterhouse: Dune*]

Red Chasm Sietch—Red Chasm Sietch was the old, poor sietch to which Ghabhean al-Fali took Jessica after the two of them had escaped from Arrakeen, in 10,216, following the unsuccessful assassination attempt against Jessica orchestrated by Regent Alia Atreides and Ziarenko Javid. [*Children of Dune*]

Reenol—Reenol was a Bene Gesserit planet captured by the Honored Matres in the early 153rd century. [*Chapterhouse: Dune*]

Renditai—Renditai was the site of a minor skirmish in which Bene Gesserit Supreme Bashar Miles Teg was victorious. Many of the soldiers who had served under Teg at Renditai settled on Gammu afterwards, and many of these aided Teg after he had escaped from the Harkonen no-globe and was approaching the city of Ysai. [*Heretics of Dune*]

residual poison—a poison that can be countered only by the repeated administration of the antidote, residual poison was invented by Harkonnen Mentat Piter de Vries and was administered to Atreides Mentat Thufir Hawat after Hawat was captured by the Harkonnens in 10,191. [*Dune*]

Reverend Mother—A Reverend Mother is a member of the Bene Gesserit or a Fremen Sayyadina who has elevated herself to a higher state of consciousness and awareness through having successfully ingested and transmuted the Water of Life, a spice derivative that is fatal to those who cannot successfully transmute it. In the 153rd century, by which time the availability of mélange from the Bene Tleilax had increased the human lifespan to 300–400 years, it took some postulates 50 years to become Reverend Mothers. [*Dune, Heretics of Dune*]

Richese—The fourth planet orbiting Eridani A, Richese, with Ix, escaped the more severe effects of the Butlerian Jihad and was home to a machine culture noted for miniaturization in the 102nd century, the time of Muad'Dib. *The Last Jihad*, by Sumer and Kautman, examines the forces that allowed Richese and Ix to evade the Butlerian Jihad's anti-machine proscriptions. [*Dune*]

Riddles of Arrakis—Riddles of Arrakis is a volume authored by Harq al-Ada. [*Children of Dune*]

Roc—Roc is a planet in the Scattering. Honored Matres from Roc are especially dangerous as they can kill with any moveable part of their bodies. Great Honored Matre/Reverend Mother Superior Murbella was from Roc. [*Chapterhouse: Dune*]

Roitiro (15,193–15,536)—Roitiro was the Miles Teg clone's childhood friend Yorgi's father. [*Chapterhouse: Dune*]

Romo—Sabine Teg, Bene Gesserit Supreme Bashar Miles Teg's younger brother, was poisoned on the planet Romo. [*Heretics of Dune*]

Rossak—Rossak was a stopping point in the migration of the Zensunni Wanderers (the Fremen). A poison from Rossak was the illuminating substance used by the Bene Gesserit to create Reverend Mothers prior to the discovery of the Water of Life on Arrakis. [*Dune*]

Roxbrough, Reverend Mother Janet
(14,862–15,178)—Large-boned, fair
Bene Gesserit Reverend Mother Janet
Roxbrough was Loschy Teg's wife and
Bene Gesserit Supreme Bashar Miles
Teg's mother. Born and raised on Ler-
naeus, she was a Bene Gesserit heretic
who had taught her son secrets that
should only be taught to a Bene
Gesserit acolyte, including the Bene
Gesserit Imprinters' secrets of seduc-
tion. [*Heretics of Dune*]

Royal Cart—Activated and steered
by Emperor Leto II's thoughts, the
Royal Cart was an Ixian machine that
supported Leto II's five-ton weight
and enabled him to move about in his
Citadel fortress. Equipped with suspensors, the Royal Cart was also the
vehicle in which Leto II travelled on
the Royal Road. [*God Emperor of
Dune*]

Royal Road—The Royal Road was
the highway that stretched from Emperor Leto II's Citadel fortress in the
Sareer to the festival city of Onn.
[*God Emperor of Dune*]

Rugi, Princess (10,184–10,266)—One
of Emperor Shaddam IV's and
Anirul's five daughters, Rugi accompanied Shaddam IV into retirement
on Salusa Secundus in 10,193. [*Dune*]

Saajid (10,159–10,207)—An ally of
Korba's in the Fremen conspiracy
against Muad'Dib, Saajid was a dissident Fremen Naib who attended
Korba's trial, precided over by Alia,
in 10,207. [*Dune Messiah*]

Sabanda, Reverend Mother (15,182–
15,234)—Reverend Mother Sabanda
was a Bene Gesserit teacher captured
by the Honored Matres in the early
153rd century. Rather than divulge
any information, she committed suicide while being interrogated. [*Chapterhouse: Dune*]

Sabiha (10,199–10,253)—Namri's niece,
a citizen of Jacurutu, and one of Leto
Atreides II's guards in Jacurutu, Sabiha
was a young woman whom Leto II
saw as a potential lover in his prescient
visions. He hypnotized her into falling
asleep in order to escape from Jacurutu
into the Tanzerouft. Sabiha was exiled
from Jacurutu to Shuloch for having
allowed Leto II to escape, and she was
then Leto II's guard in Shuloch as well.
[*Children of Dune*]

Salat, Placido (15,194–15,556)—One
of history's great chefs, large, beefy,
florid Placido Salat was the teaching
chef at the Bene Gesserit school in
Central, on Chapterhouse, in 15,244.
[*Chapterhouse: Dune*]

Salusa Secundus—The third planet
orbiting Gamma Waiping and the second stopping point in the migrations
of the Zensunni Wanderers (the Fremen), who spent nine generations as
slaves there, Salusa Secundus was also
the homeworld of House Corrino, the
Imperial House, prior to House Corrino's relocation to Kaitain. It subsequently became the Emperor's prison
planet, and its harsh environment became the breeding ground for the

Emperor's Sardaukar troops. Emperor Shaddam IV retired to Salusa Secundus in 10,193. In 10,207 sandworms were smuggled off of Arrakis by dissident Freman and transported to Salusa Secundus in the hope that Arrakis' mélange monopoly might thus be broken. [*Dune, Children of Dune*]

sandcrawler—Also known as a spice factory, a sandcrawler was a huge machine designed to search for and collect mélange on the surface of Arrakis. It used centrifugal force to separate the spice from sand. [*Dune*]

sand dancers—In the early 103rd century sand dancers were groups of pilgrims, often numbering fifty, who were tethered together with elacca ropes and who danced for days on end outside Regent Alia Atreides' temple seeking a state of ecstasy. [*Children of Dune*]

sandworm—Also known as "Shai-Hulud," the sandworm was the dominant lifeform on Arrakis. Sandworms were introduced to Arrakis, then a water planet, as sand trout and eventually changed the ecology of Arrakis until it was arid enough to support the mature sandworm. Most of the sand on Arrais was created by sandworm activity. Sandworms can be over 400 meters long, and a large sandworm, which was capable of swallowing a spice harvester whole, controlled a territory of 300 to 400 square kilometers. Sandworms are attracted by rhythmic vibrations and by an activated shield but avoid water, which is poisonous

to them. Luring them with thumpers and mounting and controlling them with maker hooks, the Fremen used sandworms for transportation and, in their 10,193 attack on Arrakeen, as assault vehicles. The sandworm lifecycle had transformed Arrakis into the extremely arid planet on which the adult sandworm could survive. Sandworms begin as microscopic sand plankton, which are eaten by the mature worm. Survivors become sand trout or little makers, hand-sized, half-plant-half-animal organisms that join together to encyst underground the water that once existed on Arrakis. The sand trout then secrete a catalyst that creates the chemical reaction that produces a spice blow, an underground explosion in which the encysted water is transformed into mélange. Most sand trout are killed in the spice blow, but those that survive enter a six-year semi-dormant cyst-hibernation period to emerge as small (10 meters long) sandworms. The sandworm digestive system had produced most of the oxygen that was a component of Arrakis' atmosphere, which was 23% oxygen. In 10,207 sandworms were smuggled off Arrakis by dissident Fremen and transported to Salusa Secundus in the hope that Arrakis' mélange monopoly might thus be broken. By the 138th century the mutated Emperor Leto II was the only surviving sandworm on Arrakis. On his death in the Idaho River in 13,726 Leto II disintegrated into numerous sand trout that eventually grew into mature sandworms that each possessed within them a pearl of Leto II's consciousness, thus returning the sandworm to Arrakis. By the 153rd century the Rakian priests of the Church of Shai-hulud, the Divided God, had forbidden the use of sandworms as vehicles. A sandworm was smuggled off Rakis to Chapterhouse prior to the destruction of Rakis by the Honored Matres in 15,232. The first new, small (one meter long) sandworms appeared on Chapterhouse in 15,245. Their small size was attributed the Chapterhouse's still-high moisture levels. One of these small sandworm was in the hold of the Chapterhouse no-ship that Duncan Idaho ghola number 4 launched into the space beyond the known universe later that year. [*Dune, Childern of Dune, God Emperor of Dune, Heretics of Dune, Chapterhouse: Dune*]

sapho juice—A high-energy drug extracted from the barrier roots of Ecaz, sapho juice is commonly used by Mentats to enhance their computational abilities. Users develop cranberry-colored stains on their lips and teeth. [*Dune*]

Sardaukar—The Sardaukar were the merciless, incredibly tough and capable, politically naïve soldier-fanatics of the Padishah Emperors who had survived the harsh conditions on Salusa Secundus, the Emperors' prison planet. Ten legions of Sardaukar assisted Baron Vladimir Harkonnen's troops in defeating the Atreides forces on Arrakis in 10,191, by which time the still-

formidable Sardaukar had had their strength sapped by overconfidence and the sustaining mystique of their warrior religion undermined by cynicism. In 10,193 the Sardaukar retired to Salusa Secundus with Emperor Shaddam IV, and in 10,216 Sardaukar officers trained Laza tigers on Salusa Secundus to attack and kill Leto Atreides II and Ghanima on Arrakis. The ranks of Sardaukar officers, in descending order, are Bashar, Colonel, Burseg, Bator, Levenbrech, and Lieutenant. [*Dune, Children of Dune*]

Sareer—In the 138th century the Sareer was the last desert remaining on Arrakis. Bordering the Forbidden Forest and 500 by 1500 kilometers in area, it was the location of Emperor Leto II's Citadel fortress. [*God Emperor of Dune*]

"The Sayings of Muad'Dib"—"The Sayings of Muad'Dib" is one of the many volumes authored by Princess Irulan. [*Dune*]

sayyadina—A sayyadina is a novice female aspirant in the Fremen religious hierarchy. [*Dune*]

scanlyzers—Scanlyzers were the lethal element of a defensive system used in the 153rd century that could turn any flesh crossing their field into small chunks of meat. [*Heretics of Dune*]

The Scattering—The Scattering was the outpouring of freedom-and-adventure-seeking humanity from the known universe to the greater universe beyond that was precipitated by the 3,508 years of severe repression that had preceded Emperor Leto II's death in 13,726. *See* **Sisterhood Scattering**. [*Chapterhouse: Dune*]

Schwangyu, Reverend Mother (15,082–15,229)—a Bene Gesserit Instructor and commander of the Gammu Keep, old and wizened, wrinkled, small, skinny, wide-mouthed, astigmatic, abrupt, insular Reverend Mother Schwangyu had openly protested against the Bene Gesserit ghola project. In 15,229 she conspired with the Tleilaxu to have a Face Dancer disguised as Bene Gesserit Supreme Bashar Miles Teg kill Duncan Idaho ghola number 4, but this assassination attempt was thwarted by Teg and Reverend Mother Lucilla. Schwangyu was brain-probed and killed in the subsequent Tleilaxu attack on the Gammu keep. She had not had the opportunity to share her recent memories with another Reverend Mother immediately prior to her death.[*Heretics of Dune*, *Chapterhouse: Dune*]

Scytale (10,087–10,207)—A Tleilaxu Face Dancer, and as such able to assume any humanoid shape as well as the persona of anyone thus imitated, Scytale was a participant in the 10,205–07 conspiracy against Muad'Dib, crafted on Wallach IX, that also involved Reverend Mother Gauis Helen Mohiam, Edric, and Princess Irulan. He furthered this conspiracy by assuming the name Zaal and meeting Farok, a former companion of Paul Atreides (Muad'Dib) and a former Bashar in Muad'Dib's Jihad, in a suburb of Arrakeen. During this meeting he received information on the Fremen conspiracy against Muad'Dib on Arrakis from Farok's son, a human distrans, and thus became a distrans himself. After Farok then introduced Scytale to Otheym's daughter Lichna, Scytale killed Farok with a poisoned needle and assumed Farok's identity in leaving with Lichna, whom he later also poisoned and whose body he left in the desert. In 10,207 Scytale disguised himself as one of Edric's aides to attend an interview in Arrakeen between Paul and Edric that was also audited by Stilgar. He subsequently disguised himself as Lichna to secure an interview with Paul Muad'Dib in order to request that Paul bring Chani to Otheym's house so that Otheym could reveal to them a conspiracy against them being hatched by the Fremen. Scytale as Lichna then requested and received asylum in Paul's Keep. Seeing through Scytale's disguise, however, Paul subsequently visited Otheym's house alone. Still disguised as Lichna, Scytale later accompanied Chani—with Paul, Bijaz, Hayt, Alia, Edric, Mohiam, Stilgar, Harah, and Irulan—when she returned to the desert, to Sietch Tabr, to give birth. On Chani's death in childbirth and the ghola Hayt's consequent recovery of his original Duncan Idaho persona, Scytale revealed his true identity to Paul and offered him a bargain—the dead Chani similarly restored (as was Hayt/Idaho) to

Paul in return for his Empire—while simultaneously threatening to murder Paul's children, the newborn twins Leto II and Ghanima, if Paul should reject the bargain. However, the blind Paul then perceived the entire scene from his infant son Leto II's perspective and killed Scytale with a hurled crysknife. In the 153rd century one of Scytale's clone's was a Tleilaxu Masheikh of the innermost khel and the youngest of Tleilaxu Master of Masters Tylwyth Waff's nine councilors. See **Scytale's clone**. [*Dune Messiah, Heretics of Dune*]

Scytale's clone (15,006–15,315)—Reproduced in a Tleilaxu axlotl tank from cells harvested from a previous, living Scytale clone—and thus a clone and not a ghola—the Scytale clone of the 153rd century had memories that dated back to the time of Muad'Dib, the 102nd and 103rd centuries. Slight, gray-skinned, tiny-mouthed, sharp-toothed, and narrow-faced, the Scytale clone was in the 153rd century the youngest Master in the Tleilaxu's highest kehl and carried surgically implanted in his breast a nullentropy capsule that contained the cells of fellow Tleilaxu Masters, of Face Dancers, of technical specialists, and of such historical figures as Paul Atreides, Chani, Duncan Idaho, Thufir Hawat, Gurney Hallek, and Stilgar—all of whom could be reproduced as gholas or clones with access to Tleilaxu axlotl technology. A Bene Gesserit spy ship picked up the Scy-tale clone as he was escaping in a no-ship from Junction when it fell to the Honored Matres, and he was subsequently held captive in the Chapterhouse no-ship that the Miles Teg clone had stolen from Gammu, with Duncan Idaho clone number 4 and Murbella, from 15,232 to 15,245. He was the only surviving Tleilaxu in the Old Empire after the Honored Matres had destroyed all the Bene Tleilax planets following their destruction of Rakis in 15,232. He did not believe the Bene Gesserit's false claim that they shared the Bene Tleilax's Great Belief, but he was nevertheless in 15,245 taken from the Chapterhouse no-ship to Central, where he saw Sheeana Brugh and the first small (one meter long) sandworm to appear on Chapterhouse. Later that year he escaped from Chapterhouse—with Duncan Idaho ghola number 4, Sheeana, Bene Gesserit Proctor Garimi, the Rabbi, Rebecca, some Futrars, and a sandworm—when the Idaho ghola launched the Chapterhouse no-ship into the space beyond the known universe. See **Scytale**. [*Chapterhouse: Dune*]

Secher Nbiw—"Secher Nbiw" means "Golden Path" in the Fremen tongue. It was the trigger phrase, spoken by Leto Atreides II, that released Ghanima from the self-imposed hypnotic suggestion that had compelled her to believe that Leto II had been slain by the Laza tigers. [*Children of Dune*]

Second Interspace Migrations—Despite the widespread belief that the

Jews had died out shortly after the Second Interspace Migrations, a secret society of insular, unassimilated Jews existed on Gammu and elsewhere in the 153rd century. [*Chapterhouse: Dune*]

Second Moon—Notable for the muad'dib or kangaroo mouse markings on its surface, Second Moon is the smaller of Arrakis' two satellites. [*Dune*]

Secret Israel—Secret Israel was the clandestine society of insular, unassimilated Jews that existed on Gammu and elsewhere in the 153rd century. [*Chapterhouse: Dune*]

Semboule Treaty—Emperor Paul Muad'Dib (Paul Atreides) signed the Semboule Treaty in Sietch Tabr in 10,207. [*Dune Messiah*]

Sembu—Muad'Dib's Jihad conquered the planet Sembu in 10,207. [*Dune Messiah*]

semuta—A narcotic derived by crystal extraction from the burned residue of Ecaz's elacca wood, semuta produces a state of timeless, sustained ecstasy when used while the addict is listening to semuta music, a sequence of atonal vibrations. [*Dune*]

semuta music—Atonal vibrations that produce ecstasy in a semuta user, semuta music is played on a rebec. [*Dune, Dune Messiah*]

Seprek—Seprek was the planet on which Nayla had served in a garrison prior to becoming a member of Emperor Leto II's Imperial Guard. [*God Emperor of Dune*]

Setuse (13,707–13,726)—One of Siona Ibn Faud al-Seyefa Atreides' ten companions in the theft in 13,726 of The Stolen Journals from Emperor Leto II's Citadel fortress in the Sareer, Setuse was killed by a pack of D-wolves in Arrakis' Forbidden Forest following the raid on the Citadel. [*God Emperor of Dune*]

70 Opiuchi A—70 Ophiuchi A is the star about which Sikun orbits. [*Dune*]

Shaddam IV, Emperor (10,119–10,202)—Husband to Anirul and father to Princesses Irulan, Chalice, Wensicia, Josifa, and Rugi, red-haired, baritone-voiced Emperor Shaddam IV succeeded his father, Emperor Elrood IX, when Elrood IX succumbed to chaumurky in 10,156. Shaddam IV was the 81st member of House Corrino to occupy the Golden Lion Throne, and he usually appeared in public wearing a Sardaukar uniform to emphasize that his authority as Emperor was backed by the military might epitomized by his most capable soldiers. In 10,191 he conspired with Baron Vladimir Harkonnen to destroy the Atreides by ordering them to relocate from their secure base on Caladan to Arrakis, the former Harkonnen fief, where they would be more vulnerable. He also provided the Baron with two legions of Sardaukar disguised in Harkonnen uniforms that were successfully deployed against the Atreides on Arrakis. In 10,193 he was forced to go to Arrakis with five legions of Sardaukar to attempt to oversee the subjugation of the Fremen revolt against Arrakis' Harkonnen governor, Count Glossu "Beast" Rabban. However, the Harkonnen troops and the Sardaukar on Arrakis were defeated by the Fremen, led by Paul Muad'Dib (Paul Atreides), and Shaddam IV was compelled to relinquish the throne to Paul and to give Paul his eldest daughter, Irulan, in marriage as a condition of his surrender. He then retired to Salusa Secundus with his four youngest daughters. His reign officially ended in 10,196, when it was replaced by the Regency established in Irulan's name. [*Dune*]

Shadout—"Shadout" is a fremen title that means "well-dipper." [*Dune*]

Shafqat, Mujahid (10,171–10,223)— One of the Other Ones, Mujahid Shafqat had seen Namri's family's marks carved on the Shield Wall at Jalahud-Din. [*Children of Dune*]

The Shah-Nama—The Shah-Nama was the half-legendary First Book of the Zensunni Wanderers (the Fremen). [*Dune*]

Shai-Hulud—"Shai-hulud" was a Fremen term for the sandworm of Arrakis. When written in capital letters or spoken in a certain tone the term also refers to an earth god of Fremen superstitions. By the 153rd century the priests of Rakis preached that the planet's sandworms should

be referred to as Shai-hulud, the Divided God, but Sheeana Brugh confounded them by insisting that Shaihulud and Shaitan were the same. *See also* **sandworm**. [*Dune, Heretics of Dune*]

Shaitan—"Shaitan" was a Fremen term for the sandworm of Arrakis. By the 153rd century the priests of Rakis preached that the planet's sandworms should be referred to as Shai-hulud, the Divided God, but Sheeana Brugh confounded them by insisting that Shai-hulud and Shaitan were the same. *See also* **sandworm**. [*Dune, Heretics of Dune*]

Shakkad the Wise (9,006–9,118)— The geriartric properties of mélange were discovered during the reign of Shakkad the Wise. [*Children of Dune*]

Shalus (10,192–10,254)—Shalus was Regent Alia Atreides' new Dame of Chambers in 10,217. [*Children of Dune*]

Shamir (10,166–10,191)—Shamir was a Fremen who was ordered by Dr. Liet Kynes to fetch coffee in the underground Imperial Ecological Testing Station to which Paul Atreides and Lady Jessica had escaped in fleeing Arrakeen in 10,191. He failed to return when the Station was then attacked by Sardaukar in Harkonnen uniforms. [*Dune*]

sharia-a—The sharia-a describes the superstitious rituals of the Missionaria Protectiva's panoplia propheticus. [*Dune*]

The Shariat—The Shariat is the secret religious body of the Bene Tleilax. [*Heretics of Dune*]

Sheba (prehistoric)—Sheba was a distant ancestor of the Atreides and one of the personae inhabiting Ghanima's consciousness. [*Children of Dune*]

Sheeana Brugh (15,215–15,568)—Born on Rakis and raised to distrust the Rakian priests, slender, dark-skinned, brown-haired, long-necked, wide-mouthed, ingenuous, bright, responsive, precocious Sheeana Brugh first exhibited the ability to summon and control the sandworms in 15,223, when she commanded the worm that had just orphaned her by consuming her entire village (which had been situated atop a pre-spice mass) and all its inhabitants. She was immediately adopted by the priests of Rakis. In 15,227 she ordered them to stop sacrificing people to the sandworms, and the priests obeyed. Seeing her then as someone who would intercede with the priests on their behalf, the people of Rakis began praying to Sheeana rather than to Shai-hulud or to Shai-tan. By 15,229 Sheeana had taught herself to use Voice to command the Rakian priests, who obeyed her in any case. After coming under Senior Security Mother Darwi Odrade's care in 15,232 she decided that she wanted to become a Bene Gesserit Reverend Mother. That same year she, Odrade, and Tleilaxu Master of Masters Tylwyth Waff went into the desert near Dar-es-Balat to summon and ride a sandworm, which took them to the ruined wall that had once bordered Emperor Leto II's Sareer and to the site of an ancient, dry, subterrainean Fremen water-storage basin, attached to what once had been Sietch Tabr, where Leto II had hidden a vast hoard of mélange. Subsequently, Waff had two new Face Dancers demonstrate Honored Matre sexual amplification techniques for Sheeana, Odrade, and Bene Gesserit Reverend Mother Superior Alva Mavis Taraza. A week later Sheeana again went into the desert near Dar-es-Balat to summon a worm, accompanied by Waff, Odrade, Taraza, and Rakian priest Tulushan; however, the party was attacked in the desert by Honored Matres in ornithopters, Taraza was killed, and Sheena escaped into the desert with Odrade, who had absorbed Taraza's memories. Sheeana and Odrade rode a worm to Wind Trap, where they met Bene Gesssrit Supreme Bashar Miles Teg, Reverend Mother Lucilla, Bene Gesserit Bashar Alef Burzmali, and Duncan Idaho ghola number 4; and, just prior to the destruction of Rakis, Odrade took the ghola and a sandworm, with Lucilla, Sheeana, and Honored Matre Murbella, to Chapter House on a no-ship from the Scattering that had been captured by Teg. However, Sheeana's billions of worshippers believed that she had died in the destruction of Rakis. By 15,243, when she was stationed at Chapterhouse's Desert Watch Center, Sheeana had become a tall, austere woman and the youngest woman ever to have endured the Spice Agony to become a Bene Gesserit Reverend Mother. She was given to sexual excesses as an adult, was immune to Honored Matre sexual bonding, and practiced Honored Matre sexual amplification techniques despite Bene Gesserit inhibitions against doing so. In 15,244 she was interviewed by Reverend Mother Superior Odrade at the Desert Watch Center and was invited to replace Reverend Mother Tamalane on the Bene Gesserit Council, which she did in 15,245. In 15,245 she also observed Murbella undergo the Spice Agony and brought a small (one meter long) sandworm, the first to appear on Chapterhouse, from the Desert Watch Center to Central. Using an ancient Atreides hand code, she had secretly discussed with Ducan Idaho ghola number 4 the possibility of sexually imprinting the Teg clone as a more humane means of activating his original person and memories, and in 15,245 she did restore the Teg clone's original persona and memories by attempting to sexually imprint him, an act that succeeded by awakening the 11-year-old clone's strong resistance to sexual imprinting. Sheeana then shared other memories with Reverend Mother Tamalane prior to Tamalane's, Reverend Mother Tortujla's, and Odrade's trip to Junction to parlay with the Honored Matres. She subsequently returned to the Desert Watch Center to acquire a worm to place in the Chapterhouse no-ship's cargo hold, stealing Odrade's Van Gogh (*Cottages at Cordeville*) in the process, and then escaped from the known universe in the no-ship with Idaho ghola number 4, the sandworm, some Futars, the Rabbi, Rebecca, Scytale, and Bene Gesserit Proctor Garimi. One of Sheeana's ancestors, a Zensunni Master, had led the Fremen migration to Arrakis. [*Heretics of Dune, Chapterhouse: Dune*]

shere—Shere is a drug that enables one to refrain from divulging information while under the influence of an Ixian probe or a T-probe. [*Heretics of Dune*]

shield—A protective field produced by a Holtzman generator, a shield permits entry only to objects travelling a low velocities. Thus, it protects its wearer against projectile weapons but not against a slow sword or knife thrust. It can be shorted out only by a shire-sized electric field. However, intersection of an active shield by a lasgun beam produces subatomic fusion, which is indistinguishable from a nuclear detonation. During the reign of Emperor Leto II (10,218–13,726), shields were banned throughout the empire and it was a capital offense to possess a shield. By the 153rd century shields were out of fashion in the known universe and were maintained by some societies for sporting purposes only. [*Dune, God Emperor of Dune, Heretics of Dune*]

shield wall—The shield wall was a mountainous geological feature in the northern hemisphere of Arrakis that protected the area in which Arrakeen was located from the full force of a coriolis storm. [*Dune*]

Shien-san-Shao—"Shien-san-Shao" was the Ixian term for the religion of Muad'Dib. It suggested the intensity and insanity of those who believed they could bring the universe to paradise at the point of a crysknife. [*Children of Dune*]

Shimoom (10,164–10,193)—Shimoom was a member of Stilgar's band of forty Fremen who found Paul Atreides and Lady Jessica at Tuono Basin after the 10,191 fall of Arrakeen to the Harkonnens. [*Dune*]

Shishakli (110,167–10,201)—A citizen of Stilgar's Sietch Tabr and a Fedaykin squad leader, Shishakli handed Paul Atreides the maker hooks when Paul first mounted a sandworm without assistance in 10,193. [*Dune*]

Shoab (10,169–10,199)—Stilgar's wife Tharthar's brother, Shoab was one of the many Fremen warriors who in 10,193 wanted Paul Muad'Dib to challenge Stilgar to a duel to the death for leadership of the Fremen Council of Leaders. [*Children of Dune*]

Shoel—Shoel was Rebecca's intimate name for her Truthsayer husband Sholem. [*Chapterhouse: Dune*]

Sholem (14,930–15,207)—Also known as Shoel, Sholem was a Jew, a Truthsayer, and Rebecca's husband. [*Chapterhouse: Dune*]

Shrine of the Crysknife—In the 138th century the Shrine of the Crysknife was a place of worship on Giedi Prime maintained by the Cult of Alia. [*God Emperor of Dune*]

Shuloch—In the 103rd century Shuloch was the poor, secret desert sietch in Arrakis' Tanzerouft inhabited by the Cast Out, smugglers who had escaped when Jacurutu was destroyed. In 10,207, at The Preacher's urging, citizens of Shuloch began to sell sand trout and sandworms to be exported to other worlds. In 10,217, after Leto Atreides II had escaped from it, Shulock was shut down on Alia's orders by members of Prince Farad'n's household guard. However, rebel Fremen soon returned to it, and Leto II brought Gurney Hallek and The Preacher back to Shuloch in 10,218. One of Emperor Leto II's 103rd century brides came from Shuloch. By the 138th century Shuloch had evolved into the quiet little town of Goygoa. *See* **Goygoa**. [*Children of Dune, God Emperor of Dune*]

Siaynoq—Also known as the Feast of Leto, Siaynoq was the sexually-charged decennial ritual in which Emperor Leto II was worshipped by his Fish Speakers in the festival city of Onn. Three chosen Fish Speakers from each planet in the Imperium participated in Siaynoq. (The word "siaynoq" signifies giving honor to one who speaks with sincerity and derives from the Fremen name "Sihaya," the Recording Angel who interrogates the dead.) By the 153rd century Siaynoq had devolved into a frantic, almost rythmless ritual dance, related to the Fremen way of sandwalking, that often ended in bloodshed—the "Dance Diversion," in which the performers were usually killed. [*God Emperor of Dune, Heretics of Dune*]

Sibia (15,021–15,215)—Sibia was Senior Security Mother/Reverend Mother Superior Darwi Odrade's loving foster mother on Gammu. [*Heretics of Dune*]

sietch—A Chakobsa word meaning "a meeting place in time of danger," a sietch was any cave warren on Arrakis inhabited by a Fremen tribal community. A Fremen sietch often had a population of 10,000, as did Stilgar's Sietch Tabr. There were about 2,000 such sietches on Arrakis in the 102nd century, the time of Muad'Dib. [*Dune*]

Sietch Abbir—Sietch Abbir was a Fremen sietch that had once been ruled by the Cadelam family. [*Children of Dune*]

Sietch Makab—In 10,207 Alia ordered the executions of Korba, the other Fremen traitors to Muad'Dib, Edric, and Reverend Mother Gaius Helen Mohiam at Sietch Makab. [*Dune Messiah*]

Sietch Tabr—Sietch Tabr was the cave warren enclave of some 2,000 families governed by Stilgar in the late 102nd century. Paul Atreides and Lady Jessica found sanctuary in Sietch Tabr after Stilgar's band of forty Fremen discovered them in Tuono Basin shortly after the 10,191 fall of Arrakeen to the Harkennens, and it is there that Jessica ingested and transmuted the Water of Life to become a Bene Gesserit Reverend Mother. In 10,207 Chani—with Paul, Alia, Hayt, Bijaz, Irulan, Edric, Reverend Mother Gaius Helen Mohiam, Scytale disguised as Lichna, Stilgar, and Harah—returned to Sietch Tabr to give birth to her twins, Leto Atreides II and Ghanima. Leto II and Ghanima were raised in Siietch Tabr, where they were guarded by Stilgar. Sietch Tabr was neutral territory in the conflict between Regent Alia Ateides and the rebel Fremen in the early 103rd century. In the Famine Times that followed the death of Emperor Leto II in 13,726, the Fish Speakers found and subsequently squandered a vast mélange hoard Leto II had hidden at Seitch Tabr. In 15,232 Bene Gesserit Senior Security Mother Darwi Odrade discovered another 90,000 long tons of mélange at Sietch Tabr and a message for the Bene Gesserit, predicting their eventual demise, that Emperor Leto II had inscribed on the walls. [*Dune, Dune Messiah, Children of Dune, Heretics of Dune*]

Sigma Draconis—The Battle of Corrin was fought in space near Sigma Draconis in 88 B.G. (Before Guild). [*Dune, Chapterhouse: Dune*]

sihaya—A Fremen word meaning "desert springtime," "sihaya" was Paul Atreides' intimate name for his lover

Chani. Also, in Fremen mythology Sihaya is the Recording Angel who interrogates the newly dead. "Sihaya" is the root word for "Siaynoq." [*Dune, God Emperor of Dune*]

Sikun—Sikun is a planet orbiting 70 Ophiuchi A. The akarso is a plant native to Sikun. [*Dune*]

sink—A sink is a habitable lowland area on Arrakis that is protected from coriolis storms by the higher ground surrounding it. [*Dune*]

Siona Ibn Faud al-Seyefa Atreides (13,705–13,801)—A descendant of Harq al-Ada and Ghanima (whom she resembled), Moneo's only child, and the end result of Emperor Leto II's breeding program, lanky, dark-haired, oval-faced, large-mouthed, beautiful, swift, and rebellious Siona Ibn Faud al-Seyefa Atreides was the only one of eleven rebel raiders to escape being killed by a pack of pursuing D-wolves in Arrakis' Forbidden Forest after having stolen two ridulian crystal paper volumes, The Stolen Journals, and the complete plans for the Citadel from Emperor Leto II's Citadel fortress in the Sareer in 13,726. Later that year she was flown with Duncan Idaho ghola number 3, with whom Leto II wanted her to mate, to Goygoa by a squad of Fish Speakers and was flown the next day to Leto II's Citadel. Moneo subsequently flew her to the Little Citadel, where Leto II determined that she was ready to be tested, and he then took her into the Sareer.

During the test Leto II taught Siona how to survive in the desert and allowed her, when her stillsuit catch-pockets were empty, after five days, to nurse water mixed with spice-essence from the curled flaps of the cowl near his face. This infusion of mélange acted on her Atreides genes to bestow on her Leto II's vision of his Golden Path and the horrible extinction of humanity that it prevents. It also revealed to her that she had been bred to be invisible to Leto II's prescient awareness. While in the Sareer with him, Siona learned as well that water was Leto II's only physical weakness. After surviving Leto II's test Siona was made Commander of the Fish Speakers but was given only one trooper to command, Nayla. Moneo subsequently sent Siona, Nayla, and Idaho ghola number 3 to Tuono Village so that they would miss Leto II's marriage to Hwi Noree, which was to have occurred in Tabur Village, but Leto II then changed the location of his nuptials to Tuono Village. The morning of the wedding ceremony Siona, Nayla, Idaho ghola number 3, some Museum Fremen, and some other Fish Speakers scaled the wall separating Tuono Village from the Royal Road in order to intercept Leto II's Royal Cart and entourage. As the Royal Cart crossed over the Idaho River, Siona ordered Nayla to use her lasgun to sever the bridge supports and to disable the suspensors on Leto II's Royal Cart, and Leto II, Hwi Noree, and Moneo tumbled to their deaths. Siona is reputedly the author of "The Welbeck Fragment." [*God Emperor of Dune*]

sip-well—A sip-well is a form of soak, unknown on Arrakis, where water can be drawn through a straw. [*Dune*]

Sirafa (14,881–15,252)—Dark, seam-faced, green-eyed, gray haired, apparently old Sirafa was a Gammu native who assisted Bene Gesserit Bashar Alef Burzmali in rescuing Bene Gesserit Supreme Bashar Miles Teg, Reverend Mother Lucilla, and Duncan Idaho ghola number 4 from the Harkonnen no-globe. She had previously killed Pira—an Honored Matre playfem and a fifth-stage adept in the Order of Hormu—so that Lucilla could assume Pira's identity. [*Heretics of Dune*]

Sisterhood Scattering—Following the destruction of Rakis in 15,232, the Sisterhood Scattering entailed the sending out of numerous Bene Gesserit cells, each of which had an allotment of sand trout and mélange, into the universe beyond the Old Empire to colonize new planets in a desperate attempt to avoid the extermination of the Bene Gesserit by the Honored Matres. [*Chapterhouse: Dune*]

Skar—A common name on Gammu in the 153rd century, Skar was the pseudonym used by Bene Gesserit Bashar Alef Burzmali in disguising himself as a Gammu field hand and the client of Reverend Mother Lucilla, who was disguised as an Honored Matre playfem, to facilitate Lucilla's escape from Gammu. [*Heretics of Dune*]

sligs—A slowly creeping cross between giant slugs and pigs, sligs were a product of the Tleilaxu axlotl tanks traded by the Tleilaxu through CHOAM. [*Heretics of Dune*]

soak—A soak is an area, unknown on Arrakis, where water seeps to the surface or close enough to the surface to be found by digging. [*Dune*]

Society of the Faithful—Created by Regent Alia Atriedes, the green-robed Society of the Faithful was the most powerful governing force in the Imperium in 10,216. [*Children of Dune*]

solari—The solari was the official monetary unit of the Empire in the 102nd century, the time of Muad'Dib. Its value was determined at quatricentennial negotiations involving the Spacing Guild, the Landsaard, and the Emperor. [*Dune*]

Solitz (15,172–15,247)—Solitz was a tall, bone-thin Suk doctor working for those from the Scattering who examined Bene Gesserit Supreme Bashar Miles Teg in Yasi. The diamond tattoo on his forehead was orange instead of the customary black. [*Heretics of Dune*]

"Songs of Muad'Dib"—"Songs of Muad'Dib" is one of the many volumes authored by Princess Irulan. [*Dune*]

Soo-Soo (10,141–10,193)—Soo-Soo was the nickname of the Guild Bank representative and financial advisor to the Water Peddlers Union who backed down when Dr. Liet Kynes challenged him to a duel during Lady Jessica's 10,191 dinner party in Arrakeen. His Geidi Prime speech pattern revealed to Jessica that he was a Harkonnen agent. [*Dune*]

"Soo-soo sook"—"Soo-soo sook" was the cry of the water peddlers of Arrakis. [*Dune*]

soostones—Tumors that occur in the abraded carapace of the cholister, a monoped sea creature native to Buzzell, soostones are one of the most valued jewels in the universe. Eyeball-sized, perfectly round, and milky-yet-radiant, they were often used as currency in high-level business transactions in the 153rd century. [*Heretics of Dune, Chapterhouse: Dune*]

Spacing Guild—*See* **Guild, the Spacing**. [*Dune*]

spice—Spice is the popular term for the drug mélange. *See* **mélange**. [*Dune*]

Spice Agony—The Spice Agony is a Bene Gesserit term for the physical and emotional pain a Bene Gesserit must endure in transmuting the Water of Life to become a Reverend Mother. [*Chapterhouse: Dune*]

spice factory—*See* **sandcrawler**. [*Dune*]

Spider Queen—Spider Queen was Reverend Mother Superior Darwi Odrade's term for Great Honored Matre Dama. [*Chapterhouse: Dune*]

star jewels—Star jewels were a commodity traded through CHOAM that brought wealth to the Bene Gesserit and to five Houses Minor in the 138th century. [*God Emperor of Dune*]

station mothers—Station mothers are Bene Gesserit sisters who are permitted to live out a lifetime with one mated breeding partner. [*Heretics of Dune*]

Stilgar (10,153–10,238)—A Fremen Naib and the leader of Sietch Tabr in 10,191, the tall, bearded, dark-haired Stilgar was Chani's uncle. He and his band of forty Fremen, including Chani, found Paul Atreides and Lady Jessica in the desert after the fall of Arrakeen in 10,191 and took them in, rather than murder them for their water, because Stilgar had previously received a distrans message from Dr. Liet Kynes ordering him to rescue Paul and because Jessica offered to teach him and his Fremen band the Bene Gesserit style of unarmed combat. On Liet Kynes' death in 10,191 Stilgar became the head of the Fremen Council of Leaders. He officially swore allegiance to Paul in Cave of Birds in 10,193. He became Governor of Arrakis and took Harah as one of his wives later that year, after Paul and the Fremen had retaken Arrakeen and Paul had become Emperor, and he had become Emperor Paul

Muad'Dib's Minister of State by 10,207. In that year he received Bijaz from Paul near Otheym's house in the suburbs of Arrakeen just before a stone burner was detonated in Otheym's dwelling. Escaping with Bijaz in time to avoid injury, Stilgar returned to the scene to find a blinded Paul. Subsequently he served at first as prosecuting attorney in Korba's trial, presided over by Regent Alia Atreides, but was during the trial also appointed Korba's council by Paul. Afterwards he accompanied Chani—with Paul, Bijaz, Hayt, Alia, Edric, Reverend Mother Gaius Helen Mohiam, Scytale disguised as Lichna, Harah, and Irulan—when she returned to the desert, to Sietch Tabr, to give birth. After Chani's death in childbirth Stilgar executed Edric and Mohiam on Alia's orders. He guarded Paul and Chani's twins, Leto II and Ghanima, while they were raised in Sietch Tabr, from 10,207 to 10,216. He was present when Jessica landed in Arrakeen in 10,216 after a twenty-three year absence from Arrakis. Shortly thereafter Leto II took him into the desert, near the Attendant, and ordered him to flee from Sietch Tabr with Ghanima should Leto II be slain in at that location. In 10,217 he was goaded by outrageous insults into killing Alia's husband Hayt in Sietch Tabr after Hayt had assassinated Alia's lover Ziarenko Javid. He then fled from Alia's vengeance into the desert, to the Fremen rebels, with Ghanima, Harah, Irulan, and many

others from Sietch Tabr. In the desert he met and murdered Alia's agent Buer Agarves. However, he was subsequently abducted, with Ghanima and Irulan, by kidnappers employed by Alia and returned to Arrakeen, where he was imprisoned. After Leto II became Emperor in 10,218, Stilgar returned to Sietch Tabr with Gurney Hallek. He wrote the "Preface" to Princess Irulan's "Muad'Dib, the Man" and is the author of *The Commentaries*. [*Dune, Dune Messiah, Children of Dune*]

stillsuit—A garment invented and worn by the Fremen on Arrakis, a stillsuit was a body-enclosing micro-sandwich that reclaimed the body's moisture and dissipated heat. Reclaimed moisture was made available to the wearer by tubes connected to water catch-pockets. The stillsuit also reclaimed salt, and the wearer's urine and feces were processed in the thigh pads. Use of a stillsuit reduced the wearer's water loss to less than a thimbleful per day. In the late 102nd and early 103rd centuries, during the reigns of Emperor Paul Muad'Dib and his sister Regent Alia Atreides, garments that appeared to be but were not stillsuits became the fashion in the Empire. [*Dune, Children of Dune*]

stilltent—A stilltent was a small, sealable tent made of micro-sandwich fabric and used on Arrakis that reclaimed the moisture expelled by its inhabitants. [*Dune*]

Stiros (15,108–15,229)—Krustansik's uncle, wrinkled, old, scrawny, pinched-faced, dark-lipped, pale-eyed, cynical Stiros was one of Rakian High Priest Hedley Tuek's councilors and a Rakian priest who represented the "scientific community," a powerful faction in the Rakian priesthood. He had been dismissed as being evil by Sheeana Brugh the day after she was adopted by the Rakian priests because he had objected to Sheena's command that the priests stop sacrificing people to the sandworms and to her heresy of insisting that the Rakian priests' Shai-hulud was the same as the Ralkian people's Shaitan. Secretly an Ixian agent, he was killed by the Bene Gesserit during the Tleilaxu/Ixian attempt to assassinate Sheeana when she was 14 years old. [*Heretics of Dune*]

The Stolen Journals—Written by Emperor Leto II in Galach on ridulian crystal paper with an Ixian dictatel and stolen from his Citadel by Siona in 13,726, The Stolen Journals were deciphered by the Spacing Guild using the Guild Key, which was also used to decipher the ridulian crystal paper manuscripts discovered 1000 years later at Dar-es-Balat on Rakis (Arrakis). [*God Emperor of Dune*]

stone burner—A stone burner is a nuclear weapon that emits J-rays, which cause permanent blindness to anyone in close proximity to the detonation. A stone burner with enough fuel could melt its way to a planet's molten core, with catastrophic consequences. Stone burners, like other nuclear weapons, were prohibited by the Great Convention. [*Dune Messiah*]

S'tori—The ultimate enlightenment attained through Zensunni rituals, S'tori was also achieved by Reverend Mothers who succeeded in transmuting the Water of Life. [*Heretics of Dune*]

The Story of Liet Kynes—*The Story of Liet Kynes* was a volume authored by Harq al-Ada. [*Children of Dune*]

Streggi, Aloana (15,215–15,245)—Blonde, blue-eyed, curley-haired, round-faced, intelligent, bold Aloana Streggi was an Intermediate Third Stage Bene Gesserit acolyte who had created the map of Chapterhouse in Reverend Mother Superior Darwi Odrade's bedchamber that showed the desert's daily growth. In 15,244 Odrade recruited Streggi to carry the young Miles Teg clone about on her shoulders. Later that year Streggi travelled to Chapterhouse's Desert Watch Center with Odrade and Reverend Mother Tamalane. In 15,245 she went to Gammu with the Teg clone, who commanded the feint at Gammu and then the main attack at Junction from atop her shoulders. She was killed when the Honored Matres deployed their secret weapon after the apparent Bene Gesserit victory at Junction. [*Chapterhouse: Dune*]

stunner—A stunner is a slow-dart

projectile weapon firing a poison- or drug-tipped dart that is sometimes effective against a shield, depending on the shield setting and the relative motion between target and dart. [*Dune*]

subatomic fusion—Indistinguishable from a nuclear detonation, subatomic fusion occurs when a lasgun beam intersects an active shield. [*Dune*]

Subiay (10,173–10,235)—Subiay was a citizen of Stilgar's Sietch Tabr who gave birth to a baby boy in the open hajr of the desert in 10,193. [*Dune*]

Suipol (15,213–15,245)—Suipol was an efficient Bene Gesserit acolyte, ready for the Spice Agony, who accompanied Reverend Mother Superior Darwi Odrade, Reverend Mother Tanalane, and Reverend Mother Tortujla to Junction in 15,245. She was killed by the Honored Matres during the Miles Teg clone's successful attack on Junction. [*Chapterhouse: Dune*]

Sumer (10,052–10,135)—Sumer was, with Kautman, the author of *The Last Jihad*, a study that examines the forces that allowed Richese and Ix to evade the anti-machine proscriptions of the Butlerian Jihad. [*Dune*]

suspensor—Produced by the low-drain phase of a Holtzman field generator, a suspensor negates gravity within the limits prescribed by the relative mass involved and the energy consumed. [*Dune*]

Syaksa, Reverend Mother (13,623– 13,741)—Bene Gesserit Reverend Mother Syaksa believed that Emperor Leto II considered himself to be a predator in the common sense of the word. She was the principal author of the Welbeck Abridgement, a 13,726 report to the Bene Gesserit. [*God Emperor of Dune*]

Tabla Memorium—The Table Memorium of the Mahdi Spirit Club was the source of the Muad'Dib Concordance. [*Dune Messiah*]

Tabur Village—Built on the site of Sietch Tabr in the Sareer, Tabur Village was to have been the site of Emperor Leto II's marriage to Hwi Noree until Leto II suddenly relocated his nuptuals to Tuono Village. Museum Fremen tended Tabur Village's date palms, tall grasses, and truck farms. Leto II's vast spice hoard was hidden beneath Tabur Village. [*God Emperor of Dune*]

tahaddi al-burhan—A final test from which there can be no appeal, the tahaddi al-burhan is usually a test to the death or to the destruction of the subject tested. [*Dune*]

tahaddi challenge—A tahaddi challenge is a Fremen challenge to mortal combat, usually to test a compelling issue represented by the combatants. [*Dune*]

taif—Among the Fremen on Arrakis, a "taif" was a company of men held together by mutual self-interest—as opposed to an "ichwan," a band of brothers. [*Children of Dune*]

Takim (10,157–10,218)—Takim was a dissident Fremen Naib who fled Arrakis with a stolen worm in 10,207. [*Dune Messiah*]

Talmudic Zabur—*See* **Zabur, Tawrah and Talmudic.** [*Dune*]

Tamalane, Reverend Mother (14,827–15,245)—The very old, wizened, snowy-haired, shaggy-browed, narrow-faced, leather-skinned, trim, bony, cool, aloof Reverene Mother Tamalane, who preferred chairdogs to chairs, had served the Bene Gesserit order on Gammu—where in 15,221 she had replaced Reverend Mother Geasea as Duncan Idaho number 4's teacher—and, later, as Mother Commander of the Rakian Keep, until she was replaced in that post by Senior Security Mother Darwi Odrade in 15,229. She spied for the Bene Gesserit on the Rakian priests, returned to Chapterhouse, and travelled to Chapterhouse's Desert Watch Center with Reverend Mother Superior Odrade, Bene Gesserit acolyte Aloana Streggi, and their entourage in 15,244. In 15,245 she was replaced as a member of Odrade's Council by Sheeana, but she remained on the Council as an advisor. She then received both Odrade's and Sheeana's other memories in preparation for going to Junction, with Odrade and Reverend Mother Dortuja, to parlay with the Honored Matres. After observing Murbella undergo the Spice Agony in the Chapterhouse no-ship, she accompanied Odrade, Dortuja, and Bene Gesserit acolyte Suipol to Junction, where she was killed by the Honored Matres during the Miles Teg clone's successful attack on that planet. [*Heretics of Dune, Chapterhouse: Dune*]

Tandis (10,180–10,246)—A Fremen lieutenant who in 10,207 accompanied Paul Muad'Dib, Hayt, Alia, Bijaz, Edric, Reverend Mothyer Gaius Helen Mohiam, Scytale disguised as Lichna, Stilgar, Harah, Irulan, and Chani to Sietch Tabr when Chani returned to the desert to give birth to her twins, Tandis soon thereafter informed Paul that Chani had died in childbirth, that she had given birth to twins, a boy and a girl, and that Lichna wanted to speak with him. He also subsequently informed Hayt (who at this point possessed Duncan Idaho's persona) that Paul had gone into the desert to die as a blind Fremen. [*Dune Messiah*]

Tantrus—Tantrus is the god of sex worshipped by many who returned to the known universe from the Scattering in the 153rd century. [*Heretics of Dune*]

Tanzerouft—Also known as the Land of Terror, the Tanzerouft was 3,800 square kilometers of wasteland on Arrakis south of Jacurutu. [*Children of Dune*]

taqua—Among the Fremen of Arrakis, "taqua" was the fear invoked by the presence of a demon. [*Children of Dune*] *taquiyya*—Also known as *ketman* among the ancient Fremen, *taquiyya* is the practice of concealing one's identity when revealing it might be harmful. [*God Emperor of Dune*]

taqwa—In the Fremen tongue, a "taqwa" is something of great value, literally "the price of freedom." [*Dune*]

Tarahell—A world conquered by Muad'Dib's Jihad, Tarahell is the planet on which Otheym had contracted the splitting disease. The stone burner that blinded Emperor Paul Muad'Dib in Arrakeen in 10,207 had been transported from Tarahell on Korba's orders. [*Dune Messiah*]

Taraza, Reverend Mother Superior Alma Mavis (15,159–15,232)—Small, beautiful, oval-faced, black-haired Reverend Mother Superior Alva Mavis Taraza had been Senior Security Mother Darwi Odrade's mentor in the Bene Gesserit School on Chapter House. She subsequently worked with Bene Gesserit Supreme Bashar Miles Teg to resolve peacefully the Barandiko Incident. With Reverend Mother Bellonda and Sister Hesterion of Archives, she was the only Bene Gesserit to possess all the memories of the unbroken line of Bene Gesserit Reverend Mother Superiors. While a captive of the Honored Matres in 15,228 she met Teg on a Guild transport orbiting Gammu, ordered him to reawaken Duncan Idaho ghola number 4's original persona, and warned him that attempts would be made to

kill the ghola. She was then rescued from captivity by Teg. After the 15,229 Tleilaxu attempt to assassinate the ghola, she met with Tleilaxu Master of Masters Tylwyth Waff in a Guild no-ship and threatened to inform the Honored Matres that they had been infiltrated by Tleilaxu Face Dancers if the Bene Tleilax would not share all that they knew about the Honored Matres with the Bene Gesserit. Waff insincerely offered to share this information, but Taraza then falsely offered to share Atreides genetic material with the Bene Tleilax in return for a fully-operational axlotl tank, and Waff initially refused. However, Taraza learned from this meeting that the Bene Tleilax considered Emperor Leto II to have been God's prophet, pretended to share this belief, and on this supposed mutual ground agreed to bargain with the Tleilaxu. After Odrade had committed the Bene Gesserit to serving as missionaries for the Bene Tleilax, Taraza went to Rakis, met again with Waff, and offered to give the Tleilaxu Odrade as an Atreides breeder. A week later she, Waff, Odrade, Rakian priest Tulushan, and Sheeana Brugh went to the desert near Dar-es-Balat, where Sheeana was to summon a sandworm, but the party was attacked by Honored Matres in ornithopters and Taraza was mortally wounded; however, she managed to pass her other memories to Odrade before she died. Odrade then realized that the goal of Taraza's machinations had been to goad the Honored Matres into destroying Rakis and its sand-worms. The Bene Gesserit believe that Taraza had saved the Sisterhood and was the best Reverend Mother Superior in Bene Gesserit history. [*Heretics of Dune, Chapterhouse: Dune*]

Tariq, Assan (10,202–10,217)—One of the Cast Out of Shuloch, nubbin-nosed, flat-faced, innocent-looking, bright-eyed, saucy, cynical Assan Tariq was Muriz's son and the young guide who led The Preacher into Arrakeen in 10,216. As a test of his man-hood, earlier that year he had slain with a crysknife a half-dozen Fremen pilgrims and guides who had discovered Shulock. In 10,217 he and The Preacher encountered in the Tanzer-ouft Leto Atreides II, who had already merged with the sand trout and acquired super-human strength, super-human speed, and command over Arrakis' sandworms. During Leto II's and the Preacher's subsequent struggle of prescient visions Tariq activated a pseudo-shield in an attempt to attract and madden a sandworm that would then kill both Leto II and The Preacher, but he was slain by Leto II. [*Children of Dune*]

Tasmin (10,165–10,207)—Tasmin was a dissident Fremen Naib who at-tended the trial of Korba, precided over by Alia, in 10,207. [*Dune Messiah*]

tau—In the Fremen tongue, the "tau" is the oneness of the Fremen sietch community, which is enhanced by the Fremen's spice diet and by the tau

orgy precipitated by sharing the transmuted (and thus no longer poi-sonous) Water of Life. [*Dune*]

Taw (13,701–13,760)—Taw was an aide to Nayla who witnessed Siona Ibn Faud al-Seyefa Atreides' 13,726 interview with Ixian Ambassador to Arrakis Iyo Kobat in Onn. [*God Emperor of Dune*]

Tawrah Zabur—*See* **Zabur, Tawrah and Talmudic**. [*Dune*]

Tawsuoko, Sister (13,682–13,778)—With Sister Chenoeh, Sister Tawsuoko reported to the Bene Gesserit in 13,726 that Emperor Leto II had executed nine historians in 12,334 for their pre-tentious lies. [*God Emperor of Dune*]

Tecrube (10,167–10,244)—Tecrube was the whiskered, shaven-headed Fremen who served as the Clerk of the Assemblage in Emperor Paul Muad'Dib's Imperial Court in Arra-keen in 10,207. [*Dune Messiah*]

Tedah riagrimi—*Tedah riagrimi* was a Fremen phrase designating "the agony that opens the mind." [*God Emperor of Dune*]

Teg, Bene Gesserit Supreme Bashar Miles Teg (14,923–15,232)—Loschy Teg's and Bene Gesserit Reverend Mother Janet Roxbrough's son, and Senior Security Mother Darwi Odrade's father, the very tall, old, gray-haired, regal, square-shouldered, narrow-waisted, thin-mouthed, narrow-faced, highly-moral, utilitarian, imposing Miles Teg was a philosophical Mentat, a retired Bene Gesserit Supreme Bashar, and an Atreides with a very strong resemblance to Duke Leto. His favorite alcoholic beverage was Danian Marinette, and he disliked synthetic fabrics and chairdogs. At the age of twelve he had been sent to school on the Bene Gesserit planet Lampadas. He had subsequently worked with Reverend Mother Superior Alva Mavis Taraza to resolve peacefully the Barandiko Incident, and he had delivered victories to the Bene Gessrit at the Battle of Markow, where his reputation had compelled the enemy to surrender, at Arbelough, where he had joined the troops at the front to bolster their morale, at Kroinin, where he had broken the anti–Sisterhood forces, and at Renditai, where he had won a minor skirmish. He was called out of retirement in 15,219 to guard the Bene Gesserit Keep on Gammu and to serve as one of Duncan Idaho Ghola number 4's teachers, instructing the ghola in weapons mastery, military tactics, and planetary defenses. While she was a captive of the Honored Matres, Taraza met Teg in 15,228 on a Guild transport orbiting Gammu, ordered him to reawaken Duncan Idaho ghola number 4's original persona, and warned him that attempts would be made to kill the ghola. Teg then rescued Taraza from captivity and returned to Gammu. In 15,229 he saved the ghola and Reverend Mother Lucilla from an attack by a Tleilaxu Face Dancer

disguised as Teg whom Reverend Mother Schwangyu's minions had allowed into the Keep. To evade Schwangyu's treachery Teg then led the ghola and Lucilla into the forest northeast of the Gammu Keep and to an ancient Harkonnen no-globe his batman Patrin had discovered as a teenager and kept a secret for over two hundred years. While hidden in the no-globe for three months, Teg restored the ghola's original Duncan Idaho persona by subjecting the ghola to intense physical and emotional pain. With the assistance of Bene Gesserit Bashar Alef Burzmali, who had been Teg's favorite student, Teg, Lucilla, and the ghola escaped from the no-globe. However, in covering Lucilla's and the ghola's escape Teg was captured by attacking forces from the Scattering and subjected to a T-probe. The agony produced by the T-probe elevated Teg to a new level of ability—endowing him with super-human speed, a knowledge of things around him before those things occurred, and the ability to perceive no-ships and no-globes— and he employed these new abilities to kill his three interrogators and escape to Ysai, where he met Field Marshal Jafa Muzzafar, a regional commander from the Scattering who took Teg to a deserted bank and introduced him to an ancient, wrinkled Honored Matre. However, Teg escaped again, using his new abilities to slaughter Muzzafar, the Honored Matre, and the other fifty inhabitants of the building. He then met Professor Delnay in an upscale Ysai restaurant, and Delnay had him disguise himself as a Bordano overseer to get him safely through the Yasi streets to a bar where Teg met many veterans who had served under him at Renditai. Assisted by the most trustworthy of the veterans, Teg then captured a no-ship from the Scattering; rescued Lucilla, Burzmali, and the ghola; and took them, with Honored Matre Murbella, in the captured no-ship to Rakis, where he met Reverend Mother Superior Odrade and Sheeana Brugh, instructed Burzmali to command Rakis' defenses, and ordered Odrade to take the ghola, Sheeana, Murbella, and a captured sandworm to Chapterhouse. Teg was killed when the Honored Matres destroyed Rakis in a failed attempt to assassinate the ghola. *See also* **Teg Clone, Bene Gesserit Supreme Bashar Miles**. [*Heretics of Dune*]

Teg Clone, Bene Gesserit Supreme Bashar Miles (15,234–15,625)—Referred to as "ghola Teg" by many of the Bene Gesserit, the Miles Teg produced in a Bene Gesserit axlotl tank in 15,234—the first infant delivered from the first Bene Gesserit axlotl tank—was a clone, not a ghola, because he was created from cells harvested as fingernail scrapings from his neck by Reverend Mother Superior Darwi Odrade while he was alive, not from cells harvested from a cadaver. Precocious as a child, he was born and raised on Chapterhouse in the no-ship the original Teg had stolen from Gammu. When he was seven he began to study the history of his own life. He also was trained in weapons mastery by Duncan Idaho ghola number 4, another captive in the Chapterhouse no-ship, and in the deepest Bene Gesserit teachings by Odrade. When he was eleven his original persona and memories were restored in the no-ship by Sheeana Brugh—who restored them by having sex with the young clone, whose original persona had been trained by his mother to resist sexual imprinting—and he immediately exhibited the super-human speed the original Teg had acquired at the end of his life. In a subsequent war council with Odrade, Reverend Mother Bellonda, and Reverend Mother Tamalane, the Teg clone proposed a feint at Gammu as a prelude to an attack on the Honored Matre headquarters on Junction while Odrade was there, ostensibly negotiating with Great Honored Matre Dama, as his spy. Accompanied by Bene Gesserit acolyte Aloana Streggi, who carried the young clone about on her shoulders, he attacked Gammu successfully due to his ability to perceive the Honored Matre's defensive no-ships—a talent he continued to keep secret so that the Bene Gesserit would not be aware that he had it. After defeating Gammu's no-ship defenses the Teg clone landed near Yasi (formerly Barony) to punish the Honored Matres on the ground.

After rescuing the Rabbi and Rebecca from their no-chamber on Gammu he attacked the Honored Matres at Junction, riding on Streggi's shoulders again while commanding the ground battle. Despite winning the battle for Junction, he was taken prisoner when his forces were all suddenly killed by the Honored Matres' secret weapon. He was released from captivity by Honored Matre/Reverend Mother Murbella when Murbella killed Great Honored Matre Longo to become the Great Honored Matre and then absorbed the deceased Odrade's most recent other memories to become the Bene Gesserit Reverend Mother Superior as well. See also **Teg, Bene Gesserit Supreme Bashar Miles**. [*Chapterhouse: Dune*]

Teg, Dimela (14,961–15,310)—Firus' husband and Bene Gesserit Supreme Bashar Miles Teg's eldest daughter, Dimela Teg lived with Teg as a part of his entourage-in-retirement on Lernaeus. [*Heretics of Dune*]

Teg, Loschy (14,852–15,177)—A minor functionary in CHOAM, thin, dark-eyed, narrow-faced, black-haired Loschy Teg was Reverend Mother Janet Roxbrough's husband and Bene Gesserit Supreme Bashar Miles Teg's father. [*Heretics of Dune*]

Teg, Sabine (14,926–15,081)—Sabine Teg was Bene Gesserit Supreme Bashar Miles Teg's younger brother. He was poisoned to death on Romo. [*Heretics of Dune*]

Teishar (13,646–13,730)—Sunken-eyed, darkly-wrinkled, wizened, crabbed, bent, ugly, and avaricious Teishar was a 138th-century Museum Fremen, an aide to Garum of Tuono, who surreptitiously sold a plastic copy of a crysknife to Siona Ibn Faud al-Seyefa Atreides and Topri in Onn. [*God Emperor of Dune*]

Thalim—Thalim is the star about which Tleilax orbits. [*Dune*]

Tharthar (10,171–10,235)—One of Stilgar's wives and a citizen of Sietch Tabr, small, dark Tharthar warned Lady Jessica in 10,193 that the Fremen wanted Paul to challenge Stilgar to a duel to the death in order for Paul to wrest command of the Fremen from Stilgar. [*Dune*]

Thatta—Thatta was a character from Fremen mythology who, with Shakir Ali, saw a vision of the City of Tombs. [*Children of Dune*]

Theta Shalish—Theta Shalish is the star about which Chusuk orbits. [*Dune*]

Theta Shaowei—Theta Shaowei is the star about which Hagal orbits. [*Dune*]

thorses—Six-legged pack animals, thorses were the main beasts of burden throughout the Empire in the 138th century. [*God Emperor of Dune*]

thumper—A spring-driven mechanism with a clapper at one end that creates thumping vibrations when driven into the ground and activated, the thumper was used by the Fremen to attract a sandworm. A thumper is among the tools in the fremkit that Dr. Wellington Yueh left for Paul Atreides and Lady Jessica in the ornithopter in which Kinet and Czigo transport them to the Arrakeen desert in 10,191. [*Dune*]

Thurgrod—Thurgrod was a planet the Fremen inhabited during their migrations. [*Children of Dune*]

Tibana (9th century B.G.)—Probably a native of IV Aunbus, Tibana was an apologist for Socratic Christianity during the second reign of Dalamak. [*Dune Messiah*]

tidal basin—A tidal basin was a desert depression on Arrakis that had filled with dust. Large tidal basins could have currents and tides. [*Dune*]

Tleilax—The homeworld of the Tleilaxu, a training center for Mentats, and the source of "twisted" Mentats, Tleilax is the only planet orbiting the star Thalim. Bandalong is Tleilax's capital city. Piter de Vries was trained on Tleilax. [*Dune, Heretics of Dune*]

Tleilaxu—Based on their homeworld Tleilax and also known as the Bene Tleilax, the Tleilaxu are a secretive society that allows only its male members to appear publicly. No Bene Tleilax female has ever been seen away from the protection of the core Tleilaxu planets. Certain Tleilaxu are Face Dancers, Jadacha hermaphrodites who have the chameleon-like ability to assume the physical appearance and the psyche of anyone they choose to mimic. The Face Dancers are subservient to the Tleilaxu Masters. Bene Gesserit Truthsayers cannot read the Tleilaxu. The Tleilaxu code of honor mandates that a victim must always be allowed a means of escape. Since the 103rd century, the time of Muad'Dib, the Tleilaxu masters had achieved a kind of serial immortality by restoring their original personae and memories in clone or ghola iterations of themselves produced in axlotl tanks. In 13,726 fifty Tleilaxu Face Dancers unsuccessfully attempted to assassinate Emperor Leto II on the Royal Road to Onn. As a consequence, the Tleilaxu Ambassador to Arrakis, Duro Nunepi, was publicly flogged and Theilax was given no mélange allotment for the next ten years. By the 153rd century the Tleilaxu—who had by then been fashioning their deceptive image as vile, dirty, stupid, detestable, predictable creatures for millennia— produced the bulk of the universe's mélange in their axlotl tanks, which were secretly Tleilaxu females connected to mechanisms that precisely controlled chemical balances and limited variables, and had become— with the Bene Gesserit, the Guild, and Ix—one of the most powerful forces in the known universe. They hoped to monopolize mélange production through an alliance with the priests of Rakis, and they saw Emperor Leto II as having been God's prophet whose message only they have heard. All of the Bene Tleilax planets were destroyed by the Honored Matres shortly after the destruction of Rakis in 15,232; Scytale was the only Theilaxu Master in the known universe to survive this genocide. [*Dune Messiah, God Emperor of Dune, Heretics of Dune, Chapterhouse: Dune*]

Tleilaxu-Contact Element—The Tleilaxu-Contact Element was the splinter group of the rebellion against Emperor Leto II on Arrakis that had participated in the 13,726 Tleilaxu/rebel attack on the Ixian Embassy in Onn. [*God Emperor of Dune*]

Tleilaxu eyes—Tleilaxu eyes are metallic orbs that enable a blind man to see. The Fremen believe that uniting such metal eyes with flesh is sinful and that Tleilaxu eyes enslave their users. The ghola Hayt arrived in Emperor Paul Muad'Dib's Imperial Court in 10,207 outfited with Tleilaxu eyes that were intended to remind Paul of the ghola's Tleilaxu origin. [*Dune Messiah*]

toil of the shaduf—To the Fremen of Arrakis, toil of the shaduf was agricultural work of a very menial kind that simultaneously occurred in Another World where it symbolized cultivating the richness of the soul. [*Children of Dune*]

Tolstoy, Count Leo Nikolayevich (prehistoric)—Count Leo Nickolayevich Tolstoy was a writer of ancient Earth. [*Chapterhouse: Dune*]

Topri (13,688–13,736)—A minor functionary in Onn city services and a member of Siona Ibn Faud al-Seyefa Atreides' rebellion against Emperor Leto II recruited by Ulot, fat, nervous, pug-nosed, thin-lipped, green-eyed, faithless, clumsy Topri was actually Moneo's spy on Siona. When Siona realized that Topri was her father's spy she dismissed him from the rebellion by having him deliver to Moneo the message that she had accepted Leto II's challenge and the rules of combat that he had prescribed. [*God Emperor of Dune*]

Torg the Younger (10,496–17,163)—In the 153rd century Torg the Younger was a Tleilaxu Masheikh of the innermost Khel and one of Master of Masters Tylwyth Waff's nine concillors. [*Heretics of Dune*]

Tormsa—*See* **Ambitorm**. [*Heretics of Dune*]

T-probe—A T-probe is a machine that can reveal the contents of a mind even after death, until the individual brain cells die. It is similar to an Ixian probe but is not manufactured on IX but in the Scattering. The drug shere protects one from the effects of a T-probe, but not as effectively as it protects one from the effects of an Ixian probe. The T-probe also enables its user to order the body of its victim to perform any bodily function. [*Heretics of Dune*]

Trebo (15,226–15,602)—Golden-haired, golden-skinned Trebo was a young man whom Duncan Idaho ghola number 4 had sent to Sheeana in 15,244 so that Sheeana could complete his training in sexual amplification techniques. [*Chapterhouse: Dune*]

truthsayer—A truthsayer is a Bene Gesserit Reverend Mother who can enter truthtrance, through the use of awareness spectrum narcotics, to detect falsehood or insincerity. Reverend Mother Gaius Helen Mohiam was Emperor Shaddam IV's truthsayer. [*Dune*]

truthtrance—a semi-hypnotic state induced through the ingestion of an awareness spectrum narcotic, truthtrance enables the user to detect if another is speaking the truth. [*Dune*]

Tsimpay (15,208–15,574)—Brown-haired, heavy-browed, narrow-faced, fit, austere Tsimpay was in the 153rd century the Bene Gesserit leader in Pondrille, a postulant center on the way from Central to the Desert Watch Center on Chapterhouse. [*Chapterhouse: Dune*]

Tsimpo—Tsimpo was a garrison village in the 102nd century that served as a buffer outpost for Carthag, the capital of Arrakis under the Harkonnens. [*Dune*]

Tuek, Esmar (10,135–10,191)—The father of Staban Tuek, an ancestor to Hedley Tuek, and a rugged, scar-faced spice smuggler who attended Lady Jessica's 10,191 dinner party in Arrakeen, Esmar Tuek seemed on that occasion to be a follower or ally of Dr. Liet Kynes. He was killed in the hallway of the Arrakeen palace by Dr. Wellington Yueh two days later. [*Dune*]

Tuek, Hedley (15,042–15,232)—A descendant of Esmar Tuek, square-faced, thick-mouthed, heavy-chinned, bushy-browed, blue-eyed Hedley Tuek wore his silky, gray hair to his shoulders. He was in the early 153rd century the High Priest of Rakis and, as such, the planet's titular ruler. He gave his High Priest quarters to Sheeana Brugh the day after she was adopted by the Ralkian priesthood. In 15,232 he futilely resisted Senior Security Mother Darwi Odrade's effort to transfer guardianship of Sheeana from the Rakian priests to the Bene Gesserit on Arrakis and was subsequently killed by Tleilaxu Master of Masters Tylwyth Waff and replaced by a new Tleilaxu Face Dancer who mimicked Tuek so thoroughly that he eventually came to believe that he was Tuek. Thus, the Face Dancer mimic could no longer be controlled by Waff and ultimately allied himself and the Rakian priesthood with the Bene Gesserit. [*Heretics of Dune*]

Tuek, Staban (10,155–10,222)—The son of Esmar Tuek, shaggy-browed Staban Tuek was the spice smuggler with whom Gurney Hallek and seventy-four Atreides soldiers enlisted after the fall of Arrakeen to the Harkonnens in 10,191. [*Dune*]

Tulushan (15,206–15,232)—Tulushan was a darkly handsome, young Rakian priest who in 15,232 accompanied Reverend Mother Superior Alma Mavis Taraza, Senior Security Mother Darwi Odrade, Tleilaxu Master of Masters Tylwyth Waff, and Sheeana Brugh to the desert near Dar-es-Balat where Sheeana was to summon a worm, but the party was attacked by Honored Matres in ornithopters. Tulushan was later killed in the destruction of Rakis. [*Heretics of Dune*]

tunyou vine—A plant that has absolutely no smell, the tunyon vine grew in Emperor Leto II's Citadel fortress. [*God Emperor of Dune*]

Tuono Basin—Tuono Basin was the desert location on Arrakis, some fifteen kilometers from Sietch Tabr, where Stilgar and his troop of forty Fremen found Paul Atreides and Lady Jessica after the fall of Arrakeen to the Harkonnens in 10,191. [*Dune*]

Tuono Village—Tuono Village was the small village of Museum Fremen at the edge of the Sareer to which Moneo sent Duncan Idaho ghola number 3, Siona Ibn Faud al-Seyefa Atreides, and Nayla so that they would miss Emperor Leto II's 13,726 wedding to Hwi Noree, which was to have occurred in Tabur Village. However, Leto II subsequently changed the location of his nuptuals to Tuono Village and was assassinated by Nayla, acting on Siona's orders, while on his way to the ceremony. [*God Emperor of Dune*]

Tupile—Tupile was the general term for a small number of planets, the Tupile Entente, on which defeated Houses of the Imperium could find sanctuary. Its location was known only to the Spacing Guild, and its inviolability was protected under the Guild Peace. [*Dune, Dune Messiah*]

Tupile Treaty—The Tupile Treaty of 10,207 was an accord between Emperor Paul Muad'Dib's Imperium and the Spacing Guild that maintained the secrecy of the locations of the planets in the Tupile Entente. [*Dune Messiah*]

Turok (10,166–10,191)—Befriended by Duncan Idaho as he lay dying, Turok was a Fremen courier who was waylaid and killed by the Harkonnens in 10,191 while attempting to warn the Atreides of a band of Harkonnen mercenaries disguised as Fremen. [*Dune*]

Tykanik, Bashar (10,166–10,244)— Bashar Tykanik was a blocky, thicktoothed, square-faced aide to Princess Wensicia who was privy to Wensicia's 10,216 plot to use Laza tigers to assassinate Leto Atreides II and Ghanima and then to place her son Prince Farad'n on the throne. He was ordered by Wensicia to pretend to embrace the religion of Muad'Dib so as to influence Farad'n to embrace it in earnest, and at Wensicia's behest he had The Preacher brought to Salusa Secundus, ostensibly to interpret Farad'n's dreams, but in reality to interest Farad'n further in the religion of Muad'Dib. Tykanik was subsequently convinced that the Corrino spy in Regent Alia Atreides' court, Ziarenko Javid, who had become Alia's lover, was a double agent. In 10,218 he accompanied Farad'n and Jessica from Salusa Secundus to Arrakis, where he formed an uneasy friendship of distrust with Stilgar. [*Children of Dune*]

Uliet (10,124–10,160)—Uliet was a Fremen who deliberately fell on his own knife rather than kill Pardot Kynes, which he had been ordered to do when Kynes was taken to a sietch near Wind Pass after he had saved three Fremen youths from six shielded and fully-armed Harkonnens. [*Dune*]

Ulot (13,697–13,726)—One of Siona Ibn Faud al-Seyefa Atreides' ten companions in the theft in 13,726 of The Stolen Journals from Emperor Leto II's Citadel fortress in the Sareer, Ulot was killed by a pack of D-wolves in Arrakis' Forbidden Forest following the raid on the Citadel. Ulot had previously recruited the spy Topri into Siona's rebellion against Leto II. [*God Emperor of Dune*]

Umbu (10,167–10,207)—Umbu was a dissident Fremen Naib who attended the trial of Korba, presided over by Alia, in 10,207. [*Dune Messiah*]

umma—In the Fremen tongue, the umma is the brotherhood of prophets. It is a derisive term in the Imperium generally, where it refers to any wild person given to fanatical predictions. During the reigns of Emperor Paul Muad'Dib and his sister Regent Alia Atreides, the "umma" was also a personal revelation often experienced by a Fremen on Hajj. [*Dune, Children of Dune*]

Umphrud (15,118–15,232)—Fat, hedonistic Umphrud was a priest of Rakis and one of High Priest Hedley Tuek's councilors. He was killed in the destriuction of Rakis. [*Heretics of Dune*]

uroshnor—A meaningless sound, "uroshnor" is one of several words that the Bene Gesserit implant into the subconscious of certain individuals they hope to control. The victim of this control is temporarily immobilized upon hearing the word. Lady Margot Fenring implanted the word "uroshnor" in Feyd-Rautha Rabban Harkonnen's subconscious on Giedi Prime in 10,191. [*Dune*]

Usul—A Fremen word that means "the base of the pillar," "Usul" was the secret Fremen name bestowed on Paul Atreides in Cave of the Ridges after Paul had killed Jamis during a tahaddi challenge in 10,191. [*Dune*]

Valefor, Ziarenka (10,193–10,218)—A Fremen, Ziarenka Valefor was the chief of Regent Alia Atreides' guardian amazons in 10,216. After being convinced by the persona of the Baron Harkonnen inhabiting her consciousness that she should take Ziarenko Javid as her lover, Alia ordered Valefor to bring Javid to her private chamber. Alia subsequently ordered

Valefor to assassinate Hayt while transporting him from Arrakeen to Sietch Tabr, but Hayt suspected this treachery and flew himself to Sietch Tabr alone. [*Children of Dune*]

Van Gogh, Vincent (prehistoric)— Vincent van Gogh was a painter of ancient Earth. Reverend Mother Superior Darwi Odrade kept van Gogh's *Cottages at Cordeville* in her bedchamber on Chapterhouse. The painting was stolen by Sheeana Brugh in 15,245 and transported out of the known universe in the no-ship in which Sheeana, Duncan Idaho ghola number 4, the Rabbi, Rebecca, Scytale, Bene Gesserit Proctor Garimi, a sandworm, and some Futars escaped from Chapterhouse. [*Chapterhouse: Dune*]

Varota (10,030–10,111)—A native of Chusuk, Varota was a legendary manufacturer of balisets. Gurney Hallek owned a baliset that may have been made by Varota or by a student of Varota. [*Dune*]

Venport, Aurelius (118–40 B.G.)— An ancestor of Emperor Leto II, Aurelius Venport was erroneously believed to have designed the first Guild ship, which was actually designed by his mistress Norma Cenva. [*God Emperor of Dune*]

Verite—A narcotic derived from a plant native to Ecaz, verite makes it impossible for the person to whom it is administered to speak a falsehood. [*Dune*]

Voice—The Voice is a Bene Gesserit technique that enables the adept to control another through selected tonal shadings of the vocal chords. [*Dune*]

"The Void"—"The Void" was the title of a disturbing black plaz sculpture created by Sheeana Brugh at the Desert Watch Center on Chapterhouse in 15,244. [*Chapterhouse: Dune*]

Vreeb, Rebeth (14,190–14,267)—A well-known 143rd-century poet, Rebeth Vreeb gave an oral reading of the recordings made by Emperor Leto II, in Paul Atreides voice, that were found in an ancient Ixian no-globe ar Dar-es-Balat on Rakis (Arrakis). [*God Emperor of Dune*]

Waff, Master of Masters Tylwyth (10,348–15,232)—Short, round-faced, small-eyed, sharp-toothed, pugnosed, pipe-voiced Tylwyth Waff was a Sufi and Zensunni priest and the Tleilaxu Mahai, the Master of Masters, in the 153rd century. In 15,219 he met an Honored Matre on neutral ground and killed her and a colleague with a poisoned dart so that two Face Dancers could mimic and replace them. He subsequently had sex with a Face Dancer mimicking an Honored Matre and experienced first hand Honored Matre sexual amplification techniques, after which he immediately killed the Face Dancer. In 15,229, after the failed Tleilaxu attempt to assassinate Duncan Idaho ghola number 4 in the Gammu Keep, he met Reverend Mother Superior Alma Mavis Taraza in a Guild no-ship and agreed, insincerely, to share with the Bene Gesserit all that the Bene Tleilax knew about the Honored Matres in return for Taraza's promise that the Bene Gesserit would not inform the Honored Matres that they had been infiltrated by Face Dancers. He initially refused Taraza's offer to trade Atreides genetic material for a fully operational axlotl tank, but in their conversation he had revealed to Taraza that the Bene Tleilax consider Leto II to have been God's prophet; Taraza pretended to share this belief, and on this supposed mutual ground Waff agreed to bargain with the Bene Gesserit. In 15,232, with Rakian High Priest Hedley Tuek's knowledge, Waff evesdropped on Tuek's and Bene Gesserit Reverend Senior Security Mother Darwi Odrade's conversation about the "Atreides Manifesto" and Sheeana Brugh's future; then, at Odrade's invitation, he joined them and killed Tuek with a poisoned dart before he could be apprehended by Odrade, who broke both his arms in subduing him. Odrade then convinced Waff that the Bene Tleilax and the Bene Gesserit could be allies because the Bene Gesserit shared the Tleilaxu's Great Belief, even though this was not true. Waff, Sheeana, and Odrade then went into the desert near Dar-es-Balat to summon and ride a sandworm, which took them to a ruined wall that had once bordered Emperor Leto II's Sareer and to the site of an ancient, dry, subterranean Fremen water storage basin, attached to what had once been Sietch Tabr, where Leto II had hidden a vast horde of mélange. After they returned to Keen, Odrade allied the Bene Gesserit with the Bene Tleilax—against the Honored Matres of the Scattering—by striking a bargain with Waff that was based on Waff's misapprehension that the Bene Gesserit shared the Tleilaxu Great Belief. Waff then had two Face Dancers demonstrate Honored Matre sexual amplification techniques for Taraza, Odrade, and Sheeana. A week later Waff, Taraza, Odrade, Sheeana, and Rakian priest Tulushan again went to the desert near Dar-es-Balat to summon a worm, but the party was attacked by Honored Matres in ornithopters. Waff was killed in the destruction of Rakis. [*Heretics of Dune*]

wali—A wali is an untried Fremen youth. [*Dune*]

Wallach IX—The ninth planet orbiting Laoujin, Wallach IX is the location of the Bene Gesserit Mother School. Lady Jessica was educated on Wallach IX, and the 10,205–07 conspiracy against Emperor Paul Muad'Dib involving Reverend Mother Gaius Helen Mohiam, Princess Irulan, Edric, and Scytale was hatched there. Wallach IX was captured by the Honored Matres in the early 153rd century. [*Dune, Dune Messiah, Chapterhouse: Dune*]

Walli, Senior Acolyte Assistant (15,213–15,578)—Large-eyed, freckeled, almost-albino Bene Gesserit Senior Acolyte Assistant Walli assumed command of Chapterhouse's Desert Watch Center in 15,245, when Sheeana Brugh joined Reverend Mother Superior Darwi Odrade's Council. Walli was aware that Sheeana was immune to Honored Matre sexual bonding. [*Chapterhouse: Dune*]

Wallport—In the 138th century Wallport was a town visible in the distance from the balcony of Emperor Leto II's Little Citadel in the Sareer. [*God Emperor of Dune*]

War of Assassins—A limited form of warfare permitted under the Great Convention, the War of Assassins was intended to reduce the involvement of innocent bystanders. Its rules prescribe formal declarations of intent and limit the weapons that can be used. [*Dune*]

Water of Death—When the Water of Life is poured onto a pre-spice mass, it becomes the Water of Death, which had the capacity to kill all of the sandtrout on Arrakis and thus, eventually, all of the sandworms. As mélange is a by-product of the sandworm lifecycle, introducing the Water of Death to a pre-spice mass would eventually end spice production on Arrakis. [*Dune*]

Water of Life—The liquid exhalation of a dying, drowned sandworm, the Water of Life is a poison that some Bene Gesserit can transmute into a non-lethal awareness spectrum nar-

cotic within their bodies. The altered narcotic is then used in the Fremen sietch tau orgy. A Bene Gesserit who successfully transmutes the Water of Life for the first time becomes a Reverend Mother in the process. If added to a pre-spice mass, the Water of Life would cause a chain reaction that would kill all of the sandtrout on Arrakis, thus making the sandworms extinct. [*Dune*]

The Way—The Way is the major thoroughfare in Central on Chapterhouse. In the early 153rd century it was a straight avenue twelve kilometers long that reached from the square of Reverend Mother Darwi Odrade's tower to the southern outskirts of Central's urban area. [*Chapterhouse: Dune*]

Weapon—The Weapon was a small black tube that, when charged, could cut a swath of bloodless death across the arc of its limited range. Only 300 units of the Weapon remained in the Honored Matres' arsenal when they fled the Scattering to return to the Old Empire in the early 153rd century, and the Honored Matres then attempted unsuccessfully to have the scientists of Ix duplicate the Weapon. The Honored Matres used the last charge of the Weapon that they possessed to kill nearly all of the Bene Gesserit force, led by the Miles Teg clone, that had captured Junction in 15,245. [*Chapterhouse: Dune*]

weirding way—The weirding way is the Bene Gesserit style of unarmed combat that Lady Jessica promised to teach to the Fremen in return for her life when she and Paul Atreides were found by Stilgar's troop in Tuono Basin in 10,191. [*Dune*]

The Welbeck Abridgement—Authored by Bene Gesserit Reverend Mothers Syaksa, Yitob, Mamulut, Eknekosk, and Akeli, The Welbeck Abridgement was a report to the Bene Gesserit on the state of the Empire in 13,726. [*God Emperor of Dune*]

"The Welbeck Fragment"—Ostensibly authored by Siona Ibn Faud al-Seyefa Atreides, "The Welbeck Fragment" contains a dialogue between Siona and her father Moneo that occurred during Siona's teens at the Fish Speakers' School in the festival city of Onn. [*God Emperor of Dune*]

Wensicia, Princess (10,180–10,265)—One of Emperor Shaddam IV's and Anirul's five daughters, Princess Wensicia accompanied Shaddam IV into retirement on Salusa Secundus in 10,193. She was fair-haired and had a heart-shaped face. The widow of Dalak and Prince Farad'n's mother, she plotted in 10,216 to assassinate Leto Atreides II and Ghanima with Laza tigers trained on Salusa Secundus and then to place Farad'n on the throne. (She was intimate with a Sardaukar Laza tiger trainer whom she later had the tigers kill to assure that her plot would remain a secret.) Later she had her aide Basha Tyekanik convert to the religion of Muad'Dib and trans-port The Preacher from Arrakis to Salusa Secundus in order to interest Farad'n in that religion—as a way to ingratiate him with the Fremen. She subsequently was convinced that her spy in Alia's court, Ziarenko Javid, who had become Alia's lover, was now a double agent. Angered by his mother's plot to assassinate Leto Atreides II and Ghanima, Farad'n agreed to banish Wensicia, which he did, in return for Jessica's offer to teach him the Bene Gesserit way. [*Dune, Children of Dune*]

Windsack—Windsack was the Arrakeen village near which Pardot Kynes saved three Fremen youths from being killed by six fully armed and shielded Harkonnens, an act that gained Kynes admittance to a Fremen sietch near Wind Pass. After merging with the sand trout in 10,217, Leto Atreides II destroyed the qanats at Windsack—and at Gara Rulen, Old Gap, and Harg—to set back the ecological transformation of Arrakis. [*Dune, Children of Dune*]

Wind Trap—Wind Trap was the location on Rakis where Bene Gesserit Supreme Bashar Miles Teg, Reverend Mother Lucilla, Bene Gesserit Bashar Burzmali, and Duncan Idaho ghola number 4 met Reverend Mother Superior Darwi Odrade and Sheeana Brugh in 15,232. [*Heretics of Dune*]

"The Wisdom of Muad'Dib"—"The Wisdom of Muad'Dib" is one of the many volumes authored by Princess Irulan. [*Dune*]

Wose (11,347–16,492)—Wose was the Tleilaxu envoy to Rakis when Rakian High Priest Hedly Tuek's father had been Rakian High Priest. [*Heretics of Dune*]

Wose—Wose was the pseudonym used by Duncan Idaho ghola number 4 when he was disguised as a Tleilaxu Master after his escape with Reverend Mother Lucilla from the Harkonnen no-globe on Gammu. [*Heretics of Dune*]

Yaghist—"Yaghist" is the land of the unruled in Islamiyat, the ancient, secret language of the Bene Tleilax. [*Heretics of Dune, Chapterhouse: Dune*]

Yake, Othwi (13,682–13,726)—Sandy-haired, narrow-faced, unpleasant Othwi Yake was the assistant to former Ixian Ambassador to Arrakis Iyo Kobat who in 13,726 sent a message to Bene Gesserit Reverend Mothers Tertius Eileen Anteac and Marcus Claire Luseyal informing them that Emperor Leto II would be assassinated by the Tleilaxu on his way to Onn and that the Ixian Embassy on Arrakis had been infiltrated by Tleilaxu Face Dancers. Yake was later appointed first assistant to the new Ixian Ambassador to Arrakis, Hwi Noree, but by the time he received this appointment he had already been murdered and replaced by a Tleilaxu Face Dancer. [*God Emperor of Dune*]

Yali—A yali was a citizen's personal quarters in a Fremen sietch. [*Dune*]

Yar (15,126–15,232)—Square-faced, beady-eyed Yar was the Gammu native in league with the Honored Matres from the Scattering who interrogated Bene Gesserit Supreme Bashar Miles Teg with a T-probe after Teg had been captured in Reverend Mother Lucilla's and Duncan Idaho ghola number 4's escape from the Harkonnen no-globe. Teg killed him in escaping from the T-probe's influence after the agony it had caused had lifted Teg to a new level of ability. [*Heretics of Dune*]

Yitob, Reverend Mother (13,654–13,761)—Bene Gesserit Reverend Mother Yitob was an author of the Welbeck Abridgement, a 13,726 report to the Bene Gesserit on the state of the Empire. [*God Emperor of Dune*]

Yorgi (15,233–15,589)—Roitiro's son, Yorgi was the Miles Teg clone's childhood friend on Chapterhouse. [*Chapterhouse: Dune*]

Ysai—Named Barony in the 102nd century, when it had been the capital city on Giedi Prime, Ysai was still one of Gammu's major cities in the 153rd century, when it was a repellant, sprawling mass of warrens surrounding the ancient, massive Keep. [*Heretics of Dune*]

Yueh, Doctor Wellington (10,082–10,191)—Purple-lipped, mustachioed, high-voiced Doctor Wellington Yueh had a buttery complexion, long, ebony hair that he kept bound in a silver Suk school ring, and a black diamond tattoo of Imperial Conditioning on his forehead. He graduated from the Suk School in 10,112 and subsequently married Wanna Marcus, a Bene Gesserit. While secretly an agent for Baron Vladimir Harkonnen, who had discovered a way to break Yueh's Imperial Conditioning and thus to make him an assassin and a traitor to Duke Leto Atreides, Yueh was physician to the Atreides and young Paul Atreides' teacher from 10,185 to 10,191. In 10,191 Yueh killed Esmar Tuek and the Shadout Mapes in sabotaging the Atreides' Arrakeen Palace shield generators. He then drugged Duke Leto and handed him over to the Harkonnens, but he was stabbed to death hours later by Piter De Vries. Motivated by his desire to kill the Baron—who had had Wanna captured, tortured, and executed—Yueh had placed a poison-filled false tooth in Duke Leto's mouth after drugging him, in the hope that Leto would murder the Baron with it once the Baron got close enough to gloat over him, but the Baron narrowly escaped this assassination attempt. To secure Leto's cooperation, Yueh had promised to save Paul and Lady Jessica from the Harkonnens by hiding them among the Fremen. He had also conveyed Leto's ducal signet ring to Paul by placing it, with a fremkit, in the ornithopter that was to take Paul and Jessica to the desert to die. [*Dune*]

Zaal—Zall was the pseudonym used by Scytale when he met Farok in a suburb of Arrakeen in 10,207 to further the Bene Gesserit/Spacing Guild/Tleilaxu conspiracy against Emperor Paul Muad'Dib. [*Dune Messiah*]

Zabulon—Emperor Paul Muad'Dib's Jihad conquered the planet Zabulon in 10,207. [*Dune Messiah*]

Zabur, the Tawrah and Talmudic—The Tawrah and Talmudic Zabur surviving on Salusa Secundus is one of the Ancient Teachings that shaped the dominant religious beliefs of the Imperium in the 102nd century, the time of Muad'Dib. [*Dune*]

zaha—On Arrakis, zaha was the morning siesta. [*Children of Dune*]

Zarr Sadus—The Zarr Sadus were the Fremen of Arrakis who, in the early 103rd century, followed The Preacher and refused to submit to the priests of the religion of Muad'Dib. Hayt acknowledged to Jessica that he was one of the Zarr Sadus on Salusa Secundus. [*Children of Dune*]

Zebataleph (10,171–10,218)—Blond-bearded, thin-faced, jolly, ruthless Zebataleph was the second son of a Fremen Naib and a priest in the religion of Muad'Dib. He was one of Regent Alia Atreides' Society of the Faithful and greeted Jessica on her arrival in Arrakeen, after her twenty-three year absence from Arrakis, in 10,216. [*Children of Dune*]

Zen Hekiganshu—The Zen Hekiganshu of III Delta Pavonis is one of the Ancient Teachings that shaped the dominant religious beliefs of the Imperium in the 102nd century, the time of Muad'Dib. [*Dune*]

Zensunni—The Zensunni were the followers of the sect led by Ali Ben Ohashi that broke away from the teachings of Moameth in about 1,381. The Zensunni creed denied objective function of all mental activity. The Fremen of Arrakis were descendants of the Zensunni. [*Dune, Dune Messiah*]

Ziamad   (10,150–10,222)—Ziamad was Namri's uncle and a citizen of Jacurutu. [*Children of Dune*]

Index